A DULL ROAR

(What I Did On My Summer Deracination 2006)

Henry Rollins

de·rac·i·nate (d-rs-nt)
tr.v. de·rac·i·nat·ed, de·rac·i·nat·ing, de·rac·i·nates
1. To pull out by the roots; uproot.
2. To displace from one's native or accustomed environment.
de·raci·nation n.

A DULL ROAR © 2006 Henry Rollins
Third Printing

Published by
2.13.61
7510 Sunset Blvd #602
Los Angeles, CA 90046
www.21361.com / www.henryrollins.com

Design: Dave Chapple www.chappledesign.com

2.13.61

Thanks: Carol, Heidi, Road Manager Mike,
Mitch Bury of Adams Mass.

For Ginger, always.

JOE COLE 04.10.61 – 12.19.91

APRIL 2006

"The first to start and the last to quit, the loser runs longest but unknown.
Here I am setting up for the last one. I am nothing but my will."
(From *Also Ran*, Rollins Band lyric.)

04-01-06 LA CA: I should explain what this story is all about. I can only tell you about it up to a certain point because I don't know how it's going to end. I can tell you how it started though:

Several months ago, Chris Haskett (old pal from DC & guitar player in the Rollins Band) and I started e-mailing back and forth about doing some music together. It had been a long time since we'd worked together. I was enthusiastic. I didn't have anyone to play with and wanted to do something. You can get as strange as you want with Chris and he's completely cool with it.

Whenever I was in NYC, where he lives, we would get together and talk about what kind of stuff we wanted to do. Months went by and we had not really got a lot happening. Schedules and everything else seemed to keep the project on a back burner.

At one point Chris asked what I thought about playing with what we call "the other two," who are Melvin Gibbs and Sim Cain. I liked the idea but it comes with baggage. When you have played with people for a decade and then not played with them for almost that long, there's no way there's not stuff to deal with. We had parted ways as a band in the autumn of 1997 in Osaka, Japan. At that time I thought we had come to the end of what we could do together as a band and

I didn't know if that had changed. I didn't know why it would have. Our conversation would eventually stray onto other topics as there's always something to talk about with Chris. His mind is a warehouse of information and he's quite brilliant.

A few months ago I was in NYC again and Chris said he had been talking to Melvin and did I want to get together with them and talk about music? I don't remember what I said but that night I was at Chris' place and there was Melvin. I had not seen him for years. He looked the same, except for very long dreadlocks.

We talked around the topic for awhile and then Chris finally asked Melvin what he thought about playing with the two of us. He said he was into it. That surprised me and moved me a great deal.

You might be wondering why there's been no mention of Sim Cain. No one had talked to Sim yet as he was in New Jersey and not in the neighborhood. Chris, Melvin and I talked about Sim and then it sounded like "reunion" and everyone kind of backed off and changed the topic.

At some point, I am not sure exactly when, Chris made contact with Sim and asked if he would be interested in jamming with him and Melvin on some old songs. Sim said ok and Chris booked time.

I waited eagerly to hear from Chris about how it went. He got back to me and said it sounded pretty good and that everyone's mood was great. He asked what I thought the next move should be. I thought they should practice a little more and see if it still felt good to them and, if it did, I would go in there and jam with them. After that we could see how it was and go from there.

In a few months, I had gone from thinking it would be a bad idea to a good one and I thought about it all the time. So, to get to the point, the men worked on many songs and got them together. On 02-17-06, I walked into Ultra Sound on 30th Street for band practice. This would be the first time these four people were in the same room since late 1997. I wasn't nervous. I was actually looking forward to it. These guys are some of the finest people I have ever met.

I finally figured out what room we were booked into as no one there seemed to want to help me. Melvin and Chris were there. Sim was out getting some sticks and would return in a moment. I had not seen Sim since Osaka, 1997.

Then Sim Cain walked in and we hugged. I was so happy to see him. I have known him for 20 years. He sat down behind the drums and then all the old jokes started up again and it was as if I had not been away from these guys at all. It was very strange.

I had my mic with me. I plugged in and looked at the list of songs they had ready to play. I asked if they wanted to do *Volume 4*. Sim just started counting in and all of a sudden we were playing. We played for almost three hours. At one point, we all sat down and I asked what they thought. Everyone said it was feeling good. I then asked if we were really doing this. I said I am in if they are in and willing to do what it takes to really kill it. All agreed. It was on. There was one detail we had not worked out yet—our soundman and very important member Theo Van Rock, the Low End Ranger. Chris said he'd put in the call and see what he said.

We left practice promising to keep in touch and to start developing a schedule that would hopefully have us in fighting shape by August.

Jetlag has its teeth in me. More tomorrow.

04-02-06 LA CA: 1946 hrs. So, like I was saying, we left it there. The guys would keep practicing and I would get back to them as soon as I could. Chris got in touch days later and said he had talked to Theo and reported that he sounded good but was slightly vague and would not commit. Theo said he would talk to me when I got to Amsterdam in a few weeks. That's Theo. He's going to do what he says he's going to do. If that's what he said, you can just stop asking about it. Once he says it, it stays said, if you know what I mean. I promised to get back to the others after I had met with him.

On March 21st, I did a show at the Paradiso in Amsterdam Holland. This is the venue where I turned 22. I hit the stage and sitting right in front of me, dead center, was Theo. We just grinned at each other and then I got to work. After the show, he and I talked for about an hour. He wanted to hear it from me, see me say it. That's Theo. I told him it was the real thing or I wouldn't be doing it. I said it was going to be great and everyone was in but him. He said he was in. I told him I would keep in touch.

I don't know how many bands count the soundman as a member but in this one we do. The Rollins Band is five people. Theo is as much a part of the sound as any of us. I didn't want to announce the thing without knowing if he was in or out. I was happy he was in because to me, it wouldn't be the thing without him. It would just be a thing. A good thing but not the thing.

After he left, I wrote all the others: "You have a FOH sound man. His name is Theo Van Rock. He's in 100%. Get ready for the return of the Low End Ranger, motherfuckers." So, that was it. We were back.

There is a feeling I get when playing with these guys that I have never felt with anyone else.

Later on as we were heading to Belgia (I have renamed Belgium), Road Manager Mike and I started planning potential tour ideas and schedules. The two of us have spent hours all over the world plotting our next move as the miles pass underneath the bus wheels.

A few nights later, we were in London talking to Paul Boswell, who has been booking me since Black Flag. He was happy about the news and promised to start looking around to see what interest, if any, there would be.

I don't know if anyone will care about us getting together to play. I announced it on my site the other day and got a few happy letters. Management has been putting the word out to people and apparently there's interest with promoters and venues. I am going to enjoy the next four months.

It is now April. I have decided to go into a very hard training regimen that will ratchet up as the weeks pass by so when it's August and time to play, I will hopefully be in shape.

I was just in NYC for press and did three nights of practice. The first one was a little strange. I flew from Dublin, Ireland to NYC. I went right to the hotel, changed and ran to band practice, which was right down the street. I ran in, hit it with the band for a good while and then had to run back to the hotel for two + hours of phone press. I caught the first one as I was opening the door of my room. That's how I like to keep my schedule. I did the press and then grabbed some sleep and got up around 0500 hrs. to get ready for more press. The next two nights of practice were good and only got better.

There's a certain level of hostility and animal intensity that I can only achieve with these guys. I had a good time with the Mother Superior guys. They are good men and good players all of them. It was good but different. There just wasn't the malevolent drive that propels this unit. It was surging though my body on the second night of practice. There's nothing like it. It felt like getting an internal organ re-installed. It makes me feel alive and invincible.

So, now I'm back in LA about to shoot the next month of the IFC show. It's the second of four or five months of shows. IFC has the option to ask for a fifth month if they want. It would be great if they didn't want it. I could be done in July and have less to think about while getting ready for the August shows. Also, I don't always get along with the production team. Doesn't matter. I get through most things. I like doing the show and think we're doing good work but the relationship with them is at times trying. They're not bad people but they get me wound up sometimes.

Being back with the band puts me in a certain mindset that is unique to working with them. It's perfect for the training I plan on doing and the training I plan on doing is perfect for the music we'll be playing.

The way I live is based on the work I do. I don't know many people and the ones I see with any regularity are those I work with. I see people I grew up with when I can. They are great and I always value the time with them. Past that, it's all about the work, the schedule, the deadlines and the delivery. It's pretty much all I care about. I live alone and I don't want for company. It's very rare there's someone at my house besides the people who maintain it when I am not here. I

Henry Rollins

9

am thinking about the band rituals coming up and living in NYC for weeks at a time again. I have a lot of memories in Manhattan. The pain I will be putting my body through will put me into that perfect space. Pain has always pushed me to good stuff. Without pain, life isn't real to me.

Chest workout. Hi rep bench, hi rep dumbbell press, ab work. 1 can minestrone soup, spinach and salmon salad, tomato soup, 1 qt. carrot juice, some bread.

04-03-06 LA CA: 2102 hrs. Today was pretty damn cool. We had the New York Dolls on the IFC show today. They played really well and the new song they played, *Dance Like A Monkey*, sounded great. I talked to Sylvain Sylvain a lot between shots. They are very cool people. It's a blast seeing these bands play and be one of only a few people in the room. The band's bass player is Sammi Yaffa from Hanoi Rocks. I told him about the time I saw Hanoi play in summer 1984 at the Electric Ballroom where guitar player Nasty got hit in the temple by a drumstick and it knocked him out. He remembered the show. It was a real kick seeing those guys play up close. I had always wanted to meet David Johansen and now I have been on his radio show and he's been on my TV show. That's pretty cool.

I gave my manager's son a ride back to his house. I have never been in a car with him alone. He's old enough to sit in the front so we drove back through downtown and talked about stuff. He's a very cool kid. I asked him if there was a kid in his class who was a spazz and he said of course. I asked him how he treats the kid and he said he always makes sure to invite him to his birthday party. I think that's really cool. I was that kid when I was in school. It was good to hear what the guy has to say for himself. He's 11 or 12 and I think he's going to be a smart and well-adjusted young man.

We got to his house and I hung out with him and his sister for a little while and when I tried to leave his sister didn't want me to go and she held onto my ankle so I stuck around for awhile longer. It's no problem, I like them very much and they like me. I have known them all their lives. I have a lot of work tomorrow and I have to start somehow getting myself wound down so I can sleep. Unless I am really tired, it's a problem getting to sleep.

Oatmeal, 1 can minestrone soup, spinach and salmon salad, water, coffee ? cups.

04-04-06 LA CA: 2325 hrs. Today was long. I went to work at the IFC show. I did all the Teeing Off segments and then interviewed Eddie Izzard. I had not talked to him in a long time. I think the last time I saw him was when we were both in the parking lot of the Canyon Country Store a few years ago.

I have seen Eddie do his show and have seen him in movies but have never seen him speak on topics and he was very interesting. To me at least, it's interesting to get a take on what's happening here from a European's perspective. There's a lot about Europe that is very appealing to me. It's not as dreary, money-centered and ready to start a war as America is it seems to me. They do crazy things like take care of the environment and care about kids and value education. America must freak them out.

Anyway, Eddie was a good interview and I must say I was a little surprised. I know the guy is brilliant and I have spent time with the guy and he's friendly enough but I didn't know if he would be forthcoming in an interview situation and he was right into it. The interviews and putting up with the producers are the only hard parts of doing this show.

So we had as good a day as one can get in that environment. The producers get my heart rate up a bit and can be frustrating at times but they are good people and work very hard. I am a motherfucker and work very hard so we have a few things in common and it works for now. I can tell it's going to be a very long season.

I had to move very quickly to get to the radio station in time for the show but I did it with about half an hour to spare. Being on the air and playing music makes all the rest of the day's bullshit disappear. I love that show. It's always over too fast. I just get it going and there's only 40 minutes left. Tomorrow is long and starts early so I better hit it.

Bagel, cream cheese, fish, vegetable, veg. burrito, water, coffee.

Henry Rollins   **11**

04-05-06 LA CA: 2123 hrs. Today was office work. Tomorrow I interview PT Anderson. I am looking forward to that. I am a true fan and have seen all his films more than once. I hope he's cool.

I take this as a sign of how much of a right on individual I am. I have a cold and didn't even break to figure that out until yesterday when they told me my voice sounded rough. It was then that I noticed that I felt bad. That's pretty cool that I am unaware of it. That's working hard. I like that. I like it when I get run down. I would rather not be run down but I know I am working my ass off when I am feeling bad. It's a small badge. I only like myself when I am overworking. It's the only way I can stand myself and can justify food. There's only one way to achieve—overachieve.

I bought good food at the market and will push my body right through this. It's one of the things I learned from my father who used to work some insane hours. He would do that thing where he worked all night at the office, walk into the men's room, shave, put on a new shirt and work the next day. He once told me that you can eat your way through exhaustion. It kind of works. You can stick it out for several more hours so you can get it all done but then you have to put it down. I was running from press to band practice back to press etc., so I was asking for it. I also worked out tonight and that hurt but there's no way I'm not getting the training in. I have to really stay on the training this summer. It's not hard for me to stick with it. I don't have a lot else going on outside of the work.

Chest pt. 2. Oatmeal, 2 protein bars, spinach and salmon salad, carrot juice, water, coffee 1 cup.

04-06-06 LA CA: 2208 hrs. I'm beat. I don't know how I pulled off a workout but I did. There's nothing like the wave of fear that assaults me when I think of the band and all that we need to do to get it together. Failure is a motivator. Knowing I am going to fail anyway at least gives me a sense of humor about it all and allows resolve to take the lead in front of ambition. Going down swinging is what I reckon the last half of my life is all about.

I interviewed PT Anderson today and am happy to say that he was great. I can call myself a true fan. I have seen all his films at least 2-3 times each and have them all on DVD. He's weeks away from starting work on a film called <u>There Will Be Blood</u> which is based on an Upton Sinclair novel. Daniel Day-Lewis is the lead. It will be interesting to see how PT directs him. He said that project will take a long time to shoot and edit.

I am sorry but I am too tired and burnt to write. Weeks ago, I made April 1st my finish line. If I could get to April 1st, I'd be alright. All the stuff I had lined up to that date had me stressed but good. So, got to the 1st and there was a momentary exhalation and then I looked up and saw the wall rise again in front of me. It's fucked up but it's the only way I can see to honestly approach life. Either work too much and be crazy or don't bother.

Biceps / triceps, abs. Bagel, cream cheese, fish, vegetable, veg. burrito, water, coffee 1 cup.

04-07-06 LA CA: 2137 hrs. We have a good practice schedule for next week in NYC. I am eager to get in there and start making a set. We will be at it like we used to. Four to five hours a day in a small room. I have work every day at the office and a lot to do when I get back to the house at night. I am not stressing about it. I can do it if I talk to as few people as possible and stay focused. I am all about the training and the work. I have some talking shows coming up, writing for different projects, a deadline on the retail version of Fanatic! and other stuff. People stress me out and make me mad. It's not their fault, it's mine but at least I know enough to stay to myself and get the work done.

I am thinking about August shows with the band. I don't know where we're playing and I don't know who we're playing with. It doesn't matter to me. Fucked up club, festival, doesn't matter. If I had my way, it would be the middle slot on someone else's tour so I could focus on killing them every night. That's the only way to get the music to really do what it needs to do. It needs to be played with the intent to destroy. I am not interested in harmony. I am not interested in getting along. Conflict and confrontation are better. They are honest attitudes that are foremost in my thinking.

There's nothing in these shows for me besides the opportunity to aspire to excellence, the opportunity to walk the halls of discipline and to defy. This is way better than when I was young. I am supposed to be soft and middle-aged now. I am supposed to have calmed down and settled into a comfortable lifestyle. Money and privilege should have ruined me by now.

I don't want to be touched. I don't want to be loved or understood. Fuck that. I want what comes to those who dare. That's it. I have three and a half months to train before the first shows. I need to temper myself. There's a few thousand push-ups I have to do before then. The wait will make me stronger. This is real life for me. The rest is bullshit.

Shoulder workout. Overhead press, straight legged row, front raises. 1 serving oatmeal, 1 can tomato soup, spinach and salmon salad, 1 qt. carrot juice, water, coffee 1 cup.

04-08-06 LA CA: 2244 hrs. Back at the house after a long day. Shoulders too thrashed to do shoulder night pt. II. I was going to do a ton of calisthenics tonight but I'll get some good sleep and do it all tomorrow evening.

Today I interviewed Bill Maher and Jeff Bridges. They were both different and good interviews. I have always admired Bill Maher's intelligence and speed. He said a lot of cool stuff today. He makes sense hard and fast. The interview was over quickly. I don't think he wanted to be there all that much. I know it was one of his only days off. He was cool but I think he wanted to get back to what he was doing and I can totally understand that. It will be an interesting interview. Jeff Bridges was really cool as well. He's a very humble and earnest man. I am truly a fan of his so it was easy to do the interview. I have not had any guest I didn't want on the show so all the interviews are sincere. It was cool to talk about his role as President in <u>The Contender</u>. Past that, I got back here and felt pretty used up. Now it's late. I am going to do some journal writing to strengthen myself from the inside.

I am listening to the first Buzzcocks album. I play this album too much. Earlier I listened to an old Japanese pressing of the Damned's <u>Machine Gun Etiquette</u> on Chiswick. Hard to find. This pressing was very noisy and not all that great.

There were no messages on the machine when I got in. I always count that as a plus. I recently shut down the e-mail at the radio show site as well as the IFC one. It was mostly 50+ pieces of spam a day and a few real letters. I can't keep up with the mail and it's rarely anything that is of any importance, like when people start writing in to ask what to do if they can't get to sleep. I would like to answer less mail. It's not that I hate the people who pay attention to what I do, they're great, it's just better not to exchange letters. I just want to do the work and that's it.

1 serving oatmeal, 1 vegetable sandwich, 1 bagel w/ cream cheese, 1 can minestrone soup, water, coffee 2 cups.

04-09-06 LA CA: 2010 hrs. Not much happening today besides what I make happen. I finished up all the work for the upcoming radio show.

I will be going to NYC soon for band practice and I'm looking forward to getting back into the room with the guys and starting this thing up. This next batch of practices will make us see what we need to do to get the thing up to speed.

I hope these guys are into it. They can be very adult sometimes. A little too adult for me. There's a lot of things that spring up when I am with them. There's that feeling I get when I go out months later with the woman I don't go out with anymore and I remember immediately why I don't go out with her anymore. There's a little of that but that's alright. I just have to hope they are as intense on all this shit as I am. I'll take half as intense, that'll do.

Looking forward to being in NYC. Being in LA is like being asleep for me. Days can go by and if I'm not careful, I won't notice. NYC makes you work. You have to be aware all the time in NYC. It takes me a day to get back to that. It's one of the reasons I want to get out of here all the time. The older I get, the harder I want to push things. My body fails where it didn't used to. Having trained for so many years I am very aware of even the slightest change. Any shows we do are going to be very hard on me. The knees, never very good to begin with, are not what they used to be. The only thing that is stronger than it used to be is my resolve and knowledge of the field. I know what it takes more than ever and I know what I need to do to prepare for it. I learned a lot getting ready for the <u>Rise Above</u> tour but I will be training much harder for this one.

What else is there to do? Relax? That's what gets people in my line of work. It's their rage and discontent that ripped their lives open and gave them access to the vitality and essence of it all and then they are so easily bought off. You give some of these guys some money and some females and they turn into fucking house cats. If they were going to be so completely overrun and defeated so quickly, then no one should have listened the first time around. I see a lot of that.

I will never, ever, get out of survival mode. I will always be desperate. Desperation and dread keep it real. It's why I walk my old streets as often as I can. I keep coming back around, keep wading back into the place I came from. Never forget. Never take anything for granted. And never EVER think any of this is going to last longer than a tour, a film shoot, a week or a month at best. It's like climbing a mountain with no hope of reaching the summit. It's not like there isn't a summit. It's not a matter of never becoming enlightened because you're always on the way to becoming enlightened. There's a summit—I just lack what it takes to get there. I will die en route. That's how I see it.

If I am not at odds with at least some of it all the time, then I will surely fail without honor.

The name of my radio show is *Harmony In My Head*. It's a great Buzzcocks song and it reflects the fact that there's only two genres of music. Good and bad. That being said, I don't want harmony in my life. I don't trust it. It can't last. It's something you turn your back on knowing you should not have. There is no evidence in my life experience to tell me that to be anything less than being grimly prepared to confront at all times on all levels is the only way to be.

Leg workout. 1 serving oatmeal, 1 can bean soup, spinach salad, 1 veg burrito, handful of crackers, carrot juice, water, coffee 1 cup.

04-10-06 LA CA: 2331 hrs. This day is always hard. Joe Cole would be a 45 year old man today. I just can't see it. I wonder how he would be at this age? What would he have learned in all the years that have passed? I think he would have made a great actor. He was on his way and gaining some momentum. He was talented in the strangest ways. Not exactly book smart but smart. Kind of a fuck up but with true charisma. He died for nothing. He died for America's dysfunctional bullshit. He died in America's War on America. He died and I lived. I don't get it. There's no such thing as fate, god, hell, any of it. That stuff is only for people who can't handle the truth so I don't care about it. I will always wonder why it was him and not me. It was almost both of us. One bullet missed me by a few inches, it would have hit me on the left side around the heart. The detectives had me stand where I was standing and then lined up where the bullet lodged in the doorjamb.

I had a lot of press today:

0830 - Stephanie Miller phoner from office

0915 - WRAT radio phoner from office

1030 - Connecticut Post phoner from office

1240 - Car arrives at office to take you to Current TV

1300 - Current TV, hair/makeup, interview, promos for show

It went alright. As good as it ever goes. I was hoping for more with the Stephanie Miller show. I think she's great and I listen to her all the time. When I talked to her she just bantered on about how I should train her and that I'm in shape, etc. It was off-putting. I am sure she meant no harm but it sucked. She asked about my recent interview with Ozzy for the IFC show and her voice impression guy started doing an Ozzy impression and they all started kinda bagging on the guy. I know they were just doing their little morning radio thing and I was pretty cool about it but they were more into making fun of him than hearing me say that he's a good guy. It was not a good time and I will still listen to her show with great interest as a fan but don't want to be on it again.

I did the rest of the press and it was fine. I went on Al Gore's Current TV. It's a cool set up. It's a small operation, very much like the IFC show. I talked about some topics blah blah blah. I do my best in these situations but never have any idea of how I really come off.

That was basically most of the day. I got some stuff done at the office. Mostly tied up the loose ends on the radio show. NYC is looming and I am looking forward to how it will be to work through these songs over and over. After these practice sessions are over, we'll know what we need to do. One of the things we may need to do is not play together again.

Calisthenics. Oatmeal, 1 piece coffee cake, 1 veg. burrito, 1 ice cream bar, water, coffee 2 cups.

04-11-06 LA CA: 2335 hrs. Nothing. I got nothing. I did office. I sat in traffic. I went and did the radio show and came back here. The radio show was good, over too quickly as usual but good. I just want to get out the door to NYC and get this going. I remember being in NYC about 11 years ago starting on the songwriting that would eventually produce the <u>Come In And Burn</u> album. I was sub-letting a place on 3rd around 31st. When I wasn't at the gym or the practice room, I was working on the book <u>Eye Scream</u>. Work on the book was hard. The workouts were bad and the songs weren't coming. Every time I think of the NYC practices coming up, I think of those times. I don't want to get into that defeatist mindset that gets to me but as much as I love NYC, it also holds a lot of sadness and failure for me. I had some extremely bad times there. There have been some very difficult times being in that band and a lot of the worst times were in NYC when we were trying to make that album work. Now we will be revisiting those songs every day. All that was wrong with them, lacking with them and inherently fucked up about them will be back to remind me at hundreds of dollars a day in rental bills. Who else is paying for all this

merriment? You?! It's why they make Rolaids.
1 cup yoghurt. 1 can tomato soup, spinach and salmon salad, carrot juice, water, coffee 1 cup.

04-12-06 LA CA: 2313 hrs. I think I'm good to go now. Did a long day at the office and then went to a meeting for a film. The director and producer have mild interest in me so I went down the road to the meeting. I never know how those things are supposed to go. I went right from the office: T shirt, baggy pants, unshaven, tired. Fuck it. The people at the meeting were really cool. The film is not <u>Citizen Kane</u> by a long shot but it would be a month of work and the pay is ok. It is supposed to shoot in Vancouver B.C., which is a fine place to me and it's always great to be living somewhere else. If the thing happens, I'll write about it. As far as I know, it's an extreme maybe but perhaps I'll hear something about it next week or never. I am always up for the work. I am always looking for a job. I like the legitimacy of employment. I don't consider myself an actor. If I am, I'm not a good one. Films for me are gainful employment and I am happy for the opportunity to work. I don't care if the movie isn't any good. It's not art to me. It's work and I'll gladly take it. When I am on the set, I give it all I have and take the task very seriously but I don't take myself seriously. For an industry that relies so heavily on illusion, there is more than enough brutality and heartbreaking truth to be found within it.

You're in and all is well. Then you're not in. While you're in, you wonder how long it will be until you're not in anymore and what you'll do then. I see my face all over this town at the moment. Billboard, posters, everywhere. That's April. That's for now. We have about another nine to twelve shoot days left for this season of the show on IFC. That's nine to twelve days of work and lunch. Will I ever see these people again after those days are over? I have no idea. Will I have a tour to go on next year? Can you tell me? I wish you could. But you can't. I have lived job to job, by my wits and desperation for over twenty-five years now. Never once did it ever occur to me to take it easy. I have always done what I wanted but never thought that I had "made it" or done much more than the best I could. That's why I save, live below my means and take outside jobs when I can to look out for myself. Who will feed me? Who will care? I have that answer and it's always on my mind.

There are not many friendships in the entertainment business. I am talking about the business of entertainment. I am not talking about in the band room or whatever. I am talking about where the money moves from one place to the other and the cooks enter the kitchen. Management, agents, those who you do the tango with, can be good people but the glue of the relationship is money.

I have always made the books and records I wanted to make. Following that truth and sticking to it has been mixed with good and bad parts. If you really want to go out and do it, you have to take what comes. And it comes. A box arrives. It is full of books I have written. They are well used, underlined in places and dog-eared. On top of the books is a letter explaining that the books are now mine again. The sender saw me on television and is completely disgusted with me and wants me to read my own books so I can remember when I had some integrity. This happens. This is part of it. The Sea of Consequence. Slings, arrows, adulation, appreciation, all mixed in a blender and served up. They are the things you must distance yourself from in order to do exactly as you want. You can hear what they say but you can't listen with any great deal of concern. This business has taught me to be very single-minded and direct. There is only one direction.

1 cup yoghurt, 1 can tomato soup, crackers, spinach and salmon salad, carrot juice, water, coffee 2 cups.

04-13-06 NYC NY: It's a little past midnight so technically it's the 14th. I got in a little while ago. I just ate some soup I bought at the store down the street from the hotel. I hope I can get my head down soon.

I was in the car on the way into the city and saw an ad for the IFC show on the top of a cab. I got out at the hotel and some people standing in front ran up to shake my hand. People are very friendly to me here for some reason. People talk to me on almost every block when I am walking. I know NYC is a very hard place. I have had some good times here and some not so good ones as well. It was never the place that was bad to me, it was just the bullshit I was going through.

New York City is one of the planet's greatest attractions—an incredible invention. Sometimes when I walk around here, I feel, I don't know if lucky is the right word but something like it. I have never felt like I belonged anywhere, not even in the city I grew up in, DC. I think about it all the time. There's something about the streets in NYC that makes me feel I'm in the right place. Not a feeling of belonging but the feeling that I can get it done and I am free. In those expanses of time I walk endless blocks uptown, downtown and cross-town, I feel like I am in the middle of a fascinating story that's writing itself in real time right in front of me. I am never here for very long so that feeling rarely has time to wear off.

I think it comes down to the strength of the people here. That thing that is so "New York" about them, their backbone, personality and abundant charisma—it always inspires me. I like being in it for a few days. I have written some good stuff in this city. I have done some of the best shows in my life here and that means a lot. New Yorkers are a dream audience. That last Town Hall show, what a blast it was. I don't know many people here. Mainly the ones in the band. It's better that way.

1 cup yoghurt, spinach and salmon salad, carrot juice, water, air plane meal of crab cakes, 1 can of soup, coffee 2 cups.

04-14-06 Brooklyn NY: 2210 hrs. At Melvin's place in Brooklyn. We walked through a Hasidic neighborhood tonight on the way to a market on Broadway. It was raining and the men had these amazing plastic protectors for their Shtreimel hats (yes, I had to look that up. I wanted to be respectful). I only saw one person besides Melvin and me who were not Hasidic until we got to Broadway. I don't know anything about them. They looked very serious and somewhat grim. In the lobby of one of the apartments we passed, I saw some girls jumping rope. One man asked us if we could turn off his gas line. Melvin said that because of the holiday they are celebrating right now, hold on, I'll look it up. Ok, I guess it's Passover. Shows you how much I know about religious holidays. Anyway, Melvin said they can't do any work after sundown and needed us to do it for him. We declined and kept moving. Their trip seems really heavy. With outfits like that, you're definitely not trying to blend in.

We had a good time at band practice today. We hit pretty much all the material. We did *Shame* and *Shine*. I have not done *Shine* since 1994. It felt pretty good the 2nd time we played it. *Shame* sounded pretty good too. It was the first time I had done that one since 1997. I am doing some slightly different phrasing on the lines. It's been so long it feels like a new song to me. I don't think anyone in the audience would be able to tell but it makes more sense the way I was doing it today.

I'm going to be living at Melvin's tonight and tomorrow night. I have some nights at a hotel lined up for later in the week. It's always interesting to check out what Melvin is reading. When we were on the road, he would read the most hyper-intellectual material. His bookshelves have some serious reading material. Melvin cooked up some great vegetarian food for dinner and we hung out and listened to music and all of a sudden it was late.

Band practice, ab crunches, push-ups. 2 cups yoghurt, protein bar, water, veg. meal, sesame bars, 1 small glass Orangina, coffee 2 cups.

04-15-06 Brooklyn NY: 2311 hrs. At Melvin's place listening to this CD he turned me onto called <u>Ahaando</u> by Les Tambours de Brazza. Incredible. I can't wait to get a copy of this to Ian, he's going to flip when he hears it.

Band practice was pretty good today. It was a little rushed and a little blown through I thought. Sim Cain had to leave to take a train out to the Jersey shore to play in a band he does shows with all the time called The Fairlanes. He has three sets with them tonight. He had a few last night as well and he's playing with them again on Sunday. He's busting his ass at band practice and I know he's rippin' it with The Fairlanes as well. I don't know where's he getting the energy

A Dull Roar

from. We'll have a good practice on Monday. I am going to work hard on Sunday to re-learn some arrangements that have been confusing me on *Shine* and *Almost Real*. I was better on them today but I still need a lot of work.

Melvin and I went into Manhattan on the train today. It was packed. The NY train experience is like nothing else. The humanity! Manhattan is one thing. Brooklyn is a whole other world to me. We walked to a small store that makes food in the back. I got some rice and beans and we walked back to his building. As we got closer, I asked him what he saw of the September 11th attacks. He said he was in his place when the first one hit and he felt the building shake. His girlfriend was on the roof to see the 2nd plane hit. He said the smell lasted about a week and it was awful. He said we should go up to his roof and check out the sunset and I could eat up there. We looked up and saw some people up there and I instinctively pulled back from that idea and said I was cool to eat in his place. Of course we went up to the roof. The view was amazing. One of the guys from the group of people who were up there saw me and started yelling my name. All his friends started staring. He came over and we shook hands. I think he was a little drunk. Seemed like a nice enough guy but he kept yelling out that he never thought he'd meet me or something and I got that feeling like I wanted to bolt. I felt stupid standing there. I said again to Melvin that I would rather just eat in his place and we turned around and went back down the stairs. Melvin said if it were him, he wouldn't have given a fuck and sat down and eaten the food. He's not as self-conscious as I am. I just wanted to eat the fucking food and get it over with. Melvin is absolutely right. I know I am way too tightly wound. People are cool but my instinct is to leave them alone. When I hang out with the guys in the band, a lot of their friends will come over to talk to them, they know a lot of people wherever we go. When someone comes over to talk to one of them, I just freeze. It's the strangest thing. It's very hard for me to meet people. In a lot of situations, I feel I am not where I am supposed to be. Like on that roof. I shouldn't have been there. It's their building, their roof. I always feel better on my own. I understand and trust alone more than anything or anyone.

People are really great to me in New York though. It's an amazing place. I am looking forward to walking around Manhattan this week.

Band practice, ab crunches, push-ups. 1 cup yoghurt, hummus, wheat flat bread, sesame bars, water, rice and beans, 1 bottle diet soda, coffee 2 cups.

04-16-06 NYC NY: 2258 hrs. In the hotel room. Today was bad and will factor mightily in the weeks coming up. I was walking to the market around 1330 hrs. today and my right foot came down a little crooked or something and I fell really hard. Like when you see a drunk guy really hit the deck. I went down hard. First thing that hit the ground was my right wrist. I heard a bone break. I got up and a couple of people asked me if I was alright and someone asked, "Aren't you Henry Rollins?"

I knew my wrist was broken but I had walked a long way to the market so I was determined to get some food. My hand started going numb. I knew this fracture. I used to break this part of my wrist when I was skating in the 70's. Same place every time. Hurts like a bastard. Takes weeks to heal.

I hate to admit this but while walking around the market, I was almost in tears knowing that I was not going to be able to train the way I wanted to for the shows. I got my food and left the market. I went to a drugstore and bought a bandage and wrapped my wrist and started back to the hotel.

By the time I got back here, I was in a lot of pain. I took some aspirin and re-wrapped my wrist. I had work to do so I got into it and soon realized I was going to have to do something different to type. I have to kind of freeze my right hand and plunk it straight down on the keys. I have about a month to work on my technique.

Nothing was going to stop me from working out. I went down to the gym in the basement and hit it as best I could. I did dumbbell presses with my left hand, a lot of sit-ups and some reps on the fake bench press thing hotel gyms have. I did a lot of ab crunches off the bench as well. Then I ran for awhile and went back to my room and ate.

The hand hurts like a bastard and it will for some time. I guess I'll do a lot of running, leg and ab work and dumbbell stuff with my left hand. I will do what I can to work the right arm. I guess it could have been worse. I was really looking forward to this training period and now it won't be what I hoped for. Another setback. I have to remember what Seneca said about adversity: that the warrior sees adversity as exercise. Ok, so this is exercise.

On my way back to the hotel, I passed an old man sitting in a doorway puking on his legs. It hurts like hell to type. Perhaps it will let up a little tomorrow.

I am glad I was alone when this happened. All this stuff is better alone. I don't want to lean on anyone or waste their time. It's stuff like this that teaches me good lessons. I get stronger when I deal with pain and adversity alone. They are opportunities to learn. I will do the press I signed on to do and see Road Manager Mike and the band and I will get all my fucking work done and I will train somehow every day this week. It's not like I'm at Walter Reed with my arm gone. I wrote RMM about the wrist just so he would know.

Ab crunches, 1 arm dumbbell press, 1 arm Universal machine press, 15 minute run. Hummus, wheat flat bread, 1 can minestrone soup, sesame bars, water, V8 juice, coffee 1 cup.

04-17-06 NYC NY: 2348 hrs. Back from band practice. It was pretty good. The guys played well. I had some ups and downs with it. I really have to work at some of these songs. A couple of them feel somewhat familiar but not all the way ingrained yet. I'll be better tomorrow.

I wrote all day today for the IFC show. I have to hit it every day. Hopefully I can get it all done. Actually, I have no choice there. I have to get it done. I didn't get outside today except to go to band practice. Not much happened today besides work and practice. Not much to write about. I'll have more time for writing tomorrow if my wrist can take it.

Band practice. 1 protein bar, hummus, wheat flat bread, 1 bowl fat free milk and granola, fig newtons, 2 cans soup, water, V8 juice, coffee 1 cup.

04-18-06 NYC NY: 2241 hrs. Today was good as far as getting work done. We put *Also Ran* into the set and worked on *Stray* for quite a while. Some intense lyrics in those songs. We played hard and did a good five hours of work.

I came back here and watched some news and went to the gym and did an arm workout, literally one arm was all I could work out on. I ran some after that and came back here to get some writing done for the IFC show.

Looks like I got the part in that film and now management and agent woman are haggling over the pay and the dates. I don't know how it is for other low budget actors but, at least for me, what the agent says it's going to be and what it actually turns out to be are usually two wildly different things. I will hear more about what it really is tomorrow I guess and will decide if it's something I want to do.

A little while ago, I went outside to go to the store for some V8 juice and as I was stepping up onto the sidewalk after crossing the street I heard a voice behind me call out my name. A woman came up to me and said she had something for me. She gave me a card with her picture on it that had information on her new album and the show she had coming up in a few days. She said that I had written her friend back and forth a few times and gave me her name and description. I don't remember writing this person but I probably did. I told the woman that I answer all the mail and that sometimes people keep writing and it's not something I can always keep up as I am busy and really don't know anyone who writes me out of the blue. She said, "I guess I shouldn't tell her I ran into you." I then tried to explain that I meant no harm but I am not good at correspondence and it's very time consuming to answer mail as frequently as I get it. It's true. I'm like most people, busy all the time. I do my best to answer the mail but it becomes difficult when someone starts to write all the time. The last thing I want to do is write back and forth with someone but at the same time, I don't want to bum someone out when they mean no harm. You have to be very careful of other people's feelings. I don't think it's right to be hard on people who aren't in line for it. I don't know if I made myself clear to the woman but I thanked her for the card and walked off. I should have offered to walk her to her car as she was going in the same direction I was. I never think of stuff like that in time. I went to her website and left her a letter wishing her good luck with the show.

I get x-rayed in the morning. It will be good to get the arm checked out. The swelling has gone down some and it's a lot easier to type today compared to yesterday. I still have to kind of chop away at it. I should get some sleep. I have a long day tomorrow.

Band practice. 1 arm dumbbell curls, 1 arm Universal machine press, 15 minute run. Hummus, wheat flat bread, 1 can minestrone soup, sesame bars, water, V8 juice, coffee 1 cup.

04-19-06 NYC NY: 2310 hrs. In the room. I got my hand x-rayed today. The doctor and I looked at the x-ray and he said there was no sign of fracture but also said sometimes a bone doesn't show signs of fracture for some days. He said that there should be more bruising and swelling if it were a fracture. He said I probably severely sprained it and perhaps did some ligament damage. He gave me a wrist brace and sent me on my way with a referral for a doctor in LA who could do an MRI. So, that's pretty cool.

I met a great cab driver on the way back downtown. His name was Omar and he told me a story about a woman with a knife who tried to mug him in Brooklyn and how he grabbed the woman's hand and politely explained that he only had two dollars, which he gave her before she just fucked off.

I went to band practice and it was perhaps the best one yet. *Almost Real* and *Civilized* sounded really good so did *Also Ran.* We were in there a long time. I was pretty burnt when I left.

I got back here and worked on my nightly writing for IFC and came up with a good thing on what to look forward to this coming summer that might work.

Management called and said they were in final negotiations on the film. We went over the script together and made the final decision that I was going to go for it. Management hung up and got into it with the agent and the producer and called back several minutes later with more details. We went back and forth for about an hour with stuff and then we finalized everything.

So it looks like I will play the part of retired Marine Col. Dale Murphy in the film <u>Wrong Turn 2</u>. I am grateful for the work and will give it everything I have.

There were some talking shows tentatively booked for Scandinavia that I'll have to skip. There were no tickets put on sale or anything, the shows were just talked about and were waiting confirmation pending this film. So, I'll be doing two shows in England and then coming right back to Canada and finishing up the film, only breaking to do the IFC show and then right back into band practice and off on tour.

Looks like the tour will be Rollins Band and X in America for about a month. Co-headline but they close the show every night. I love that. I love X. Some of the best shows I have ever seen have been X shows—really. That being said, any band that I'm opening for, I want to vanquish every night, even if it's X. It's nothing personal. If I'm not primed to fuckin' destroy then what good is touring at all? I'm not interested in playing good time music. Never have been. I hope this tour gives me the chance to get out there and defy all expectation. It's pressure that I live for.

Band practice. 1 bowl granola w/soy milk, hummus, wheat flat bread, sesame bars, water, V8 juice, coffee 1 cup.

04-20-06 NYC NY: 2340 hrs. Scorched. Today was long. It was good to see Howard Stern and Robyn again. I think that's the best time I've ever had on that show. It was good to see Brad Balfour again as well. He is always cool to interview with. I get up in a few hours and do press right up until flight time back to LA. I didn't get to do any walking around on this trip. I practiced, trained, did press and really fucked my wrist up. I got the writing for the IFC show done so that's some pressure off.

0830-0930 - Howard Stern Show Sirius Satellite Radio in-studio

0930 - Larry Flick's morning show (entertainment based)

1015 - XM Opie & Anthony

1130 - NPR's "Wait, Wait Don't Tell Me" pre-interview phoner.

1200 - 1315 - Lunch

1330 - Interview with Brad Balfour

1415 - Google video interview 2:45 PM Int. w/Robin Milling

1830 - 2030 - Band practice

2110 - "Wait Wait Don't Tell Me" on NPR phoner from hotel.
Band practice. 1 bowl granola w/soy milk, hummus, salmon, rice, tuna wrap, sesame bars, water, V8 juice, coffee 1 cup.

04-21-06 JFK Airport: 1535 hrs. I finished press and went to the airport early. I don't mind getting to a flight really early. If I have something to write on I'm fine.

I have been working away on the 2nd draft of the Fanatic! book and I am done. Carol will be very happy to get this book out the door and to the printer. Hopefully there will be a few less typos this time around. I did a lot of phone press this morning that went alright. Sometimes you move so fast from station to station, you forget who you're talking to. An engineer in another room just keeps feeding you the next call into your headphones and you talk fairly nonstop for hours.

I am cautiously satisfied with the way the band is sounding. It is sounding good. Chris is really digging in. Always depressing to board a flight and know that I'm only going to LA. Don't really feel like writing. The thought of going back to LA and all that bullshit has somewhat muted my normal youthful effervescence.
Protein bars, minestrone soup, water, coffee.

04-22-06 LA CA: 2331 hrs. At the desk. Several hours ago I was working around the house, about to start writing up band intros for the upcoming TV shows when I got a call from of one of the IFC producers. He asked when I was planning on coming down. I asked him what for and he said that Dinosaur Jr. had finished soundchecking and were getting ready to play. I had completely forgotten that they were taping today. I put everything here on hold and got down there as soon as I could.

Henry Rollins

It's amazing how much traffic there is in Los Angeles all the time now. No matter where you go, it's bumper-to-bumper. I finally got down there and said hello to the band: J Mascis on guitar, Lou Barlow on bass and Murph on drums. Really cool guys. I had not seen this line up play for a long time.

They soundchecked *Raisans* from <u>You're Living All Over Me</u>. J's guitar level was insane, he sounds great of course, but there's a lot of it. When they were done, he looks at the monitor man and asks, "Can I get more guitar in the monitor?" I thought he was joking. He was playing a stack that was cranked and he needed more. I thought that was so cool. One of the road crew set up another one of his speaker boxes aimed at him like a wedge monitor and that seemed to do the trick. They played *Raisans* twice and then played *Forget The Swan* from their 1st album twice. They were fantastic. That rhythm section is solid as hell and J's solos were scorching. It was such a blast to see them playing in front of a few people in a small room. It's going to be great for the show.

We hung out for a little while after they were done and it was good to talk to them. They humored me by signing an Australian pressing of their album <u>Bug</u> I brought down. I wanted something to remember the event by.

I'm really glad they're playing again. It's not lame like some kinds of reunions. It's really full-on and there's nothing about it that's at all fake or distracting. They played and sounded great. *Forget The Swan* sounds much better now than it does on the record. They're all better players now.

They took off for soundcheck. They had a show at the Troubadour in Hollywood. I was on the guest list. I got back here and did some work and then hit the weights as best I could with one hand. The right hand is feeling a lot better, it allows me to type slowly but it's going to be awhile before I can do much with it.

They were going to hit stage at 2230 hrs. so I headed down there a little before that. I drove by the venue and saw all the people outside and got that feeling I do when I see a lot of people I would have to walk amongst. I realized there was no way I was going to be able to stand around there and wait to get in. I feel vulnerable with only one hand operational and seeing all those people made me want to go the other way. So, I did. I was mad at myself all the way back to the house but there was no way I was going to be able to handle it so I left. As I got farther away from the show, I started to feel better in a way because I was alone in the car and didn't have to talk to anyone or be anything except myself alone. Being myself alone is what I'm best at. I don't know who I am when I am around people.

I wrote a letter to J Mascis, thanking him and the band for playing on the show and apologizing for not having whatever it is you need to walk into a place full of people. How lame am I? I feel so out of place amongst people. I feel like I am intruding on someone else's scene. A show is anybody's scene but I can't get my head around that, even though I know it's true. In a situation like that, I am on my own, I get stared at, I hear my name being said and everything in me says I should bolt. It is unbearable. When I am walking down the street in NYC, I hear my name being said out loud almost every single block but at least I am moving there and don't have to stop.

So, I feel bad that I didn't have the discipline to stick it out and get into the venue. I really wanted to see that show but at least I got to see them play earlier.

I got back here and felt relieved. I always feel good when I am on my own. It's the time when everything makes sense. When I am amongst people too much, I tell myself that as soon as I finish whatever it is that I'm doing, I will be able to be on my own. It's the reward I give myself.

I am looking forward to tomorrow because I will be on my own all day and no one will call me and I don't have to be anywhere for anyone. Next week will be busy as hell with the IFC show and press. I am on east coast time and am tired. I have to start getting more sleep. I didn't get all the work done that I had planned for because of going to the studio. I will have to put in at least 12 hours tomorrow.

Shoulder workout. 1 bowl oatmeal, salmon, spinach, carrot juice, water, hard candy, coffee 1 cup.

04-23-06 LA CA: 1737 hrs. After the IFC show airs I always get mail feedback. All kinds of things come in. Some people like the show and some find exception with the strangest things. There's a section of the show where I take a controversial stand on something. I don't write this part but I don't mind it and most of the time it's really funny. Some people don't get the joke or apparently see no humor in the thing at all, so they write in and let me have it. Fair enough but sometimes it's a little much.

Like I said, I get a lot of mail. There are a few women who seem to have a fantasy relationship with me. They tell me what they want to do with me if they ever get the chance. Sometimes they send pictures. Most of these are people who have written before in a more conventional way. Being polite, I answer. It's no big deal to answer a letter, someone took the time to write, it's respectful to answer. But for some, it turns into something else. Some of these women are really aggressive. I am always polite but it's sometimes tricky to deal with them. It used to offend me but not anymore. Whenever I answer mail, I censor myself most of the time. I don't write anything that I'm not ok with showing up posted in some chat room. That happens a lot. I will answer someone's letter and it will get posted in several places. I answer every letter like I am writing in to a newspaper who will print whatever I write. It's not that I don't trust people. I do. I trust them to do whatever it is they get in their heads to do.

If you do what you want, or what you think is right, there's a price to pay. Good old Sec. Def. Don Rumsfeld was talking about that just the other day. He said that when you do something, some people are going to like it and some people aren't and you have to live with that. He was talking about sending in all those brave kids to get killed in Iraq. He and the others at the White House have found a way to live with it. That's just fantastic.

Sometimes when I meet people after the show, there will be a female who asks if I will hug her. It makes me cringe. I don't hate people but I am not the hugging type really and I know it's only a matter of time before one asks for a hug so they can accuse me of groping them. I am always careful to make as little contact as possible.

I remember one time I was on a shoot and the make up person was a female. She would flirt with me. The first couple of times, I didn't notice as I am not used to that kind of thing. I figured it out a few days in. At one point after she had finished telling me about a dream she had about the two of us kissing, I just sat and said nothing. She said, "It's safe to flirt with you because you don't flirt back." Safe? Flirt back? Fuck that. It was so completely unprofessional and lame. I wanted to tell her how uncomfortable it all made me but I said nothing and just got the work done and split. I never saw her again, which is great.

My wrist has taken a turn for the better. From how it feels, I think the doctor was correct and that it's not broken. It's been a week now and it feels much better. I am typing ok and it's not hurting all that bad. I did some dumbbell work with my left hand last night and will see what I can do tonight.

Shoulder workout. 1 bowl oatmeal, 2 cups yoghurt, rice crackers, water, coffee 2 cups.

04-24-06 LA CA: 2235 hrs. All I did today was finish up on the 2nd edition of <u>Fanatic!</u> and give it to Carol around quitting time. I went back and forth with the producers for the IFC show about guests and stuff. We are trying to find an address for Legs McNeil of <u>Please Kill Me</u> fame. Legs is a fascinating man with an endless amount of stories. Talk about been there and done that. He's seen everything from the beginning of Punk Rock in NYC to damn near everything else. He always has amazing stuff to talk about whenever I see him. I want him to come on the show and talk about his latest book <u>The Other Hollywood: The Uncensored Oral History of the Porn Film Industry</u>, which is, as the title states, a history of porn in America. He did an instore thing a few years ago at a bookstore around here, Book Soup maybe, where he talked about the book and what he was learning and it was insane. So hopefully something comes of that.

I waited on but didn't get a call from George Carlin. We have asked him to be on the show and he's interested but he wants to talk to me first. I have not talked to GC in a long time. I hope he calls tomorrow. He's always been someone who inspired me. I see his tour dates and it makes me jealous. Last time I was in Las Vegas I saw that he was doing so many nights there, it was like a leg of one of my tours but in only one city. I wish I could do multiple nights at one place. That would be so great to be in that kind of demand. Sometime, I should go to a couple of nights of one of his shows to see how he works from night to night, maybe I could learn a few things. Understatement.

I had a great time last year when I did all those shows at the Zipper Theater in NYC. Every night I had my show and then I would go back to my hotel room. I liked that. I like hotels more than where I live. I like being anonymous in a big building. I like that none of it's mine and I'm a stranger and it's only for a few days and I set up camp and then pack it all up and leave. I like things. I have a lot of books and records. They are my reference materials. I use them all the time. I use a lot of notebooks. I make notes on everything. That being said, I am not a stuff person. Not into clutter, although I have a lot of it around me. A lot of it is stuff people send me. Everyone wants to be read, listened to and seen. So do I. How can you blame them? I'm into access to information and getting the answers and getting onto the next thing. Having that stuff is also a pain in the ass and goes against a lot of the way I think and the way I want to be. That's why I like the hotel and bus life. I have nothing but the few items in my back pack and the tool bag I carry everything else in. I can live like that for as long as the tour lasts and never miss anything or anyone.

I am looking forward to working on that movie in Canada. I am happy to live in Canada for weeks and weeks. I can't wait. Starting in late July, I get to be out for 4 or 5 weeks, that's going to be great. I will have to find a way to get out for the autumn. Go live somewhere. Maybe go live in Vietnam for a few weeks.

I don't know what it is but I never want to stop moving. I like anything that allows me to keep a lot in a small space. I like iPods. All that music in a small box. It's perfect for a guy like me. I feel best when I am in a moving vehicle or backstage in some city anywhere in the world. I don't want to live with a woman. I don't want anyone to miss me. I don't want to call someone all the time and explain myself to them. I don't want anyone to give a fuck about me. It's just a drag. It just drags. It compromises and normalizes and makes everything only go so far. Years ago I wanted the relationship but now, I can't remember what that was like and can't pick up the scent of that trail or even see what I saw in it. I would have to look at old journal entries. All that stuff seems like someone else's thing. Feels like strangulation when you put your arms around me. Would rather be free and cold. Free and starving. Free and staring into the abyss with disintegrating eyes. Free and lost in the desert to die alone of thirst. That makes more sense to me than growing old with another human. I don't hate people. I don't want to hack them to pieces but as I get older, I only want to get on with it. Just give me the list of shows, the itinerary or whatever it is and turn me loose. I am at my best when I am working or alone. It's increasingly hard to be around people but I can work with them very well. The people who do the IFC show are all very cool people, they work incredibly hard and I respect that but I don't know them past the work we do.

One of the people who I can be around in close quarters day after day is Road Manager Mike. He's as solid as they come and I trust him more than I trust myself. He's the man.

As it is right now, I am sitting here alone in this room and want for nothing human. I don't want anyone to touch me. I don't want to call anyone, I don't want anyone calling me. I use time alone as a reward for time being out with people. What's interesting in life is all that can change in about a minute. I know that. I am not some hard ass who can't change his mind. I am fucked and better off on my own.
1 bowl oatmeal, rice crackers, sushi, hard candy, water, coffee 1 cup.

04-25-06 LA CA: 2350 hrs. Almost done with this day. Radio show was a good time as always. Nothing much to report today. I did office work and then went back to the house and then to the radio station. I don't always get a lot of writing done after the radio show as it kind of burns me out, I try hard but it's never as good as I want it to be. I don't know exactly what it is I am looking to improve. I should try to get my head down as soon as I can. Some days I can beat my misery down and some days I can't. I have press materials to go through and mark up still to prepare for the interviews I have coming up. I will be interviewing Penelope Spheeris and Perry Farrell on the 28th and want to be ready. I admire both of them very much. I have known them a long time. I have done a lot of shows with Perry and have seen his bands play many times and Penelope was one of the first people I met when I got out here all those years ago.

1 bowl oatmeal, rice crackers, salmon and spinach, 1 burrito, hard candy, water, carrot juice, coffee 1 cup.

04-26-06 LA CA: 2230 hrs. Today was long. I did a lot of phone press. The journalists were all cool but it was a lot of talking. After that, I had some writing work to do for the IFC show shoot dates coming up. We go in tomorrow and do teleprompter reads all day and then on Friday are the interviews with Perry Farrell and Penelope Spheeris. I like both of them. They have both done some really great work over the years and they both think differently so it will hopefully be interesting to interview them. I have meetings with the movie people on Saturday and then later that day, I fly to PA for a talking show that night. This is the contents of my mind. It's just a lot of schedule a lot of the time. Hit it. Hit it. Hit it. Don't be late and always be ready to do it over and over.

It's no problem. It's not a problem as long as I stay on my own and talk to as few people as possible. I don't hate people but it's better that I don't interact with them more than I have to, especially right now, with all the stuff that I have signed on for work-wise. People write to me asking for advice, to help them with their term paper, to help them with some outlandish idea they have for a website or some massive plan to "help people" and it's all very sincere and cool but I'm not the guy for the job. How can I give out advice? I write them back and tell them the truth, that I have no time to help them and I am sorry and best of luck. They're cool about it. It's all I can do to try and get it all done every day at this point. Things should slow down a little around mid-September.

It's all work I can do if I just stay on point. I can do that very easily. I live alone and I don't see anyone I don't work with. It's the only thing that interests me at this point—getting the work done. Realizing the objective and getting onto the next thing. I am not anti-people but I just don't want to hang around and talk that good time bullshit with anyone as much as I just want to get it done.

I got a letter today from a guy who doesn't like me anymore because he just figured out that I don't like the Bush Administration. I wonder how I hid that one from him for so long? He's mad at me and feels let down. Oh well. I wrote him back and told him that perhaps he shouldn't like me anymore and it's probably a good time for him to tell all his friends that I suck and to hate me. Might as well just get to the truth as quickly as possible.

A good leg workout tonight. I hit sets of squats and then immediately into ab crunches and then right into hi-rep leg presses and then back to the squats. I felt fucked afterwards but I know I got in a good one. For me, it's all about August now. It's all about the shows. I am doing work every day. Every day. No days off. Not a single one. I don't know what the hell a day off means. I really don't. A brutal schedule keeps me honest. This is the best way to be. Completely living it. Inside the machine. I don't want to know anyone and I don't want anyone to know me. I just want to wreck it. The rest—fuck it.

Leg and ab work out. 1 bowl oatmeal, rice crackers, 1 bowl rice + vegetables, hard candy, water, carrot juice, coffee 1 cup.

04-27-06 LA CA: 2201 hrs. We got a lot of work done today for the IFC show. All I did was a lot of teleprompter reads. I got news that we will be getting The Fall on the show but unfortunately I will be in San Francisco or at least on my way there for that thing I'm doing for the West Memphis Three. I don't know exactly what it is I will be doing past just being there but Damien Echols asked me to go to it and I told him I would so I am. That's a week away. My eyes are shutting on me as I write this. I got about 5 hours of sleep last night so I am pretty done.

I got a call from Ian right when I wrapped out from the T.V. show. It was good to hear from him. He and Amy are working on new songs for their band The Evens. He says it's going well but they've got a lot to do.

The next five days are flat out. A lot of flying and stuff to do. At least I got all the writing done for this set of episodes. I have to get the radio show together for Tuesday. When can I work on that? It will have to be on one of those flights or pre-show on Sunday. Whenever I'm awake with an hour to spare I can finalize it. It's almost there. I can get it all done if I stay on my own and work. It's the only way to do it. There's no temptation to procrastinate on any of this stuff. It's getting around people that sometimes becomes a task. It's one of the reasons I like traveling. It allows you to dodge people so you can get the work done. It's almost like people are the anti-work. It sometimes feels as if you have to hide from them to get anything done.

1 bowl oatmeal, rice crackers, bagel, cream cheese, 1 cookie, fish, rice, water, coffee 1 cup.

04-28-06 LA CA: 2305 hrs. Today was long and I am very tired and don't want to sleep but I have to. I have to read a script before I sleep tonight and wish I could just pass out now but I have to slug it out for at least an hour. I have been up since 0600 hrs.

In short, the interviews went really well. It was great to see Penelope Spheeris and Perry Farrell. What struck me about Penelope was how humble she is. She prefers doing documentaries and indie stuff over the big stuff. She's very punk rock. Not like she's wrecking the studio but she's just not into the bullshit and tries to keep it real. And Perry has always fascinated me. I have never met anyone like that guy. Amazing frontman and an amazing mind. He talked about the upcoming three day Lollapalooza in August. The way he has worked his way into the major label industry is interesting to me. He's a hus-

A Dull Roar

tler at heart and he has hustled the industry for decades. He's made a lot of people money so he can get listened to but he's one of the more 'street' types I have ever met. It was always cool watching Perry and Ice-T hanging out. Both of those guys have that thing. They keep it interesting, that's for sure.

So, it was a good day of work but I am too tired and burnt to write anything but the facts. The interviews leave me oddly depleted. It's a lot of work keeping that ball up in the air. In my case it's much easier to be interviewed than to do the interviewing.

1 bowl oatmeal, yoghurt, granola, rice crackers, bagel, cream cheese, 1 cookie, veg. lasagna, water, coffee 2 cups.

04-29-06 LA CA: 1832 hrs. I am out of here and on the way to the airport in about four hours. My chores around here are pretty much done and I am going to take a couple of hours to just sit still and listen to some music. At present, I am listening to the first Generation X album. When the weather warms up, there's a few albums that I always go to and this is one of them. The Rites of Spring album on Dischord is another. For me, these are warm weather listens.

I had an almost three hour meeting earlier today with Joe Lynch, who is the director of Wrong Turn 2. I like Joe. I like his enthusiasm, I like the work he's put into the set up for the film. He's got a lot of energy and I am looking forward to working with him. We went over my part and the different aspects of the character. I think we see the guy the same way. There wasn't anything he said that made me wince or cringe. I think we'll have a good time.

I take work on a film or anything else I sign on for with great seriousness. I don't take myself seriously in a film. I just give it all I have.

I will be flying all night to get to PA. I will get in tomorrow morning and have a few hours to turn it around before I get picked up and taken to the venue. I hit stage and then go back to the room for a few hours of no sleep and then back to the airport and back out here.

I am restless and keyed up. I am not trying to complain. This week was a blur between the radio show and the IFC show. That's how I like it. I like the blur and the constant activity. At least I think I do. It's all I know at this point. It doesn't occur to me to do it any other way. It keeps me away from myself and most of the time that's a good thing.

Damn, it just hit me that I haven't worked out yet. I will change up in a few minutes and do a one-arm chest work out and do some ab work as well. Well, so much for hanging out with this cup of coffee and the music. It's better, I was getting distracted by thinking about going to the airport soon anyway.

1 bowl oatmeal, rice crackers, salmon, spinach, tomato soup, hard candy, 1 cookie, water, carrot juice, coffee 2 cups.

04-30-06 Erie PA: 2338 hrs. I have to use part of this entry for the Dispatches entry on my website because I am too tired to write up both. I have to get my head down as soon as I can. I have to be up at 0400 to start making my way back to LA.

Today was a drag up until show time. The flight out of LA was packed out and I was in a small seat next to a large man who took up a good part of mine. The flight was over an hour late getting out because of rudder problems. I missed my flight in PA and had to get on another one three hours later, screwing up my hoped for afternoon nap scenario. I fell out at the gate in Detroit and woke up a little before flight time. I got a little bit of sleep in the room before pick up time. By stage time, I was good to go though. I always am. I am always good enough to get out there and fear of failure and desire to do well takes care of the rest.

So, it was a good show I think. The students were really cool and hung in with me the whole time. I watched a little news before I went out to the venue. I wanted to talk about the President at the Correspondent's dinner the other night but it made me too sick to go off on it. To see Bush with that guy all made up to look like him sharing the podium, doing his funny Bush impression was sickening. They should have both been covered in the blood of soldiers and the press core should have been calling for their fucking heads.

In a few hours, I get up, go back to LA and somehow go to band practice. I am looking forward to it but it's going to be a long day and Northwest Airlines is really lame. Off I go, of course.

None of this stuff is easy but it's a lot less difficult doing it alone. It would be much harder to have to call some girlfriend and check in. I don't mind the bad sleep and the flights being fucked—that's travel. What I do have going for me is that I am alone and don't have to be anything for anyone. It's the only way I can see pulling all this off.

Tomorrow, basically a few hours from now, will be hard work all the way to quitting time.

Protein bars, hummus, pita bread, vegetables, water, coffee ? cups.

MAY 2006

05-01-06 LA CA: 2331 hrs. Got in from PA. Met up with the band guys and we went to the office. From there we went to Cole Rehearsal to get ready for our performance on the IFC show tomorrow. I felt washed out but I woke up at band practice. We played the songs we will do for the show tomorrow over and over. *Volume 4, All I Want, Burned Beyond Recognition, Starve.* It sounded good but we didn't stay in there very long as everyone was a little baked from the flights.

After that we all went to eat dinner and hung out. Chris is staying at my place and Melvin is staying at the office. Sim is off in the wilds of Los Angeles.

Tomorrow's performance will be the first time the band has played in front of anyone besides Road Manager Mike since Osaka Japan 1997. It's a small slice of history which will no doubt be lost upon the crew shooting the footage.

So, another period of time spent with the band in the practice room. How many years of my life have I spent in those places? Anyway, it sounded good again. Whenever I am away from it, I sometimes wonder if we can pull this off but when we're in there doing it, it sounds really great to me. I hope I am not fooling myself. Management will be at the thing tomorrow and he has seen this band play many times so we'll see what he has to say.

I started in PA this morning and it's been a long day and I am not good for much writing-wise. Tomorrow will be a test.

Band practice. 1 tostada, hard candy, water, coffee 1 cup.

05-02-06 LA CA: 2310 hrs. I learned some things today while we were taping the songs for the show about how I will have to train for the tour. We have been practicing hard and I have been training but a few songs into the taping, I could feel my legs weakening. I also felt some instability in my abdominal and lumbar regions. I see now how I have to train. I have to cane my body with reps. I have to batter my body with medium weight and high reps.

We played well I think. We played *Volume 4* two times, *All I Want* three times, *Burned Beyond Recognition* three times and *Starve* once. We hit it hard and I was drenched and tired. It was nothing like band practice. I am going to up the training as the weeks go by. I will really need it to realize the objective. My body needs a shake up. My body needs to be beaten into shape. I am in pretty good shape but not in tour shape so that's what I will be working on. Glad we had this time to check it out.

Management was at the taping and I asked him what he thought and he liked it. We still have a ways to go and I have a lot of work to do.

Never be satisfied. Satisfaction is a dead end. It's nowhere. I am an enemy of satisfaction. I'll take dissatisfaction any time. Anything that will motivate me to improve. There's nothing like my own limitations to inspire and infuriate me. I suck—so I have to work harder to achieve half of what others do. I am not good at anything—so I have to do it over and over again until it is beaten into my skull. I understand that pain hurts and I can take a lot of it. It's one thing I'm good at. Another thing I am good at is sticking out the bad choices I have made over and over in my life. Bad choices that have cost me days, weeks, wages, self-respect and who knows what else. I can stick it out though. I put myself up to something and as soon as I see the mistake I have made and what it's going to take to see it through, I just do it and take the beating. Record deals with motherfuckers, tours that were poorly booked by pieces of shit, I just do it.

That's how I'm going to train. I am going to train knowing I am a weak piece of mediocre shit and I will beat myself into an animal state where I can take any fucking thing. That's when it's real. When you stop articulating it and start surviving it. That's when you know you're onto something.

Did the radio show tonight. It was a good one but it started out strange. Evan Shapiro, who is my boss at IFC, has a show on Indie 103 once a month and it ends when mine begins. I didn't know that. I walked up to the door of the studio to go in and start setting up and saw all these people in there. I checked my watch and we were about three minutes out. I went right into panic mode. The people came out and one of them was Evan, who is a really cool guy. He very casually asked how the taping went and I can barely answer him because Engineer X and I are throwing CDs around, trying to get the intro music ready and the first song up because we're now on in less than a minute. I said "fine" as I'm weaving around the people who were still in the room and throwing my notes up and trying to plug my headphones in. We barely got it together in time but we did. Evan probably thinks I'm some kind of jerk but at that moment, there's nothing more important than the show. I was told later that he was supposed to hang around and talk to me about something during my show. Not tonight.

I have to get up in a few hours and do 3.5 hours of phone press and then get fitted for a body mold at 1500 hrs. for the film. I have no idea what that's all about but if it's interesting, I will report tomorrow. My schedule prevents me from watching the Daniel Johnston taping that goes down tomorrow afternoon but I can't get out of this fitting.

I am tired but happy that we played well today. It's good to be alone. The more time I spend by myself, the better I am. I fucking hate everything most of the time.
Band plays for TV show. 1 bowl oatmeal, 1 piece of salmon, 1 burrito, hard candy, water, coffee 2 cups.

05-03-06 LA CA: 2210 hrs. Today was long. I got up at 0600 hrs. and have been going ever since. I feel pretty good for some reason. This was the press schedule that was waiting for me:

0900: Broken Newz
0915: Hip Online
0930: Movie Web
0945: Bullz Eye
1000: Groovevolt
1020: Crave Online
1040: Artist Direct
1100: IGN
1120: Amazon.com
1200: Shakefire

I felt pretty burnt afterwards but it wasn't all that bad. All the journalists were cool.

After press, I had time to get some office work done and chase down e-mails back and forth from management. I had to leave around 1400 hrs. to head to the Valley for the fitting for the WT2 film. I didn't bother to read what was going to happen, I figured I'd deal with whatever I had to deal with when I got there. This is what the e-mail from management said:

#1 full head and shoulders 1 inch thick hollow hydrocal positive relaxed expression.

#2 gypsona bandage 2 piece negative torso casting (standing position from under arms to crotch).

#3 clear digital photos of dale's head/face straight on, 3/4 front right, 3/4 front left, profile right and left, and back of the head (no expression).

#4 color swatches of neck and side of torso at the ribs and love handles.

#5 hair clippings from head.

I pulled into the parking lot of what looked like a self storage building, a long parking lot with a lot of metal roller doors and anonymous black glass fronts. I went to the address and walked in. There were movie posters everywhere so I figured I was in the right place. At least I hoped I was, as there was no one around and nothing had the name of the place on it. A moment later, a man came out and told me they would be ready in a few minutes and invited me in to look around.

I have never seen anything like this place in my life. It's a company that makes bodies, body parts, monsters—it was nuts. It's where they did all the creatures for *Buffy The Vampire Slayer*. They do all the bodies for *Crossing Jordan* there as well. I saw a shelf with a row of heads in different states of decay and mutilation, their faces twisted in frozen agony. I asked one of the guys what they were all about and he said it was a bunch of heads they had just made for an episode of *The Shield*.

There was a row of tables with rubber bodies on them. One massive one, entirely covered in burns, was actually half in and out of a body bag. I think this was something used in *Crossing Jordan*. There was a naked girl on the table next to the burned man. I asked if they ever use the bodies over again and was told they use them over and over. Sometimes if they get the specs for a different looking head but the body is what they need, they remove the head and put a new one on. Lance, the guy that was taking me around, said that this particular body had been through the ringer and used a lot of times.

I can't explain how strange it was to see what looked like a city morgue mixed in with monsters of all sizes, heads from *Babylon 5* and a massive shark hanging from the ceiling. It was amazing. Bodies, heads and parts all over. In a box, there was a human arm that looked so real it was hard to look at. These guys really know what they are doing.

I still didn't quite understand what they were going to do with me. Lance asked me if I had ever been body cast before and I said no. He said I was about to be. They gave me one of those unitard things to put on and told me to come back out after I had suited up. I came out and they handed me a bucket of stuff that looked kind of like mayonnaise. I asked them what it was and what I was to do with it. I was told that it was hair conditioner and it will make a layer between the unitard and the plaster and that I was going to apply it to myself in the crotch and ass area. Understood. I coated myself liberally and they did the rest. Moments later, three of them were wrapping me in strips of plaster and cloth straps soaked in water and all of a sudden I was in plaster from my armpits to my thighs. That stuff gets pretty hot. We waited a little while for the plaster to dry and then they cracked it off me.

Next they made a cast of my head. They put a rubber cap on my head and glued it to my forehead and neck. Then they covered me with I don't know exactly what but within minutes I was encased in a thick coat of something from my head all the way down to my shoulders. There were holes for my nostrils so I could breathe but past that, I couldn't see anything and could barely hear them. They would ask me now and then if I was alright and I would kind of rock forward and back to indicate yes. It was really interesting in there. It felt like the inside of my head was the entire world. While I was in there, I thought that it might be cool to spend a few days like that. I was really enjoying it when they cracked me out of it. It's a perfect mold of my head. I don't know exactly what they're going to use it for but all this made for an interesting afternoon.

This next month of training will be harder than last. Each month I will ratchet it up. I have a lot of work to do and the next few weeks will be a lot of movement. I have to look over some notes now as I am interviewing Adam Carrolla and Patton Oswalt tomorrow. I have been listening to Patton's Feeling Kinda Patton album a lot lately, he's one funny man and so is Adam. Should be a good day. No one has given me a schedule yet for when I fly to NYC on Friday. I will actually have a little time off there on Friday night. After I get in I'll go to the regular hotel, catch a workout and get some writing done. I have to get a back cover comment for Colby Buzzell's book My War done and read up on Shirin Neshat, the woman I will be doing the television show with on Sunday. Have I mentioned the TV show I'm doing in NYC on Sunday? I don't remember. I'll write about that tomorrow when I get a chance.

I have been going for it hard lately. I have been getting by on about 5 hours of sleep a night. Last night I got about 4.5. I have a long day at the studio tomorrow and then a very early flight to NYC on Friday. I will get good sleep on Friday night. Tired from the shoulder workout but feel ok. Wrist getting better and better.

I am keeping to myself and getting it done. I took the mail section on the radio show site down to cut incoming mail so I don't have to pull away from the work. Weeks ago, my goal was to get to April with all the goals reached. I did that. Now I'm trying to get to September in one piece. Or some pieces. As long as I get the shows done, I really don't care what shape I'm in at the end of it.

Shoulder workout. 1 bowl oatmeal, salmon, spinach, rice crackers, hard candy, V8 juice, water, coffee 1 cup.

05-04-06 LA CA: 2310 hrs. I have to get up at 0400 hrs. to get ready to go. I am packed and squared away. I am really tired from the day but want to get some writing done here.

Today I interviewed Adam Carrolla (the comedian who took over Howard Stern's radio slot in some markets) for the IFC show. I have met Adam many times over the years by being on his old radio show *Love Line*. He's a very funny guy and always really cool to me. We talked about what he's learning about handling morning radio. He said something interesting: he said it's a marathon, not a wind sprint and you really have to pace yourself. I have always respected Adam. He comes from real work, got a break and has never looked back. He does radio, television, he produces shows with Jimmy Kimmel. He kicks ass and I admire him. Anyway, it should be a good interview for the show.

After that I did a lot of teleprompter reads to nail down all the intros and outros for all four shows.

Around 8 pm., comedian Patton Oswalt came in. I am a big fan but have never met the man. Patton is on that TV show *King of Queens*. I have never seen it.

I am really tired and keyed up because I have to be up soon. I have a lot of work coming up. I am feeling pretty good though. I am liking the way the training is going and I will get some gym time tomorrow night in NYC. I just have to get on that plane so I can get a few hours of sleep.

1 bowl oatmeal, bagel, cream cheese, salmon, rice, rice crackers, hard candy, V8 juice, water, coffee 1 cup.

05-05-06 NYC NY: 2301 hrs. I am in the coffee place across the street from the hotel. 7th Avenue is in front of me. I am alone and The Damned's <u>Machine Gun Etiquette</u> album is in my headphones. I got here around 1500 hrs. I don't remember anything of the flight really. I slept for almost all of it. I read Colby Buzzell's book <u>My War</u> before and after I racked out.

I got out of the car and was walking into the hotel and a man who was standing next to the door recognized me, said hello, introduced himself and we shook hands. People are pretty cool to me in this city.

I went up to the desk and checked in. The man recognized me and welcomed me back. I think stuff like that is kind of cool. Same thing happened at the airport in Los Angeles hours ago. I like that I fly and live in rented spaces all over so much that I am somewhat familiar to these people. It's a small thing I have earned for myself. It's not currency but it makes me feel like I get out and into the world on my own terms which is more important to me than a lot of things.

I went up to my room and set up camp. I brought food with me so I could keep my diet fairly consistent. These rooms have small kitchens so it's cool to bring your own food and stuff.

I left the hotel near 1800 hrs. to go to the deli down the street. The sun was setting and the air was dry. It was one of those perfect NYC moments when I feel that I am in the right place at the right time. That happens to me all the time in NYC. I am not always happy to be alive. There are long expanses of time where I am not really interested in anything, even breathing. I snap out of it but sometimes it gets to me. It's been a part of my life for as long as I can remember. The point I'm trying to make is that when I am in New York City, THE City, one of the greatest inventions on the earth—I feel pretty good. I feel good that I am alive and in that moment. Nothing or nowhere in the world has New York City beat. Not the greatest museums, the greatest leaps in technology or science, or even Paris, Tokyo, London, Melbourne or St. Petersburg. New York City beats them all. I don't know if I could live here again but I hope to always come back here every year until I die.

A man just came up to me. I saw his mouth moving so I figured he was talking to me. He asked me if I was me and I said yes. He said he was very nervous and I told him he shouldn't be. He said he was from Russia and he's here studying literature. It's too bad he was so nervous, I wanted to ask him about a few Russian writers but it didn't seem like the right thing to do. He pulled out a folded piece of paper and asked me to sign it. I did. He thanked me and left. I am listening to The Damned's 3rd album <u>Machine Gun Etiquette</u>. *Smash It Up Pt. 1* has just started playing through my small speakers. This album makes me think of Washington DC.

Back to what happened outside the deli. I was walking to the deli and all of a sudden I stopped and looked towards the intersection. Around the corner is the place where we have been practicing lately. At that moment, I wanted nothing more than to be on my way to band practice. All of a sudden I felt lonely, a feeling that doesn't really happen to me anymore. I wanted to be with the guys in the room playing the songs. I can't wait until we're all back together at band practice and getting the final tightening done to the set. It's been quite an emotional ride being back with Chris, Sim, Melvin and Theo again. That we are a band again is really something amazing to me.

It sure is good being in a band again. I went a couple of years without being in one and it was strange. The workouts had no real meaning. I wasn't training for anything. I feel a lot better being in a band again. At least I have a good answer when people ask me if I am still doing music. I don't feel as old somehow. When I was talking to Perry the other day, he said that the music keeps you young and I think he's right. I told him that we were at band practice getting the rust off the machine. He said that I was making his point. Without the music, you get rusty. I do at least. It's giving me a reason to be. It's hard for me to stay focused without a goal or an objective. Being back in the band has given me a reason to hit it. It's been great so far. Sometimes it's all you need—a reason to keep going.

As the plane was approaching JFK today, I thought of DC and Ian. I thought how cool it would be if the plane was landing at Dulles

International. One of my favorite rituals is taking that shuttle ride across to the other terminal to baggage retrieval. I am always so happy when I am on that short ride because I know that soon I will be heading into DC. The ride into DC from Dulles is the best—all those trees and the smell of the air. New York is amazing but I wouldn't mind being in DC tonight. I will write Ian later tonight and tell him that I am here and check in with him. I talked to him the other day. It's always great to hear his voice. I have known him over 30 years now.

I wonder if people who have been released from prison ever walk outside and think to themselves that they have a lot of catching up to do. I get the idea that what exists outside the prison walls is somehow more real than the world they lived in behind the walls of the facility and they have to hurry up to be like everyone else on the street. I feel like that all the time. Sometimes I feel like my life is just starting and I have been woken up from a coma. That's why I travel and live all over the place. I have a lot of catching up to do. I don't know what it is that I am trying to catch up with besides my expectations and the constant rage that courses through me. I think the idea of harmony in your life is death. Fuck harmony. It's 2318 hrs. I think I'll go to the hotel gym and do a bunch of fucked calisthenics and then run very hard and very fast. I got the tentative routing for the tour dates a few hours ago. It's all the reason I need right now.

Shoulder/triceps/biceps/treadmill. 1 bowl oatmeal, protein bar, minestrone soup, sesame bars, V8 juice, water, coffee 2 cups.

05-06-06 NYC NY: 2333 hrs. Today was good. I am in the room. For some reason, the coffee place across the street closes early on Saturdays. It's one of my favorite NYC rituals, to sit in a coffee place and watch the people go by at night. It's always so animated. In an hour, so much humanity will pass in front of me. Packs of girls with their jeans painted on them, most of them with a studded belt that hangs diagonally, the men who talk to themselves and wave their hands all over the place, the groups of young men with their sports gear and gold who always seem to walk so closely together. People have so much energy in this city. I get revved up when I am here. NYC makes LA seem like a dead city, a bad idea, a failure, ruined and wait-ing for tear down. NYC, on the other hand, is crackling like bare, elec-trified wire. It's real life. High caloric burn happening to you right now. When you're here, you're in it and there's nothing you can do but deal with it. When you're in New York, you're a New Yorker. You don't have a choice. No city I've ever been to makes me feel like that.

I walked all over tonight. I have a strange attachment to this city. I used to live here and even though it was only for several months many years ago, the city holds a lot more memories than a quarter century of living in Los Angeles. If I never saw LA again, I don't think I would miss it. It's that kind of place. Nobody's city, as they say, or as the Dominick Dunne book title puts it so aptly, "Another City, Not My Own."

I used to live in the East Village when I was here. I always felt old and out of place when I lived there. I had a lot of good times there but a lot of bad too. The making of the Come In And Burn album was hard on all of us. We should have kept a few of those songs, taken a break and then come back and started again. I get a lot of letters from people who tell me they really like that record. It should have been a record and that's all but it turned into a lot more than just making a record. We spent a long time on that one and it took on a strange life of its own which took a toll on all of us.

When I am here, walking around, I sometimes get very emotion-al when I think about all the time and all the stuff I have done in this city. I get emo, man! Way emo! I wrote almost all the lyrics for Weight and CIAB here, a good deal of Eye Scream and Solipsist and put together Do I Come Here Often? as well as typed in a lot of Get In The Van. I always write and get a lot done when I am here. As soon as I get into the 212 area code, it's on and I am cooking. I wish I had a place here. I would come here all the time.

NYC's a place full of people that I walk through alone. I don't hang out with anyone anywhere really. Besides DC, I don't get to a city and call people. When the plane lands almost every single person gets on their phone and calls someone to tell them they have arrived.

I am always relieved I don't have to do that. Sometimes if I am meeting Road Manager Mike somewhere, I'll call him so we can find each other in the terminal but past that, I don't call anyone.

For me, cities are best walked through alone at night. Cities at night are some of the best places I know besides being alone in a room. I like this room I am in now. I have coffee and some music coming out of the small speakers. I am fine on my own. It's a relief. This scene would be lame with a female here. Females aren't lame but nothing ruins a good room more than a human in it with you. When I see two people walking together, holding hands or whatever, I try to remember when I did shit like that. I did. It was a long time ago.

Alone is the only thing that makes sense to me now. It's the only thing that provides relief. It's the carrot on the end of the stick. If I am good and work really hard, I will get some time to be alone in a room or in a city at night or in a place where no one recognizes me. I don't hate people. I am, in fact, a lot better with them than I used to be. A lot better. Alone is just a good thing.

I like seeing the people I work with. I never get tired of them. It's always good to be with Road Manager Mike. He's one of the best people I have ever met. I hope he comes out on every tour I'm ever on. That would be really cool. I like being around the guys in the band. It's impossible for me to express how great it's been to be back with them. I love those guys. I don't think they'll ever understand what they mean to me. Even when we weren't together, I always thought of them.

I would like to think that we could do some good shows and a good record. I don't know how long this will last but I am really liking it at the moment. Management came down to the set the other day to see the band play for the IFC show. I asked him later what he thought. He has seen this line-up play all over the place. He said it blew him away.

It feels good, the songs, the playing. It feels like it's the real thing. I don't know, perhaps I'm fooling myself. I think if we weren't hitting it, one of us would be noticing. I wrote this to the band earlier:

It's late. I am in NYC, gearing up for this TV thing Sunday.

We are going to be apart for some time. Let's remember what we are taking on in July and August. Apparently, the show in Costa Mesa went on sale and sold out. Expectation will be high.

Sim, I hope you keep doing your shows on the shore. These band shows are going to be physically intense. Chris, please keep playing all the time. I know you're busy out there and all but stay in the music as best you can, get your runs in, etc. Melvin, you play 7 days a week I know. Theo, I don't know, don't hurt your ears and stay out of trouble. Everyone, please listen to the songs now and again to keep them in your mind.

I wish we were all together here at practice. Management called me to tell me the playing we did the other day blew him away. I don't think he thought it was going to suck or anything but it knocked him out. There are going to be some people with high expectations when we hit stage. We cannot disappoint. This is us. Our music, our everything. This is what it's all about.

I am training hard and concentrating on being at peak for the shows. I don't give a fuck. I want to break motherfuckers into pieces.

I love all yall. --Henry

The wrist is getting better every day. I did hi-rep stiff legged dead-lifts with light weight tonight. It doesn't hurt to pull so there's a lot I can get done. After that I ran hard and staggered back to my room. I am going to do a lot of hi-rep exercises all the way up until the tour. I plan to just beat on my body, to temper it over several weeks with steady and controlled battering. I am going to stretch every single day.

All over the city, there are posters for the movie <u>The Proposition</u>. It's so great to see Nick Cave's name on the poster as the screenwriter. People have told me it's really great. That's one I have to get out and see without fail.

I should try and get to sleep. It's the last thing I want to do.

Deadlifts/treadmill. 1 bowl granola, soy milk, minestrone soup, ravioli soup, 2 packs peanut butter crackers, sesame bars, V8 juice, water, coffee 2 cups.

05-07-06 NYC NY: 1702 hrs. I am about an hour away from meeting up with Shirin Neshat and doing the shoot. I don't think I have explained what the show is all that well. I will do that later in the week, maybe Monday night in LA. I finished the book <u>My War</u> by Colby Buzzell, I think it's one hell of a read. It's coming out very soon in paperback. I recommend it. Colby asked me to send him a back cover thing so I sent him the following:

Colby, done with book. Really great. Here's some comments if you could use them:

I remember reading Colby's journal entries on the internet when he was filing them from Iraq. I was amazed at how heavy the material was but what really knocked me out was how sharp and vividly intense his writing was. <u>My War</u> is the real deal reportage from the ground. There's no way any reporter could have brought this back. If you care about our brave soldiers in the fray and want to get an insight into what it's really like out there, <u>My War</u> is essential reading. --Henry Rollins

Colby Buzzell went into the war in Iraq with attitude and came out with his attitude intact. In the period of time between entry and exit, he was ambushed, shot at, mortared and otherwise threatened. <u>My War</u> shows us how much the truth means and how hard it is to stand up for it anywhere. He's a brave man and his book should not go unread by anyone. --Henry Rollins

Colby Buzzell's riveting work <u>My War</u> is an essential read for anyone who wants to learn about what the Iraq War was like for the men and women on the ground. The ever-present and very real life and death situations which seem completely insane to civilians are in fact, their day-to-day existence. <u>My War</u> takes you right into the middle of it. --Henry Rollins

Colby Buzzell might very well go down as one of the greatest war time journalists of all time. <u>My War</u> is right up there with Michael Herr's <u>Dispatches</u>. Imbedded reporters are great but their range of access is limited—they don't have to shoot back. I'll take Colby's word over a journalist's any day. <u>My War</u> should be read and passed on. --Henry Rollins

Like I said, it's a hell of a read. I got to the end very quickly. It was good to just pick up a book, read it and be done. It was nothing like all the other books I have been wrestling with for the last several months. Not to say that Colby's book is light on content, it's intense as hell and real and well written, especially for a guy who just started writing. It's just that I have been reading history books for the most part and they are slow going. It takes me weeks and weeks to get through them. I have been learning a lot. I am hoping that Shirin can turn me onto some books that will help me learn more about Iran. I am very interested in that country. Besides all the things that are happening there, I think Ahmadinejad is one way and a great part of the population is another. I should get ready to do this thing.

1 bowl granola, soy milk, protein bar, sesame bars, salmon, vegetables, squid, V8 juice, water, coffee 2 cups.

05-08-06 LA CA: 2346 hrs. Back in LA and already I want to get out of here. I am still buzzing from NYC. I always write a lot and think a lot out there. Out here, it's a lot harder.

I got back from the thing with Shirin Neshat near 0200 hrs., it was an amazing time. It will take me a couple of days to find the time to detail the night because it's late and I have press and stuff all over tomorrow. I am really burnt from not sleeping and the wrist is mad at me for doing squats tonight. I wrapped it really hard and went for some sets of twenty. I am trying to beat my legs once a week with hi-rep lifts. I did sets of squats and then onto hi-rep leg press on a machine.

It's such a come down to get back from wherever I was to LA. It's a depressing place and it gets to me right away, especially coming from NYC. It would be so great to be at band practice and song writing sessions in NYC all summer. I have that film coming up in June and I want to do it but I also wish I was at band practice and training for a tour. I will get all the training done. I am on schedule pretty much. Wrist held me back a little but I am getting a lot of work done nonetheless. I am tired enough to get to sleep soon. I wanted to get a run in but I don't have it in me.

It's not all that hot out here yet but I am feeling a mood change inside me. I know I am feeling different with the band tour a reality. It's a whole other way of getting through time for me. When I know I have that unavoidable and ultimate truth coming closer and closer, everything I need to do becomes obvious. The last couple of summers, I didn't have the music tour to train for, to head towards.

I have now just figured out that I don't live life all that well. I know people who live all of each day. I wish I could sometimes but I can't. People tell me I do but I don't agree. I get through time to get to other time. As it is now, I want to get through May, get another run of episodes for the IFC show done and get into this movie. I have three talking shows this week and then that's it until the two in June. I want to do these 3 shows this week but I want to get them done so I can start getting my head around the IFC show and the movie. When I am doing the movie, I will take advantage of the fact that I'm on location to get other stuff done. I get a lot done on location shoot dates. There's not a lot else to do when not working on the film so I work like a bastard. A hotel room has always proven to be a productive environment for me. I will be training hard and writing a lot. I am looking forward to it but ultimately, it's all about the last weeks of July for band practice and then August for the tour. In September I can fall over a little but until then, it's flat out. I will be alright if I stay to myself and stay on my schedule. I can do it.
Leg workout. Protein bar, rice and shrimp, tomato soup, water, coffee 2 cups.

05-09-06 LA CA: 2333 hrs. Back from the radio show. Dispatches thing sent off to web man Tony. Today was long and the show tonight was good but a little strange as Engineer X was out sick and there was a substitute. He was cool but it wasn't Engineer X so we didn't have the hate going that we usually do. Today was long and unremarkable. It's like a lot of days I spend in LA. I work at the office all day then I go back to the house and keep working. My house looks like the office. Years ago when I got the house, it looked like a house for a little while and then it slowly started to look like the office as I will eventually turn almost any flat surface into a work space.

The next few days will hopefully be eventful. I have three shows in three days starting two nights from now. I will be driving out to the desert tomorrow to prep for a motivational speech I will deliver on

A Dull Roar

the 11th. From there I go to San Francisco to be part of a benefit for the West Memphis Three. Damien Echols wrote and asked me to be on this thing so I told him I would. It felt good to be able to say ok and pitch in.

The event happens at an art gallery. Some of Damien's art will be up and there will be people speaking: Jello, Penelope Houston of the Avengers and some others. The original date was the night I'll be in Palm Springs. I called the promoters and told them Damien wanted me to do the thing but I had another show that night. I asked them if it would be possible to move the show over one night? They checked with the gallery and they were cool with it so they moved the whole thing over just for me. Whoa! Do I have power or what?! I am glad they were able to do that because I didn't want to let Damien down.

The next night I go to Big Sur to speak at the Henry Miller Library. It's a big deal for me as Henry Miller is one of the reasons I have tried to write. I have read and re-read a lot of his stuff and it still speaks to me. I have been reading his work for almost 25 years but it feels like I have been reading him all my life. His writer's voice speaks to me very directly. He's got a lot of fans. I am looking forward to seeing the places he used to hang around in up there. I don't know much about his Big Sur period. I have not read all the books he wrote while up there but I have read some and they were good. They are good but different than his Paris era writing, which is still my favorite work of his. He was such a young maniac. It's all very inspiring. I don't know how the show will go but it's sure to be an interesting few days of travel and little sleep. Sounds good to me!

Oatmeal, tomato soup, 1 cookie, 1 ice cream bar, 1 burrito, water, 1 diet Coke, coffee 1 cup.

05-10-06 La Quinta CA: 2325 hrs. In the hotel room. I like hotel rooms better than my own room. My own bedroom is pretty cool. It is small. Wood floor and some bookshelves. I have a lot of books in there. All my F. Scott Fitzgerald is in there and Thomas Wolfe too.

There's some books I read on and off. I have some art books in there that I like to look at now and then. One is called <u>German Expressionism 1915 – 1925 The Second Generation</u>, another is <u>German Expressionism: Art And Society</u> and the other, which is my favorite is called <u>Soviet Art 1920s – 1930's</u>.

I would rather look at paintings of people than look at real people. I would rather read their work than talk to them and I'd rather see them on screen than in front of me. I like looking at those art books. I don't know a damn thing about art. I don't know anything about any of the periods or what it meant at the time. All I know is what I like to look at. I like Francis Bacon and have almost every book I have ever seen on the man and his art. A lot of the books contain images of the same paintings over and over but I don't care. I identify with the way he saw people. I think his paintings are clearer than photographs. I feel good when I look at these books. I met a woman a few years ago that I really felt something for. I told her about the books and she said that we should sit and look at them sometime. For a second there, I felt something. Whatever that thing is where you are momentarily unsure that you're alone in the world and there is possibly someone you could connect with. I felt it right when she said that. We never ended up looking at the books. I would rather have the books around than her so fuck it. Books are always, ALWAYS better than people. Things are better than people. I would rather have a DVD than someone to talk to on a long night.

Anyway, I am at this really nice resort place in La Quinta CA. It's one of those expensive resort places. The help is all over the place. Everywhere you turn, someone asks if they can do something for you. Very nice. I was here last year on the same mission. Jeremy, who heads up SpeakerCraft, asked me to do a talking show out here a year ago for his employees who are here for a three day get together. I like Jeremy. He started the company and now he's worldwide. He's a big guy with tribal tattoos and looks like trouble when in fact he's incredibly bright, funny and a good man. He asked me to come out and talk to his people this year and I said sure so here I am.

La Quinta is about 125 miles from LA. Pretty much a straight shot out the 10 E. I stupidly left at 1500 hrs. and it was a parking lot most of the way.

I listened to Randi Rhodes on Air America shredding the Administration and then when she faded out and I put on a CD I made last year when I had rented a car in DC last summer and wanted to listen to music I used to play in my car when I still lived there: UK Subs, DEVO, Teen Idles, Art Attacks. About an hour into the drive, the desert started to take over and man made structures became less and less.

All around me, there were green and brown mountains, desert scrub, countless windmills and then all of a sudden, a ridiculous looking double row of identical houses in the middle of a sea of dirt. The view out of the back of the houses is the highway. What would make you stop your car and say, "Honey, we're home!"? When I see structures like this in the middle of nowhere, it makes me think that man is just out of place on the planet and only conquers it by ruining it. It's insane to see buildings in the middle of desert sprawl, the highway littered with coke cans and signs for Burger King. At the same time, it is amazing to drive for hours on a highway and think that at one point, men had to put the road down on the ground and that it was backbreaking work that tore muscle and burned skin. Men herniated themselves and worked for years so someone could drive at 80 miles an hour for a few hours.

Hundreds of thousands of miles of road all over America. There's a lot of stories in those miles. It's one of the greatest American achievements. The American needs to go. The American can't stop moving. We are driven because we have the luxury of movement. Many Americans don't know any other way. If you took our cars away, if you limited our access to the option to go even slightly, we would freak the fuck out. Americans are screaming about the price at the pump but at the end of the day, everyone knows they would pay whatever it cost for the ability to go when they wanted to. I don't even look at the price of a gallon of gas at the pump. I just fill the car and go. What it costs is the last thing on my mind. All I know is that I want to go more than I want anything else. I want to go more than I want companionship, more than I want happiness—anything.

Many of us Americans are on the brink of insanity for a good part of our lives. We are intoxicated with freedom, opportunities, options and choices. Some of us have completely lost our minds. Many of us bang around between the borders and coasts like a fly between the window and Venetian blinds.

When I am in the American desert, I always think of Joan Didion and her California writing. Images from Play It As It Lays and Slouching Towards Bethlehem come to mind. The American desert is the American loneliness. The American savagery. A lot of people died so there can be fast food outlets and garbage stuck to cactus. People were slaughtered like locusts hit with insecticide so hundreds of years later, postcards could be sold of this barren outback. The parched crust of the American desert holds the memories of blood and scattered bones, screams and fires at night.

The American in the American desert. City smarts will not work here. This environment can kill. It humbles and troubles the American. He must move through it quickly. The American is not wanted in the American desert.

I just came back from a run. That hurt. It's still hot out there and running in it is pretty miserable. I like running because it tells you where you're failing and what you need to do. The first thing that the run told me tonight was that the burrito was a bad idea. The first mile, I wanted to vomit, have a little lie down and die. It got a little better but not much. I need to work on that middle section. More abdominal work and more work on the quads. I can do it. I know exactly what I need to do. This month, I up the amount of protein I take in and as soon as my wrist can take it, get into the push-ups every day scenario. It might take awhile but I'll get there.

Almighty Allah save me, I just turned around to look at the television that has been on with the sound off and there was Dick Cheney's daughter. It's Dick Cheney with breasts. O, vision of Hades!

A Dull Roar

This is a good room but I am not able to enjoy it all that much because my mind is on the show tomorrow night. I have made some notes which I will work on later and tomorrow as well. I am looking forward to the show but I want it to be immediate, impactful and full-on. The last thing you want to do is come off like you are putting anyone down. It's not like I'm better than anyone in that room and it's not like there's a bunch of deadbeats in there. It's not the finest line to walk but all the same, I want to be positive. Last time I talked about diet and exercise and how lucky they were to be selling a good product. SpeakerCraft gear is fucking ridiculous, super high-end, killer product. I can't wait to go out there and tell them about how much I love to work and how great it is to be in a service industry. I do love it. I love working at my company, filling the orders and rocking the people who trust us. It's great when we get together at the company and figure out how to make the prices low without sacrificing quality. It's a great challenge. This is the stuff I will talk about tomorrow night.

Back to hotel rooms. How many times in my life have I walked up to the front desk of a hotel? I wonder how many nights of my life I have spent in hotels? I like hotels. Duke Ellington loved hotel rooms. I like the anonymity of them. Ever since I was shot at, I've preferred hotel rooms over any place I've ever lived in. I like the lack of access from the outside. I get my best sleep in hotel rooms. I never sleep all that well at the house in LA. I always look forward to staying in hotel rooms. One of the best parts of doing that film next month will be living in Vancouver in a hotel room. I like that it's a temporary dwelling. I like having only a few things. When I am in a hotel room, it all makes sense. I have some notebooks, a computer, something to play music on and a door that locks. I don't really want for more. When I have my backpack and my tool bag of clothes and whatnot, I feel like that's all I want, all I need. It's a simple way to live. If I made a lot of money, or won the lottery, I would live in hotels most of the time. I would just pick a city somewhere in the world, exist there for awhile and then go exist somewhere else. There would be no need to stop. I have things. I have books and records mostly. Almost all of it sits in storage. I go and visit it sometimes.

As I get older, I want less and less. I want less and less from people too. I am not looking to make new friends. I am not looking to make new enemies either, I just want to keep everything streamlined as much as possible. Like a lot of people—I just want to go. I just want to go and go. I like going from A to B. I finish the show and the B is now the A and it's time to go. Why stop? Family? Love? Fuck it.

Run. 1 bowl oatmeal, 1 yoghurt, 1 burrito, water, carrot juice, coffee 2 cups.

05-14-06 LA CA: 1721 hrs. Where to begin? I have not had a chance to write here since Thursday night.

I did the show in La Quinta. That was Thursday night. It went alright, I guess. I had the same feeling about it as I did at the one I did last year. I think they have gotten all the use out of me they need but if they ever did ask me to come back again, I would pass. Not because I don't like Jeremy and his company, it's that I didn't feel like I was as good as I wanted to be and I have felt that way both times.

Ok, so I did that show and afterwards, talked to Bill Fold, one of the guys who was a huge part of the Rise Above album. Bill is one of the guys who puts together the Coachella Festival every year and does consultant work for SpeakerCraft and who knows what else, he's got his hands in so much intense stuff all the time. He's one of those guys whose cell phone rings nonstop. Anyway, we got to talking about the West Memphis Three and I told him about the thing at the Minna Gallery that was happening the next night and he said that he was going to go. That's Bill. He just moves on stuff. I admire him a lot. He and I talked about doing something benefit-wise for the WM3 boys. He wants to meet Lorri Davis, Damien Echols' wife.

After I was done talking with Bill, I grabbed my bags and headed for the car to drive back to LA. On my way out of the driveway, I hit the stopwatch to check my driving time against last year which was 2 hrs. 2 min. The first several minutes of the drive felt like a hair dryer was blowing in the car but then I hit a downhill part and the temperature dropped several degrees in the space of less than a mile and stayed that way all the way to my driveway, which I reached in 1 hr 59 min.

I re-packed and went to sleep as fast as I could. I was wired from the show and the drive so that took awhile but not too long. I woke up in the morning and went to the office to get some things done before I had to go to the airport to head to San Francisco for the WM3 benefit at the Minna Gallery.

I got up to SF and jumped into a cab and headed right to the gallery. I got there and walked in. Nice place. Damien's artwork was up and while still early, the place was already hopping. I did press and photos for awhile and talked to people who were hanging out. Jello Biafra came in and we talked for awhile. It's always good to see him. Soon after that, none other than Jonathan Richman came in and I talked to him for some time. He's the real deal that guy. Great player. I talked to the WM3 attorneys about the DNA testing and what's up with the case. They are optimistic but cautious and working steadily on it. They said the DNA evidence isn't giving them any Hollywood endings but it's proving to be a good thing in that none of it implicates Damien, Jesse or Jason.

As the hours went on, more people kept showing up, there was a great attendance. It's so cool that the boys have such support. People were very kind to me. San Francisco has always been good to me. I hung out and did a lot of photos. I didn't mind, people were cool and it took my mind off the depression that was eating my guts. When a wave of depression hits me, it feels like I am eating myself from the inside.

Later on in the evening, I went on stage and spoke for a little while and that was cool. Again, a great crowd. I didn't stay on there too long. Penelope Houston of the Avengers went on after me and read from Damien's book Almost Home and after that, Jello got up there and talked for a pretty long time.

I introduced Bill to Lorri so Bill could tell her about the ideas that he and I will be working on in the months to come.

Past that, I hung out, talked to a lot of people and took pictures with a whole lot of people. Usually I am nervous around people but this was alright. We were all there for the same reason and everyone there was really cool. There were only a couple of drunks there who talked to me but they knew they were wasted and didn't make me endure them for too long. That's the thing with people who really don't get that they're drunk, they think everyone they talk to is fucked up like they are.

Eventually I made my way out of there and back to my room and slept for a few hours and then went to the airport and on to Monterey.

I got to the hotel room, checked some e-mail and went to sleep. I wanted to get as much as I could as I had a 1630 pick up and my voice was not 100% from talking for so many hours the night before and not sleeping much. I could feel the lack of sleep over the last ten days or so getting to me. I woke up with enough time to get a shower/shave and stagger into the lobby to get picked up for the ride to Big Sur.

I am going to take a break from this for awhile and get some provisions for the week. I don't know all the stuff I have to do this week besides a lot of writing but it's probably best to get food for the next few days so I don't have to think about it.

Later: Back at it. I am looking at the clock. I see what the rest of the night will be. I will be here at the desk. I finished all the notes for the radio show for Tuesday and it's a good show. Before I rack tonight, I will put down some ideas for next week's show. I have to get ahead of all this stuff as best I can. I also should get some outlines done for the writing on the upcoming IFC show stuff. I will be writing all week.

Anyway, I got a ride to the Henry Miller Library via Mary Lu who is married to Magnus who runs the library. The drive from Monterey to Big Sur is incredible. Redwood trees that are at least a century old line the road and now and then they stop and you can see across to a side of a mountain covered with trees. The trees have a presence that makes them more than trees. They stand so tall and mighty and silent, they are like judges of character. To cut one down would be the wrongest thing to do. They are so imposing, I felt as if we were not driving of our own free will but only with their permission. The road is a small line of concrete in a valley of trees, it was almost as if we were driving between two walls of an ocean.

Eventually, we pulled into the library's driveway. The front lawn is where they have the show. It's a clearing in the middle of incredibly tall trees, behind the trees is a mountain wall with more trees growing out of it. The stage faces the trees and a rock wall that forms a massive curtain. I walked up on to the stage and looked out and up. It looked like I was at the bottom of a bucket made of trees. It was easily one of the most extraordinary sights I have ever seen.

I soundchecked and my voice bounced off the trees and mountain with a reverb I have never heard before.

The library itself is basically a bookstore and used to be the house of Miller's very good friend Emil White. I met Magnus there and looked around a little. I bought two Henry Miller DVDs. I have never really seen the man move so I am looking forward to checking them out when I can.

Mary Lu took me up to her house where they had some food waiting for me. We drove along a narrow and winding road with the mountain on one side and the other side dropping off to the Pacific Ocean. It would kill you if you went over, there are no guard rails, you just have to get it right every time.

We pulled off the main road and went up a very steep and narrow incline and Mary Lu informed me that this was the path that Miller would walk down to pick up his mail. I have seen a picture of him in a loin cloth pulling a cart with all his mail up that hill. She showed me the exact spot where that photo was taken. This was really great for me as I have read enough of his Big Sur era work to be well aware of his daily ritual of getting the mail. His house is owned by a private family who doesn't encourage visitors but I did see the path that leads up to it.

Mary Lu's house is amazing. It's a very small wooden structure that sits over a creek where they draw their water from. The house is powered by hydro and solar power. The views out the window are beyond belief. There's no sign of civilization, just massive trees, mountains and the ocean. On one side of the small room, there's a wood burning stove that actually belonged to Miller.

After I ate, I stood outside and tried to imagine what it would be like to live in the middle of all those trees for weeks or months on end. How would you feel about the outside world? You might never want to come out again. You could go on there and just disappear into it and just live. That would be an interesting way to finish it out if you could afford it. Just break it off, no explanation, no press release, just get a place, a four-wheel drive vehicle and be done with it. Might not be all that bad. You could go for years and not have to know what's happening in the big bad world. I could never do it but it is an interesting idea that you could willfully cut yourself off from the world and make up your own reality that wouldn't hinge on what the Bush Administration is up to. I'd rather stay in the game but all the same, it's one hell of an idea. Mary Lu has been living there for decades. She and Magnus have no plans to leave.

At 2004 hrs. I went out onto the stage and talked for a couple of hours. It was a great audience. I was told they came from all over for the show. I met people afterwards who flew in from places like the Midwest, Los Angeles, San Diego and Washington state.

I met everyone who wanted to meet me and then Mary Lu took me back to the hotel in Monterey. I slept a few hours and then went to the airport and worked on the radio show notes as I waited for the flight.

I was in seat 5A. Across from me was an older man and by the window was a female college student. She told the man she was majoring in psychology and religion. I had my ear plugs in and was trying to sleep but she talked nonstop for the entire flight. I did everything I could to drown her out including sticking my ear on the wall of the plane to fill it with the engine noise, which didn't help all that much. I dubbed her voice "the killing noise" ala Jimi Hendrix. Thankfully it was a short flight and I got out of the plane as quickly as I could and away from the Killing Noise who had by then attached itself to another victim.

I got back here and racked for a few hours and then got back to it. I got the radio show all done and listened to all the music and it sounds good.

I got a letter from a woman who is in the Army saying she was "mildly upset" about what I said about Cindy Sheehan on the IFC show last night. As I recall I said something pro Cindy. The woman in the Army said that no one forced Sheehan's son to enlist, etc. It's funny, the stuff I get complaints about is never the stuff I write, it's always, I mean always, the stuff that someone at the show has written. Anyway, I answered her letter:

"Sgt. You were mildly upset? Oh heavens! Oh no! I live in a country where the President started a fake war and got a bunch of good kids killed and mangled. I will have to pay my taxes towards all the court time ahead when his staff gets indicted and I will have to pay for their beds in prison. I have to watch an idiot take the greatest Military force in the world and exploit their talent and lives for bullshit, how do you think I feel?"

I bet she doesn't like me anymore. I'll have to live with that.

I guess there was some press or something around the WM3 benefit because I got this letter from someone who wouldn't sign their name to it:

"Hey Henry. Since your such good buddies with Demon Boy on Death Row, ask him why he had testicles in a jar in his bedroom. Where did he get them from, eBay? Come on man, read the case file............"

Incredible. Where do people get this stuff from?
Minestrone soup, salad, water, carrot juice, coffee 2 cups.

05-15-06 LA CA: 2223 hrs. At the desk. I got a lot of work done today. I wrote the first of the five things I have to write for the upcoming IFC shows. I will get one done tomorrow and another by Friday. I should be out of that and able to go over them again and tighten them up.

I put together a radio broadcast for one of the Tuesdays that I'll be gone. The first half is Buzzcocks stuff so I did some research and got all the chronology together so I can try and make sense. There were some things I didn't know, like how long bass player Garth Smith was in the band. You have to know stuff like that. The second half of the show will be Coltrane's A Love Supreme in its entirety and a cut from Kulu Se Mama and one from the Quartet Plays album. I will do the writing for it later. I just need to get the between song stuff done and Engineer X will glue it all together in post.

The President spoke tonight. It's amazing how he can talk and not say anything. All the pundits who came rushing in afterwards had much more to say than he did. Bush kept repeating that his immigration reform could in no way be considered amnesty. He said that a couple of times at least. I think that his staff thinks that if he says it enough times, everyone will just go along with it and perhaps not discuss the finer points of what he was saying, not that there was anything to be gleaned from between the lines. He talked about getting digital fingerprinting on guest workers so they can be tracked. That will take a long time and be very expensive. Until then, things will stay as normal, with bosses paying these people whatever they feel like and things will be just peachy. He's putting the National Guard at the Mexican-American border but said, "the United States is not going to militarize the southern border." Putting the National Guard at the border but not having them do anything is nothing but wasting money. I really don't think he's interested in border security. Too frustrating to dwell on.

Today I had to get a medical check up for the film. I emerged from the parking garage and walked north on La Brea towards Hollywood and came upon a car accident. A Mexican fellow in a BMW had rear-ended two black women who were driving in a Mercedes Benz. The Mexican man was young and had his West Hollywood gay thing going. He was sitting on the curb talking a mile a minute while one of the black ladies was standing in front of him with her hands stretched out wide saying, "I WISH you would get up! I wish you WOULD!" He kept sitting there saying, "I am Mexican! I am a Native

American! This is my land! You all took it from me! Well, not you all, you were brought here in ships but this is my land! I am a Mexican!" The black lady was telling him she didn't care what he was, he hit her car.

I stood and watched for a minute as this insane bit of street theater played out and then went into the building. I got through the check up and the doctor said I was in good shape and turned me loose. When I went back outside, the accident players were all still there but now there were cops, parking cops, a fire engine and an ambulance. No one was doing anything. The black ladies were smoking cigarettes and the Mexican man was leaning against a car talking to an officer. Tax dollars working hard!

I went back to the office and worked there for awhile and then went to the grocery store and then back here. I got in a good workout. I wrapped my wrist really hard and did a lot of hi-rep bench presses, dumbbell presses and a lot of ab work.

Tonight, I have been going back and forth with management and Road Manager Mike, who I think might be doing this tour with us. Oh yes, this is a few days old and it merits no short amount of attention: Road Manager Mike wrote me the other day and told me he is quitting road management. He said the work was too sporadic and when it was on, it was too routine. I completely understand. There's so many things he can do and he wants to get onto the next chapter. I understand. I understand 100%. It was unsettling to hear it though. I was onstage soon after I got the letter. I was able to put it aside until after the show but it was what I thought about most of the way back to LA as I drove across the desert. We have toured together for 8 years. We had some great times. He's one of the finest people I have ever met. I would do pretty much anything for him. Management asked if he would do this last tour in August before he moved on and he said he would. That's so cool. I hope it's true.

Anyway, we were going back and forth about details for band practice and the endless work that is part of the pre-tour build up. Where will the band practice, how can we save on this or that, how much will it cost to bring Theo over, will the money be right? I already told them that I'll do the tour for nothing if they need cash to get other things paid for. I don't give a fuck. I just want to do the shows.

Until I die, there's nothing but the work. I don't care about fame or popularity—none of that stuff means a damn thing to me. I don't care if people hate us or love us. I just want it to be real and completely intense and honest. That much can be done. What anyone else thinks of it is out of my hands and not my concern.

I can get all this done if I work every day without looking from side to side. I have no problem working split shifts. I don't think of a day/night as anything else. I finish work at the office and as I drive, I start lining up the next set of tasks I'm going to do. It's no problem. I just work and that's it. Fuck the rest. I don't want anyone calling me who's not part of the work. I don't want to talk to anyone about anything that's not on the itinerary. This is the only way I can stand myself.

Life itself is boring. Life itself is just walking death. I like discipline and repetition. I like confrontation and that which does not come easily. Here in this room alone I am good. I am good to go. I don't hate people but I would rather be alone than with anyone. I used to be different. I used to get lonely. Now I don't. It just doesn't make sense to me. Alone and working is the most honest, uncluttered and pure state I know. I am so glad I found it. I can't imagine being married. I can't imagine being any closer to anyone I know than I am now.

Sometimes I feel a temptation to move to the middle of nowhere and just finish it out in obscurity. Sometimes I want that more than anything. It's an idea I keep in my mind and pull out on long airplane flights.

Having this tour to build up to has been good for me. It's given me a reason to keep going. I don't give a fuck when I die.

Bench press, dumbbell press different types of ab work. 1 bowl oatmeal, 1 yoghurt, 1 protein bar, salmon, spinach, rice crackers, water, carrot juice, V-8 juice, coffee 2 cups.

A Dull Roar

05-16-06 LA CA: 2242 hrs. Back at the house post radio show. I thought it was a good show. It's still a good time doing the show but when I have to be in and out of town all the time, it becomes hard to keep it going. I will be gone most of June, July and August so I don't know what I'll do about that. Perhaps I'll have to stop doing the show. Before Engineer X and I did the show, we did a pre-tape for later use. I think it will be a good one. The first hour is all Buzzcocks and the second hour is Coltrane's <u>A Love Supreme</u> in its entirety plus *Chim Chim Cheree* from the <u>Quartet Plays</u> album.

Whenever I try to do something that has any permanence, like the radio show, it never works. It's not like I'm trying to make a normal life for myself but more often than not, stuff like the radio show, which I really like doing, becomes a problem because of the nature of my schedule.

That's why I like living in hotels. I like having a bag and a few things that I can walk out the door with. I don't have a lot of things besides some books and records. For me, they are more reference materials than anything else. I don't miss any items when I am away from them. A few items with me and I am good to go for however long the trip is. I don't think of being on the road as being away from anything but I sure think of being here as being away from the road.

Damn. I think I'm going to have to quit the radio show sooner than later. I'll talk to management tomorrow and see what can be done. I don't think many people listen to the show so it's not like anyone will lose any sleep over it. I am not under contract and it's a throw away time slot and I think the people who run the station would understand.

More and more now, it benefits me and the work I want to do to keep my distance from any relationships that aren't work related. I know of people who have lots of friends, some even have children. and they get a lot done. I don't have that kind of talent. The only way I can do all the things I want to do is to keep to myself as much as possible. It's not a problem. It's not like I am fighting some great temptation to live another way.

I have to be up early for press so I better try and get some sleep. I am nowhere near tired. I think I'll go into the garage and do some kind of work out and see if I can wear myself out a little.

Dumbbell flys. 1 scoop whey protein, 1 bowl oatmeal, rice crackers, 1 burrito, 2 tacos, water, V-8 juice, coffee 2 cups.

05-17-06 LA CA: 2314 hrs. Got most of my writing done. Only a little more to do. I got a tentative schedule for the band tour but I'm not allowed to show it to band members yet as part of it's still being booked. It's looking good to me though. Looks like there's a show in DC.

Training is going well. It's every night pretty much. Tonight was a lot of dumbbell work on the shoulders, barbell shrugs and ab work. Getting the training and the writing done helps my mental state. Being alone as much as I can also helps. People—I can't figure them out and I am getting tired of trying.

It is difficult for me, with great exception, to deal with people past a certain point. When it goes past the point of where I can deal with it, it's all I can do not to bolt. I did a movie with a female years ago. She was part of the crew, very cool and hard working. I talked to her now and then on the set. I recently got an e-mail from her asking what I was up to. I wrote her back and said I was doing this and that, just working away as usual. I get multiple e-mails back from her asking when we can get together, what's a good time, she needs to see me right now, what am I doing, hurry, etc. I just deleted the letters. It repelled me. I'm sure she meant no harm. Hell, I don't know what she meant, I don't care. For the most part, I regret almost every human relationship I have ever had that went past the point of casual acquaintance. That's a fucked up thing to say but it's the truth.

The older I get, the clearer things become. I know my future has only a finite amount of time. I reckon I could possibly have, if I am lucky, another two decades of functional use from my body before the joints break down too much. Rip it hard onstage, get some books read, see some countries and then do what millions before me have done and die. I am not spiritual at all. I think all that shit is fucking hilarious. Stick your karma up your ass. People kill and then go home and call it a night. Nothing happens. No god comes down to punish. Pat Robertson lies to his followers with his insane bullshit and they stay with him. They deserve each other. All those September 11th highjacker pieces of shit watched porn in their rooms the night before they went on their mission. I wonder what Allah would say about that? Shows you that at the end of the day, they were like a lot of men. Those polygamists you see in the press now must know that it's just a matter of time before they get raided. Their god won't be there for them when the ATF comes in.

Shows are coming closer and I am toughening my mind and body. Tomorrow I am going to do some uphill runs.

Front raises, side raises, barbell rows, ab curls from pull up bar, shrugs. 1 cup yoghurt, 1. scoop protein powder, 1 bowl oatmeal, rice crackers, 1 ice cream bar, minestrone soup, salmon, spinach, water, V-8 juice, coffee 2 cups.

05-18-06 LA CA: 2344 hrs. Just punched up the Dispatches thing and sent it in. I am really tired and can't stay long. I have to be up at 0700 for press. Earlier tonight I curled up on the couch because I couldn't keep my eyes open and a few minutes later the phone rang and I woke up and didn't know where I was for a second. It took me three rings to get to the phone. Thankfully it was only management. I don't get more than 1-2 calls a week here. Now and then I get a call from a woman I went out with over a year ago. She still calls to talk over the fact that we don't go out and to waste my time. I don't have that thing that tells you who is calling so when I pick up the phone I am rolling the dice. I hate it when that woman calls. I am not going to hang up on her. I don't hate her but I sure wish she wouldn't call again. If someone told me they didn't want to talk to me anymore, I would stop calling them. If I kept calling a female who didn't want me to, it would mean something different than when it's the other way around. Everyone knows that. I don't want the police dragging me away. I am not the type who gets all bent out of shape over stuff like that. It's not an "injustice" to me. I don't go along with all that bullshit about when men do something it's this but when women do the same thing it's whatever. Just deal with it. It's just life. If you want to get involved with another human, you can expect all that human stuff to happen.

Personal relationships make for friction. I like high speed low drag situations and now do all I can to be in that state as much as possible. The first thing that kills it is being close to someone. I don't remember what I ever saw in it. Like I was saying, management called and I got caught up on the schedule that came to me in bits and pieces earlier in the day. The amount of work and travel is intense but I can do it. It's what I want. I am out of here in a few days to Vancouver Canada for about ten days for wardrobe, table read, rehearsal and some shoot days. It's a very civilized shoot with a 5 day week. That means I have a weekend off in Vancouver coming up. A weekend off means I can train really hard on Friday and Saturday nights and get some good chow. Being up there will allow me to really concentrate on work. There's the film work of course but there won't be the normal distraction and sticking points like when I am here. I am working on lyrics and getting somewhere with them but I always write better when I am on the road. My life is out there, not here.

The wrist is almost 100%. I am benching light now and it's feeling good. I will get a lot of running done up there and that's one of the things I am looking forward to. I like those hour+ long runs where you sweat out completely and start thinking all kinds of strange shit because you're so deep into the run. I am almost there with the runs. I will need about a week to get to the point where I can hit that kind of run a few nights a week. I am going to try and run as many days as I can.

Depression is pushing in on me and I am pushing back at it. The training is helping. I am getting a lot of time alone at the moment and that's good as well. At the office I have had press to do but it's on the phone and it hasn't been all that long. I have about three hours of it starting at 0800. I have been working at the office all day and then taking the work back here and resuming. It's the only way I can stand myself. When I am working, I am not so fucked up and angry.

A Dull Roar

Whatever it is that's wrong with me could perhaps be neutralized or in some way lessened with medication. I know I am fucked up. It's one of the things that makes it harder and harder to be around people. I am behind a wall and I deal with the people on the other side through a very small window.

1 cup yoghurt, 1 scoop protein powder, 1 bowl oatmeal, rice crackers, 1 ice cream bar, minestrone soup, tomato soup, water, V-8 juice, coffee 2 cups.

05-19-06 LA CA: 2354 hrs. I couldn't get to sleep last night. I fell out about 0300 hrs. and dozed on and off until the alarm went off at 0700. I did phone press for over three hours and then did office work. I finished the radio show for this coming Tuesday night. I will be taping it and a couple of others on Sunday so I have to get those together tomorrow.

Tonight has been good. I did some hi-rep sets of squats and a lot of ab. work. The wrist will allow me to do push-ups on my fists, which is great. I have been doing short sets whenever I get up from this chair.

I listened to news earlier today. There's been a sudden rise in insurgent activity in Iraq and it looks like more US Forces will have to be sent in. Every time I see Cheney and Bush defend this thing it makes me mad all over again. Today Bush said his fucked approval ratings are no big deal, people are just "unsettled." I hope that someone reading this likes the job President Bush is doing. If you're reading this and you think that way, you're a fuckin' idiot. Fuck you. Get out of my country. Take the Bush family with you. What great depths of misery this administration has plunged America into. He says that knowing how to speak English will help someone in this country promote themselves in this country, like he knows a fucking thing about working a job and earning a wage, much less speaking the English language. If your child became an adult with such an alarming lack of language skills, wouldn't you feel that you had somehow failed as a parent? Can you imagine him working in the real world? He was a liability to every single company that his father got him a job at. Pathetic. And the people who stick up for him, I guess they're just idiots.

Earlier today, I thought a lot about Washington DC and my old streets. I wish I had time to go check in there before I start work on the film and the tour starts. There will be a show in DC at the 9:30 Club. I guess that will be my time in DC this summer. I don't think I'll have time to get there before September at this point. Maybe July for a couple of days. I should look to do that. Every once in awhile I like to go there and walk on the streets of my old neighborhood and see the trees.

I have trained myself to not miss anything or anyone living. I just don't. I see people when I see them and until then, I just go. I do think about my old neighborhood though. I don't think about the people there as much as I think about the streets and the way it all looks at night and the way the air smells at different times of the year. When I am there, I walk all over the place at night for hours just keeping to myself and being on my own in surroundings that I have known all my life.

There are some dead people I miss badly. I think a lot of people have that sadness. I miss Ian's mother Ginger. I am so glad we had some cool times hanging out and talking. She was always so great to me and we became closer and closer as time went on. Her kindness means more to me than I can explain. Some of her ashes are here with me in my room. I was there for some of her last hours and watching Ian handle things at the house was one of, if not the mightiest, damn thing I have ever seen. I wish I had a tenth of his strength.

1 cup yoghurt, 1 scoop protein powder, 1 bowl oatmeal, rice crackers, 1 ice cream bar, salmon, spinach, tomato soup, water, V-8 juice, coffee 2 cups.

05-20-06 LA CA: 0319 hrs. In bed. Listening to Eno's <u>Here Come The Warm Jets</u>. I think this will be the third night straight I've listened to this record. I watched some CNN and got some more details on what's happening in Iraq. There's been at least six Americans KIA in the last few days. It's so hot over there right now. Those people are so brave.

I have a few days here before I leave town. This weekend will be a great alone-athon, a misanthropathon. <u>Warm Jets</u> just finished and now I'm onto Eno's <u>Apollo</u>. This isn't bad. Being alone in a room with

A Dull Roar

some books and some music and a notebook.

As the days go by, I am getting more and more focused on the shows. I will get some good workouts done in Canada. I think it will be a cool film to work on and I'm looking forward to kicking ass for our director Joe but I am also looking forward to the time alone walking around, working out and hardening myself. As the days lead up to the first show, I will be discarding everything that doesn't matter.

I have already taken the letter section off the radio show website. I have taken down the page to reach me at IFC as well. I got too much mail. Too many voices, too many fingers tapping me on the shoulder. I don't mind when people write and I have no problem answering letters as best I can but it became too much and I don't think it's a good idea to have all those voices in your head. All these people are cool, they take the time to write and they are very kind to me. I appreciate it. But I'm not much on correspondence and most of the time, I don't want to know, I just want to go and go. I like working until failure and sleeping alone in small, anonymous rooms. Nowheres and places unfamiliar suit me.

When I was younger, I always admired those people who were alone. I never admired the family setting. Never wanted it for myself. Never wanted to start one or account to one. The closest I ever got to being around a family with any regularity was Ian's family and for that I am grateful and fortunate. That being said, it's always great to leave and not have to tell anyone where you're going or work your time around someone else's. I don't mind it for business or band and tour stuff but the idea of calling a female and asking her where she is or having to check in and tell her where I am is just nothing I want. It's cool for other people but not for me. I want to live alone and when I see that I'm starting to lose it, I will jettison my belongings, get rid of all ballast and wait it out in a place where it won't matter if my body rots.

I'd like to die outside, perhaps in a backyard so body fluids won't leak into the floorboards and damage the structure and upset the people who are going to take the place next, not to mention drive down

the resale value. I stayed in a place once where an old man had died and he stained the floor where he lay. Back of head, shoulder blades, buttocks, calves and heels pretty much. It was all polished over with floor wax. It had been there quite awhile I guess. I don't want to do that. Not caring when I die makes things pretty simple most of the time. I have been up about 22 hours straight. Should rack for awhile.
1 cup yoghurt, 1 bowl oatmeal, rice crackers, salmon, spinach, minestrone soup, water, coffee 1 cup.

05-21-06 LA CA: 0319 hrs. Keeping some strange hours that will not benefit me in the upcoming days. I have to turn this around. I stayed up late last night. Slept pretty long. At least 8 hours. That leg workout put me down pretty hard. Today, well, I guess it's yesterday, I worked on some episodes for the radio show that I will go in and tape today at 1400 hrs. I have some pretty cool ones in the can. Not many, only three but it will take care of a few weeks worth of programming. I will try to get another one together before I go down to the station. I think I can do it. After I get back from that, I have one more thing to write for the IFC show and then I have to get a workout in. I want to see that special HBO is showing tonight, "Baghdad ER" I think it's called.

I didn't watch any news at all today. I just wrote and researched music stuff. I went to the office a couple of times to get some music, mainly to get information from the liner notes that I wasn't finding on the internet. Try as I might, I can't find the exact release date for the Ruts *Babylon's Burning* single or the exact release date of their album The Crack. I was trying to do some writing on the band for one of the shows. I will get more of it done when I get to Canada. I don't have to have the notes ready for a couple of weeks. I want to get my head around my lines for the film. There's a lot I have to get memorized and I have a lot of work on Tuesday on the set for the IFC show. I do a full day there and go right to the airport and head to Vancouver. I will be a little fried when I get there but I'll be alright. Damn, that means I'll need a ride to the set in the morning. I better get on that Monday. Can't wait to get out of here. After I come back from the radio station, I'll start packing.

A Dull Roar

I didn't speak to anyone today. Not one phone call, nothing. I only saw a few people in traffic and a woman who pulled over across the street from where I live get out and vomit on the ground. I heard her talking to someone else in the car. She sounded pretty drunk. I don't wonder why I don't get lonely. I like hearing that alligators are eating people. It gives me hope.

Bench press, dumbbell bench, flys, ab. work. 1 cup yoghurt, granola, 1 bowl oatmeal, 1 burrito, 2 tacos, water, 1 diet Coke, coffee 2 cups.

05-22-06 LA CA: 2341 hrs. In bed. Just sent in the Dispatches thing to our web guy. I have to be up at 0500 hrs. to go do the TV show all day. I will be doing all the "Teeing Off" segments in a row and then interviewing Michael Chiklis from *The Shield*. I'm looking forward to that. I have met him before when we were on *Dinner For Five* together. *The Shield* is such a great show.

I went to the radio station and recorded another show for when I'm away. I finished the writing for the TV show, finished work at the office and came back here. I tried to take a nap because I couldn't keep my eyes open but a few minutes in I got too nerved up thinking about all the stuff I have to do before I leave. I went back to the office and did a final look around and then came back here, checked my pack and did some other stuff and all of a sudden it was late.

I will work all day tomorrow and then go from the set to the airport and up to Vancouver. From there, I go to the hotel. I will get up at 0600 hrs. and get ready for a full day of work on the film. I think I have the weekend off. I will catch up on sleep and get some writing done. From here on in, it's pretty flat out.

The last few days before the thing starts are hard on me. It's not exactly nervousness, it's more like compression. It seems like I'm not getting anything done, or not enough done, or not the right things done.

I have to completely throw myself into this new work. I will be on set, in film mode. I have done this many times before. I will get a lot of workout done and that will keep my spirits up. I know I can do the film and I know I can do the shows in the UK. I just want to get it going. The only way I can pull all this off is to stay alone and focus on nothing but the work. If I have to deal with more people than the ones I'm working with, I don't function well. It will be good to get out of here and into another city.

1 cup frozen yoghurt, 1 bowl oatmeal, minestrone soup, coffee 2 cups.

05-23-06 LAX: 1822 hrs. I have a 1940 hrs. board. Where we shoot the TV show is close so it was a quick ride to the airport. We did good work today, we did a lot of work today. I got up at 0500 hrs. and did a final check on my pack. I left for the studio at 0657 and got there really quickly. I always try to get to wherever I have to be a bit early so I don't have to walk in and start immediately.

I got through the teleprompter reads pretty quickly. I am getting better at reading off the teleprompter and making it feel more natural. It wasn't easy at first but I have become better at it in the last two years.

At 1400 hrs. Michael Chiklis came in for the interview. He's a very cool guy. He showed up in jeans and a t-shirt. It was a great interview. He was really energetic and his answers were really cool. They shoot *The Shield* in some hard parts of LA and he had interesting stories about dealing with the locals. A lot of the gangster types know the show and they like it when they shoot in their neighborhoods. They are working on season 6 and he said there is a possibility of another season. He said it was all up to how good the storyline is and how they're feeling. They have had the same cast and crew for the entire time. They just lost Executive Producer Scott Brazil to ALS (Amyotrophic Lateral Sclerosis) and that was hard on all of them but they have been doing 14 hour days and he said they are really burning it up. That's good news for me. I could watch that show all day.

He left and we got back to work on more teleprompter reads. I did all of those and got into a car and came here. I fly soon and get up to Vancouver around 2300 hrs. Getting into Canada with a working visa can involve a long wait. All I can hope for is that the line isn't too long in front of me. I have to be up at 0600 hrs. so this will be my third night straight of not much sleep. I am dragging ass at the moment. I will get a little sleep on the way up there.

Tomorrow is the first day of work on the film. There's a table read, hair and make up, some rehearsal and a cast dinner, I think. The name of the film is <u>Wrong Turn 2</u>. <u>WT2</u> from here on in to save time. I am "Dale" and am listed as the principal actor, which really means nothing other than your name is at the top of the list of cast members. I am usually way the fuck down there but like I said, it doesn't matter, not to me at least. I do the film stuff only for the employment aspect. I am not trying to make it in the film business. I am trying to stay fed and working.

I have always liked money. I trust money. I don't like it to have it and spend on stupid things. I like to have it because it's the last line of defense between me and America. I love America but I know that it will sell me out in a heartbeat. That's Capitalism. Capitalism doesn't care about your hard luck story. Neither does freedom. I am not angry that America will not be there for me when I get old. Actually I am happy. I am happy that I understand, without any trace of doubt whatsoever, that America will not be there for me when I need it. I don't expect anything from America—the way things are now, I don't even expect Democracy. I definitely don't expect America to be there for me when I am old and in need of some of that money I've been paying into the system all these years. It will be long gone, spent on some war or some payout on a no bid contract. Like I said, I am not mad about it. That's just the way it is.

I am saving money now to survive America later. I am in a very unstable line of work. You're in and then you're out. I have had a longer time in this field than many. Heidi at my office says that I will always be able to get work. It's a nice thought but I don't hold with that at all. My bottom line is that it can be over at any time and all I am equipped for is minimum wage work. I figure a return to that is a great possibility and perhaps even eventual but I want to stave it off as long as possible and save for that rainy day that I know is coming.

So I am always grateful for the work when it comes my way. I am not trying to be an actor. I will give this film all I've got and make Joe, the director, glad he hired me. My mission on this film: To be prepared, on time and ready to deliver exactly what our director wants, as many times as he wants it.

In a lot of scenes in <u>WT2</u>, I am not with many of the actors. That's a plus for me because most of the time, I really don't understand actors. I have met many cool actors who were great but what it is that drives someone to do it full time, I don't understand and it's sometimes hard to be around. There's been a couple of actors I've worked with who I have kept in touch with: Yul Vasquez and Jim Cody Williams. I talk to both of them now and then. Both really solid guys and good actors. I really don't know any other actors past working with them on a film. It's that kind of work for me. I hit it and then I am out. I don't go to the premier, don't know when it's going to come out. It's like a tour for me. I finish the last day and then go onto the next thing. Always onto the next thing, that's how you want to do it.
Bagel, cream cheese, fish, vegetable, protein bar, water, coffee 2 cups.

05-24-06 Vancouver Canada: 2223 hrs. In my room. Tired but feeling pretty good considering my day. After customs and immigration I finally got to my room around 0030 hrs. I was in bed, lights out, pretty soon afterwards. I had a 0600 hrs. up for an 0800 hrs. lobby. I went to the lobby for the ride to the studio and met up with some of the cast members. I met the rest of them when I got to the studio. They're all really cool. I don't know any of them from anything but then again I don't know many actors. We did a table read and then I got fitted for wardrobe, did photos for a billboard they're using in the movie and then talked to the stunt coordinator about what we'll be doing, or what will be done to me, during the film.

We blocked some scenes and rehearsed. Everyone was really good, very professional. I think I am the oldest one in the cast by many years. Everyone else seems to be in their 20s. Like I said, they're all really cool and I think we're going to do a great piece of work here. The only way I can do a film is to be surrounded by people who take it completely seriously. It makes me step up my game to the fullest. All these people are serious. I was on set until about 1700 hrs. and got back here about an hour later.

When I walked in, I was tired and wanted to pass out immediately. I changed up and hit the gym here in the hotel, which is actually really good. I hit arms and then ran for a long time. I came out from that and got some sushi at a place around the corner from the hotel. It's one of those places where the sushi goes past you on a track and you just pull plates off and eat. That place is perfect for me. That's about all the time I want to spend waiting for food. I have a feeling I will be back there soon, like tomorrow. I am up at 0600 so I better get my head down. This is a bad entry I know but I am pretty damned tired and there's still lines I need to study. It would be good to try and get about 6 hours of sleep. Damned tired.

Arm workout, run. 1 protein bar, 1 bran muffin, 1 vegetable sandwich, sushi, water, coffee 3 cups.

05-25-06 Vancouver Canada: 2325 hrs. Not a lot happened today. Went to the set very early and then was released a few hours later after working with the director on my part. Saw all the cast there today. I am still getting their names straight in my head but they're all really cool. Hit shoulders hard and ran hard as well. I'll hit legs tomorrow and skip running.

I walked around tonight. I like walking around in cities I don't live in. I like living in this hotel and working here. I like being alone on the street and alone in this room. Alone is perfect for me. Alone allows me to live almost anywhere for as long as it takes to get the work done. The older I get, the less I care where or how I live except I would rather not spend a great deal of time in Los Angeles. If I had to live here in Vancouver for a year to get whatever the work was done, it wouldn't be a problem. I don't miss anyone, want to be with anyone or want to meet anyone. Getting caught up in the lives of others is the surest way to not get the work done. Alone is better. I see some people I know once in a while and it's cool when I do but most of the time, I'd rather be on my own. On my own in a city I am not from is great. It re-enforces the alone and makes me work harder. Less distraction. It was one of the biggest appeals of doing this film, that I would be working, making my way in the world and living somewhere else. It's freedom.

A lot of people don't like the alone. I don't understand why someone would want to have their cell phone ring all the time and always be on their way to meet up with people. I don't get it. I didn't get it even when I was trying to do it when I was young. Whatever. Just do what the fuck you want to do and get on with it. No need to worry about what others are doing.

I got a letter from Road Manager Mike a few hours ago. He said that X don't want to do the New Orleans show because the show falls on the one year anniversary of the Katrina storm. I don't know any other way to say this—how fuckin' gay is that?! I wrote RMM and management and told them to see if we can do the date on our own and give some of the earnings back to the city to help scoop them out of the mud. Perhaps we can just keep enough money to pay for our expenses that day. They're going to see what they can do. I guess they have their reasons but it's lame. It comes off like they don't know the road. Like they don't know that you show up and hit it, no matter where it is, when it is or how fucked up it is. I'm all about killing them every night now. That's it. Every night, ultimate fuckin' destruction. They want to headline, they're going to have to carry that headliner weight. I wouldn't want to go on after us. It inspires me. It made me run an extra half mile earlier this evening.

Hours ago, I watched a documentary about a Marine Reserve unit from Ohio on A&E. It was called <u>Combat Diary: The Marines of Lima Company</u>. They were there for about six months and lost something like 8 men. There was a lot of footage some of them took from the engagements. Pretty intense stuff. There were a lot of interviews with the men who got back and some of them were already showing Post Traumatic Stress Disorder. One man said that everything seems dead to him now. He's in his twenties and already he's partially dead on the inside. What are you supposed to tell these guys? You can't say that it

A Dull Roar

was all for nothing. You can't tell them that they were sold out and it was a bullshit deployment. The dead paid with their lives and the living are paying with their sanity. What will make it right? Either Bush and company all go to jail or they should all lock themselves in a room and pull the pin on a grenade. It's the least they can do to atone for what they have done to America, the Military and all the families they have destroyed.

The documentary profiled a woman who lost her husband. She has two children. What's her life going to be like now? Her children don't have their father. All that pain and misery for what? So the President can walk out onto some podium, crack some bad jokes and then stagger through some awful speech.

"I can understand why people are concerned about whether or not our strategy can succeed because our progress is incremental." – President Bush

Concerned? Huh? It's what? Incremental? People voted for you? Why? Out of pity? The Dixie Chicks are not having chart success because apparently country radio and fans of that genre don't like the band's stance on President Bush. So that's where Bush's 30-something approval is. It's country music fans. Well, that clears things up. Progress? It's incremental. Be concerned. Be very concerned.

What else. There was a report on CNN yesterday about a man who is suing a church or something because he claims Christ never existed and he can prove it. What's next, kids lawyering up when they find out there's no Santa, Easter Bunny or Tooth Fairy? It's sometimes very hard to hang in there with the human race. There's so much you have to filter out now. So much you have to dodge and delete to get to the issue.

I have found a way to be cool on the street and other places when people stare at me. I tell myself that I'm dead. I'm dead so there's nothing to worry about. I'm dead to a lot of what I see, and the conversations I hear. If that's the living world then I am dead. People walking around with copies of <u>The Da Vinci Code</u>, what a laugh. I will work, train, spend as much time alone as I possibly can and keep moving for as long as I can. And also, I will be dead. I didn't want to leave that out. Dead is good. Dead is steady. Dead gets it done.

Shoulder workout, run. 2 protein bars, 1 vegetable sandwich, vegetables, sushi, water, diet Coke, coffee 2 cups.

05-26-06 Vancouver Canada: 1753 hrs. Sitting in a coffee place listening to the last of the Boston songs on my iPod. I decided to get an iPod while sitting in a Starbucks many months ago when the one way idiotic blather of someone on a cell phone next to me made me distracted enough to realize that I had to do something. Fearing I wouldn't be able to handle the difficulties of an iPod held me back. But the experience in the Starbucks was the last straw. I agree with the great philosopher Seneca on so many things and in his essay *On The Shortness Of Life,* he says that life isn't short, that we only use the time poorly. I agree—but life is too short to be put through someone else's bullshit conversation on their cell phone. Well, I found my solution and it's a beautiful thing. Now I am onto Black Sabbath *Into The Void* and I can't even hear the conversation of the people in front of me, not one single word of it.

So, as if Allah had planned it, I got an e-mail today from press woman who said the Country Music Channel wants me to come on there and talk about the state of Country Music. Like I'm the go-to guy for that?! What the fuck are they thinking? They must have interviewed every other white person in the country and are at the absolute end of the line.

I wrote back to press lady and told her that the only way I am interested in doing it is if I can ask them why the country music community doesn't like the Dixie Chicks anymore? And how such a "pro-American" demographic can be so anti-American and support President Bush and his obvious hatred and contempt for the hard working men and women of the middle class and all the fine men and women who comprise the Armed Forces? How they can be so publicly "Christian" yet so privately pro drug use? How they can support a President who, through his actions and glaring inaction, doesn't give a damn about border security and continues to support Vicente Fox and his corrupt double speaking ass? Don't they know that Mexico is the last place the drugs go before they are brought in to addict and weaken America? If only they loved America as much as I do, perhaps they might think differently. I also want to know how the country music community would be so behind Toby Keith and his song *Get Drunk And Be Somebody*? Do they think alcoholism is a good thing? I wanted to give them a chance to clarify their positions on these topics because maybe they are misunderstood by the majority of America, who is most likely not watching the Country Music Channel, who should at least have the opportunity to hear things from the source. As it is now, a lot of the conduct of the Country Music Community is a source of great humor and curiosity for millions of Americans. At a time when oil is getting more and more expensive and dangerous to procure and the Cheney Administration flatly refuses to get America off its oil addiction, why are these people wasting gas on NASCAR events? Can't they do something more constructive with their time, like getting out of credit debt and taking better care of themselves so they will stop clogging the healthcare system with their poisoned carcasses that need to be medicated and serviced due to poor food choices and ignorance? I am tired of paying for them and as Republicans, they should be able to understand that. I just want to give them a chance to clarify their positions and defend themselves. I know it may take several hours, less if they start shooting.

I slept about 8 hours last night. I must have needed it. I am getting good workouts every day at the hotel gym. It's keeping my morale up. I'll be better when we get some shooting done on the film. I am starting to get anxious.

Chest workout, run. 1 protein bar, meal: 2 pieces sushi + seafood and noodles, small meal: sushi, some olives, small piece of flat bread, water, diet Coke, coffee 2 cups.

05-27-06 Vancouver Canada: 0144 hrs. Done with Friday and on to Saturday. I did one workout and then walked around for a little while. I kept thinking that I should go down to the gym and run. I started thinking about running and within a couple of minutes, it's all I could think about and so I suited up and went for a brisk run. Only a little over three miles but it was fast and I sweated out and now I feel pretty even.

I went over my lines and will do some more in a little while. Studying my lines over and over is one of the only ways I can get to sleep. I can't wait until Monday when we start principal shooting. I just want to get it going. Rehearsal is cool but I want to get it started. Call time for Monday is 0400 hrs. Not so great but I will do what I can to be tired by Sunday evening. Perhaps I should get up early on Sunday and go for that leg workout in the evening and if I hit it hard, I will be out of gas and be good to sleep for about 5 hours. That should work.

Earlier, I encountered some of the cast members in front of the hotel. They were going to see a movie. They asked if I wanted to go with them. That's really cool of them to ask me. I declined but thanked them for inviting me. They don't know me so they don't know the fucked up loner I am.

I am, for the most part, left alone on the streets here. It's great. I get recognized here and there on the main streets but people are always really cool. Some people here who read that daily journal I keep on the site know I am here and have been writing me, asking if I want to meet up with them, women have been asking if I want to go out. It's all very friendly.

I watched the news a few hours ago and saw footage of Bush and bunk-buddy-in-low-approval-ratings Tony Blair together talking their bullshit. They know they have fucked up massively and are trying to cover their asses. The whole meeting was nothing more than a desperate attempt to pull their appalling poll numbers up. It won't work because all anyone sees now is blood all over them. They should have come out covered in the blood of soldiers. The stage should have been covered in amputated limbs full of shrapnel from IEDs. There's nothing they can do now. Rove and Cheney got their little monkey to start this shit up and bitches like Tony Blair and John Howard jumped right in because they saw the potential profit and have dreams of dominance in the Middle East too. It's never going to happen you fuck-ups.

You know why US-lead forces will never "win" over there? It's not because our forces aren't great, strong, brave, mighty, skilled or awesome, it's because the fight isn't righteous. It's not WWII. It's Vietnam, it's the Soviet-Afghan War. Of course the Russians couldn't win that one. They were there for the wrong reasons.

And it's the same thing over and over again that makes me furious: that those motherfuckers Bush, Cheney, Rumsfeld, Rove and Rice, who have never seen any war at all, have no hesitation about sending other people's children to war but won't send themselves or their own children. That's all you need to know. That's it. And that's where the bullshit walks. That's where all those neo-cons like Hannity have to shut the fuck up because they have never gone to war either and they know they're fucking pussies shouting orders from the sidelines. There's no hell hot enough for cowards. And that's what they are. I hope someone who likes these people is reading this. I am right and you are wrong. You voted for cowards and you're getting what you deserve. All those people will die like cowards and so shall you.

How come no one in the mainstream press has the stones to call these murderers, these COWARDS, on this stuff? Where's the outrage? That they got away with this fake war and got all these good people killed is the crime of the century. That's it right there. I was alive for the crime of the century. It's too bad I had to be here for this and not be able to do anything about it. To have to stand by and watch cowards, liars, and their supporters kill and maim a generation is more than I can take sometimes. I don't know what I can do. I am just a guy out here in the world. In some ways, we deserve this because we didn't stop it. Thinking about it now, I still don't know what the hell I could have done but all the same, this happened on our watch. I am angry but most of all—I am ashamed.

It's now 0237 hrs. I am listening to Television doing *Little Johnny Jewel*. I go in and out of depression. It's been with me as long as I can remember. The workouts keep it at bay. It makes it hard to be around people. I have to act when I am around people. We have a cast dinner tonight. It will be fine as they are all great but it will be hard for me. It's hard to be around people. It's at 2000 hrs. I hope it doesn't last long. That's prime time.

I don't want to kill myself but I don't care when I die. I am not trying to say I am a tough guy. I've been around tough guys and I'm not one of them. I am not brave either. I just don't give a fuck. I value other people's lives but not my own. I like to travel to fucked up places alone. It allows me to stand myself. I can stand myself when I am alone in a room. This one here is good. It's a room in a city in a country I don't come from. I like that on a lot of levels. I like that I am pulling my weight and earning my own keep and not relying on anyone. I have wanted to be self-reliant since I was very young. I mean really young, like age ten or something. It's one of the only things I am proud of—that I earn my own keep and don't borrow, always pay on time and have perfect credit. I out earn both my parents combined. I can't express how much joy that brings me. If someone was to say that is shallow, lame, stupid or boring, I would agree. It's true. Doesn't matter to me. I still like it that my work ethic fucking crushes theirs, they worked their asses off but they didn't work as hard as I do. Work is one of the things I learned from them. They were both working machines, both very intelligent and intense. But they put traditional roadblocks into their paths like marriages and children—that which gets in the way of the work. I won't do that.

I am never getting married. I will always live alone. The idea of living with a female is foreign to me. Marriage is not for everybody. Definitely not for me. I can't get past the impurity of it. Living with someone makes life a collaborative effort and in that lies all the compromise and corruption of life that is repellent to me. There is no fucking way I am going to be told what to do by a woman—unless she's my boss! When I hear about what couples have to do, like going to see a relative, I'm glad I will never have to endure the fucking hell of having to drive somewhere to watch my wife's nephew play baseball. That's your Sunday? That's all you did?! Fuck that. It's not worth anything. It's not worth a nickel or a million bucks. I hope I am alone when I die. I don't give a fuck when it happens.

1 protein bar, 2 pieces sushi + seafood and noodles, piece of tuna, water, diet Coke, coffee 2 cups.

05-28-06 Vancouver Canada: 1810 hrs. Since I have to get up at 0300 hrs. for an 0400 hrs. lobby call, I tried to wear myself out at the gym a little while ago. It was a good workout but nothing less than I should be putting myself through all the time anyway. All the same, it was a good one and I am pretty beat up.

I have been watching BBC World News because I can't stand to hear another word about movie stars having babies in Africa. It's such a waste of news time. It's not news. The Pope visiting Auschwitz isn't news either. Who cares about the Pope? Religion holds no interest for me whatsoever. All the noise made about The Da Vinci Code makes me think I'm back in 10th grade and am surrounded by immature people who have nothing better to do with themselves. The code! The secrets of the Vatican! Who gives a fuck?! It's not news! You're born, you have a few laughs, there's varying degrees of horror depending on what job you sign up for or where you're born and then you die. I can deal with that. But when I see Pat Robertson looking down the barrel of a camera, fresh from watching the Weather Channel, talking about how god told him about tsunamis hitting American coastlines, it's all I can do not to kick the television. Marines dying is news.

All those people dead in Indonesia. All those people without homes in Louisiana. Earthquakes. Floods. Cities built on fault lines. Cities built below sea level. There are some places humans aren't welcome and yet, they still go. The world does what it does and all of a sudden there's dead bodies everywhere and the living want to start building again, right where their old house was—right where that massive pool of lava is cooling. They can't handle the fact that there are some places where you just shouldn't live. Then you will hear some idiot talking about god and how these people just didn't pray hard enough or some bullshit. Why can't people learn the lesson? Your town gets flooded, you move somewhere else. I don't think that is too hard to get your head around. And definitely stop having so many fucking kids. Kids everywhere. You can't feed yourself, you're a fuck up at the workplace, you're in debt, oh, and you have four children. That's great news, thousands of years to get it right and humans still continue to miss the boat on the most basic stuff. Don't have a lot of money for food? Have less kids. Can't afford shit? Don't buy it on credit. You can't afford it, remember? What would America be like if more people lived within their means? There are some people that are really up against it and working three jobs to get by but there's a lot of people who just do stupid shit with their money. They know they're doing it too, but they still do it. If they didn't, the economy would, damn, I don't know what it would do but things would be different. If more adults started acting like adults, things would be better. Bush starts a war in Iraq. Soldiers come home to cut benefits. Families are hung out to dry. Don't start something you can't finish. Don't put people in harm's way and not take care of them when they come back. Don't talk about anything being "incremental."

I love it when I get letters from people telling me that they like my show but they don't always agree with me. That's fine. It's not there to be agreed with and I'm not a beacon of righteousness but I wonder what parts they disagree with? The parts where I call the President out on the dumbass and dangerous things he does? I'm glad there's disagreement. I like it. Makes me know I'm doing something good.

Shoulders. 1 protein bar, sushi, minestrone soup, water, coffee 1 cup.

05-29-06 Vancouver Canada: 2126 hrs. Too tired to write. Still have to go over lines. 14 hours door-to-door today. Good work though. I have to be up at 0400. I didn't sleep last night so I am a little glazed over.

Oatmeal, scrambled eggs, fruit, fish, rice, sushi, granola bars, M&Ms, water, coffee.

05-30-06 Vancouver Canada: 2126 hrs. Today was the day I had been waiting for. We did more pages of script than I have ever had to do before. I was sweating this day. It was a lot but I did it and I did it pretty well. I am holding my own in this film. This is what I always hope for, to hold my own and not be a drag to the production and the actors. I am not an actor. I'm just trying to stay fed and working all the time. I don't treat it as a "job." I give it everything I have but I don't have it like real actors do. They are trained and disciplined. I am only desperate to hang in there and stay employed. I am always looking for work. I trust work. I am nervous when I am out of work. I was very happy when I found out I had this film to do and that I would be living in a hotel in Canada for weeks. The nights are great. I don't see anyone other than people on the street and most of them leave me alone. It's good to be working. There will never be enough money in my bank account. I don't trust America. I don't trust the government. I only rely on myself. It's better that way. It's the only way. I'll take work over love or contentment or anything pretty much.

It's a great feeling to be here and working and on my own. I don't miss anyone. I don't want to meet anyone. I don't want to know anyone and I don't want anyone to know me. It's the only way I know of to be free and real. Otherwise it's all compromise.

I am relieved this day is over. I was sweating those lines for hours over many days. Our director was happy with what I did and that's great. He hired me with no audition. I want him to really be happy that he hired me. It's my goal every day. The last thing I want to be is a drag on a production.

Scrambled eggs, fruit, fish, rice, sushi, granola bars, M&Ms, water, coffee.

05-31-06 Vancouver Canada: 2317 hrs. I am pretty tired. Really tired. I have to get up at 0400 hrs. and go to the airport. I get to LA hours later and go right to IFC show set and start work. I have John C Reilly and Billy Bob Thornton interviews and some other stuff and then I am wrapped out of there. I have stuff on Friday as well. Saturday will give me a chance to catch up on some writing here. I have been tired enough post film work that I am almost falling asleep in the elevator on the way to my room. It's good work but we're all throwing pretty hard. Great cast and crew. Joe, our director, is amazing. I would work for him any time. He has my respect 100%.

I have been watching reports on New Orleans and how slow the progress is in rebuilding parts of the city. I know there are a lot of people who are home owners who are now displaced, their finances in ruin. I know. But how about this: Perhaps there are parts of the world where people aren't supposed to live. Perhaps they should not rebuild there and people should get the hint that there's not much good in building in a place where there is a chance the same disaster could very easily happen again. Maybe it's time for people to be a little more humble and not think they can control the planet. On the other hand, fuck it. If people want to rebuild their homes and they get flooded again, they will be on their own even worse than they are now.

It is clear to me, at least, that the black people who were living in the 9th Ward are no longer wanted in New Orleans. If they were, something would have been done by now after almost a year. Maybe it's time for the main stream media to tell the truth and say that the Civil Rights Movement really didn't accomplish much and America is still a racist country. Perhaps it's time to stop pretending that racism doesn't go all the way to the upper levels of government because it obviously does. One could argue that the Civil Rights Movement was not a total failure considering how things were before. That's true but the situation didn't change enough for my liking. Racism is one of the banes of my existence. It makes me furious that some people are that ignorant. Not only that—they pass it onto their children. You would have thought by 2006 we would have moved on.

There's something refreshing about honesty—even when it's something you don't want to hear. If the Bush Administration had just said they hated Saddam, wanted his oil and were going to take him out, get the oil and fuck anyone who has a problem with it there probably would have been a lot of people who would have supported that.

And in the case of New Orleans, it would be great if the President cut the crap and just said that the administration doesn't care about the poor because they don't vote Republican and are not part of their "base." The Bush Administration doesn't need black people. They have Hispanics.

New Orleans will eventually shift to a white and Hispanic demographic. It will continue to be a place where whites will come to drink, vomit and get arrested but now the Hispanics will be there to mop it up and remove the cups and beer bottles from the pool. It will be similar to when the mafia was kicked out of Las Vegas and the place turned into Disneyland.

I'm not saying all is lost and all good people should lay down and die as the treads of these blowhard cowards turn them into potting soil. I am saying it's time to deal with it as it really is. If the bad guys just had the guts to tell the truth about themselves and stop trying to convince people they represent America we would all be better off. Even they would be better off. I think more people have a problem with the lies and spin than they do with the policies and acts themselves. I hate all of it but like I said, if the Bush crooks would have only said they were jacking Iraq, a lot of people would have thought that was cool. I believe this.

PS: Evil will always prevail.

Chest, abs., long run. Scrambled eggs, fruit, fish, rice, sushi, granola bars, M&Ms, water, coffee.

JUNE 2006

06-01-06 LA CA: 2351 hrs. I have to be up at 0700 hrs. I will detail today's stuff over the weekend. I will have some time on Saturday and Sunday to write. Today was a good day of work. Interviews with Billy Bob Thornton and John C Reilly. Both were great. I have interviewed BBT before but had never met John. He was really great and I'll write about the day when I can. I am pretty tired and have been up since 0400 hrs.

Bench press, dumbbell bench, flys, ab. work. 1 cup yoghurt, granola, 1 bowl oatmeal, 1 burrito, 2 tacos, water, 1 diet Coke, coffee 2 cups.

06-02-06 LA CA: 1517 hrs. I am sitting in my small dressing room, waiting for the crew to get back from lunch and for Peaches to arrive. I am looking forward to meeting her and doing the interview. I am also interested in putting the devil's advocate question to her basically asking what she says to people who tell her that a Canadian born person who lives in Germany is out of line attacking President Bush and his policies. I am on her side all the way but really want to hear what she has to say. I'm sure that question has come her way more than once but I really want to know.

Last night was a blur. I got in and didn't get much done. As far as getting some things done here, it's all about tonight and Saturday. Tonight I am looking forward to listening to some music and getting some work done for my radio show. Getting the playlists together takes a lot of time.

There is a small bit of drama going on at the moment between the film and the IFC show, scheduling problems that I sure hope get resolved soon. As it is right now, we need two of me to get them both done because the days the agent told me I would be free from the film, I am in fact, not. It's always something with that agent. Something always goes south when dealing with her. At the moment, we are scrambling to get guests for the last episodes of the IFC show's season and it will be hard for the producers not to have some latitude on dates when wrangling guests. Of course, the film needs what they need to realize their objective too. If the information coming from the agent had been correct, I probably wouldn't have signed up for the film as the schedule wouldn't have provided me the time to do it. Now I am caught in the middle, trying to be all things for all people and it's not even my fault. This kind of thing is nothing new but it's a pain in the ass for everyone involved. These are all good people who are working really hard and trying to accommodate me. It just adds to the stress I am already having to deal with.

2350 hrs. Back at the house. Interview with Peaches was really good. She is 100%. I like her, I like what she had to say. I got out of there around 1930 hrs. and went to the grocery store. I came back here and am now in the middle of laundry and trying to get my re-pack together for my bail out to Vancouver on Sunday.

The IFC show wipes me out for other stuff, like writing, thinking, etc. We worked hard today. A lot of teleprompter reads. There's one section called "End Credits" that all has to be done in one take. If I mess up one word, I have to start over again. Usually it takes me a long time to get through that section but I did them in record time today. It was strange, I was hitting all the reads really well. I noticed I was dragging ass by the end of the day. All that stuff takes a lot of concentration.

I got back here, all burnt and see an e-mail from management. I was supposed to answer interview questions from IFC viewers via e-mail and send it all back in ten days ago. I don't remember getting this request. I looked at the questions, answered the ones I could stand, put it all in a letter back to management and told them that it was the last time I will be doing that. A lot of motherfuckers, and as Peaches has said, fatherfuckers will waste your time. If you're polite to the guy in line at the grocery store, all of a sudden he's following you to your car and you're stuck having a fucking conversation when all you want to do is go to a room and be alone. You're too cool to some companies and they figure your time is cheap and of almost disposable quantity. This must be what someone at IFC thinks about my time. Here's three of the ten questions:

-- *If a crazed gunman was holding your family hostage and threatening to kill them unless you did, would you go to a Nickleback concert?*

-- *If you could do any 3 women who they be and why?*

-- *You can pretty much tell from the backdrop they put you in front of in those publicity photos that your new show will have a very leftist view. They have you in front of a collage with pictures of Bush with devil horns and other similar images. Do you think they did all this to capture the MTV crowd? 'Rock the vote' and all that kind of crap? Or are you really going to approach it from that point of view?*

What the fuck? Is that all you could pull out? There are some simple people out there. Is it revenge? Have I offended someone over at IFC? How about that last one? A leftist point of view? How about a "I am not fucked up" point of view. This is the same kind of dumbass who thinks that 09-11-01 is the reason America went to war with Iraq.

At some point, it will become all too tiring and the good will leave the bad to go kill themselves off. Hysterical Christians with their homophobic bullshit, people like the President, all these criminal cowards, they will be the downfall of the world. Not my world though.

That's why I live alone. That's why I don't have many friends, don't want many friends. Don't want to attach, don't want to be attached to. Humans are just not worth it. Brian Eno is allowed. I am listening to <u>Here Come The Warm Jets</u> at the moment and that's all I need.

1 bowl oatmeal, bagel, cream cheese, fish, carrots, 1 slice pie, minestrone soup, rice crackers, water, coffee 2 cups.

06-03-06 LA CA: 2132 hrs. Sitting on the couch. I am listening to Flin Flon's <u>Dixie</u> LP. The LP has a different mix and sequence than the CD. I have been waiting for a chance to sit down and listen to this album carefully. Mark Robinson, who basically is Flin Flon, frequently makes two mixes for his albums. The LP mixes are usually more interesting than the CD mixes. If I didn't have to get up in a few hours, I would go to the office and make a CDR of the LP so I could compare the mixes and make notes on the differences. I pay a great deal of attention to anything Mark does musically. He's an interesting musician. I listen to one of his older bands, Unrest, a lot.

It's late and I still have a lot to do. I was hoping to sit still for an hour but I'm not going to sit any more still than this.

Something has been bugging me all day. I have been listening to the radio and reading articles on the internet about Bush and his support of a resolution to amend the Constitution to ban same sex marriage. What the fuck is important about this? He wants to amend the Constitution? I bet he hasn't even read it.

He perpetrated a pre-emptive strike in Iraq that got out of control. He's covered with soldier's blood and Condoleezza Rice's spit and he's worrying about the sanctity of marriage? Who is this supposed to appeal to who aren't stupid enough to follow him anywhere already? Knowing it won't pass in the Senate, why is he doing it? Perhaps he knows that it won't go and he wants to look like the "last good man standing" or something. It is in fact distraction. It is only to divert attention away from the tragedy of the Invasion and Occupation of Iraq and the fact that the Bush Administration is directly responsible for the deaths of thousands of Americans and who knows how many innocent Iraqis. Can't deal with the truth of that? Drink some more grape Kool Aid and shoot yourself in the mouth.

"Marriage cannot be cut off from its cultural, religious and natural roots without weakening this good influence on society."

Remember the rap from one of his lame State Of The Union Address speeches? Let's see if I can find it, I have all of the transcripts with me—you can never have too much of this guy's insult to literacy with you. Hold on. Here it is, it's from the 2004 Address. The Defense Of Marriage Act isn't good enough. He needs to crank up the stupidity and ignorance even higher!

"Congress has already taken a stand on this issue by passing the Defense of Marriage Act, signed in 1996 by President Clinton. That statute protects marriage under federal law as the union of a man and a woman, and declares that one state may not redefine marriage for other states.

Activist judges, however, have begun redefining marriage by court order, without regard for the will of the people and their elected representatives. On an issue of such great consequence, the people's voice must be heard. If judges insist on forcing their arbitrary will upon the people, the only alternative left to the people would be the constitutional process. Our nation must defend the sanctity of marriage.

The outcome of this debate is important, and so is the way we conduct it. The same moral tradition that defines marriage also teaches that each individual has dignity and value in God's sight."

So now he's all about the Sanctity Of Marriage Act. Oh snap! SOMA! SOMA for the masses! That's not going to cut it, you coward. I always thought the activist judges rap was disgusting. It's like that Fox News' idiot John Gibson and what he says about Christianity being under attack in America. Bush is basically saying that these judges better give the homophobes what they want. Only Bush would "defend" people like this.

That Bush thinks homosexuals are threatening the "institution of marriage" by wanting to get married is just so disheartening. Did you read or hear what this shitbird said today in his weekly weak address? There were some real gems. Bush said same sex marriage will change the meaning of marriage. How? Two people want to get married, what fucking business is it of yours? He stated that thousands of same sex marriage licenses have been issued in San Francisco CA. That means there's a lot of people who want nothing more than to be together for the rest of their lives.

This last bit of today's address kills me:

"America is a free society, which limits the role of government in the

lives of our citizens. This commitment of freedom, however, does not require the redefinition of one of our most basic social institutions. Our government should respect every person, and protect the institution of marriage. There is no contradiction between these responsibilities. We should also conduct this difficult debate in a manner worthy of our country, without bitterness or anger."

Be free, but you fuckin' faggots better cool the fuck out, is what he should have said and cut the crap. No contradiction between these responsibilities? It's a huge contradiction. Maybe he should go to the Mayflower Hotel where his wife is apparently staying and work on the sanctity of that marriage. I hope it's true he's having sex with Dr. Rice because I want to see how all the Fox News guys are going to turn that into the good time bullshit they sell by the ass load.

Perhaps all this will momentarily distract America from high gas prices and the Haditha Massacre? I think enough Americans are seeing the Haditha Massacre for what it is. It's overstressed soldiers who have been rotated too many days, too many times and seen too much. They are the best but they are only human and they are breaking.

I have a ritual I have been doing for years now. I get up and as soon as I can, I get to a TV or the internet and see how many Iraqis and American soldiers have died or been injured while I was sleeping. How many people were blown up and how many people have lost a member of their family. I usually don't have to wait very long to find out and rarely is there no bad news.

This "war" has fucked with me on many levels and one of the lame things I feel is that it's hard to be inspired by anything I achieve because I think of all those good men and women fighting out there and what they're going through. When I think about them it's hard for me to take what I am doing as seriously. I feel like I am just hanging around having "fun" while these people are out there laying it on the line. Basically, it cheapens anything I am trying to do. It's all in my head but all the same, it gets to me.

I still have some work to do around here and I can't concentrate on this. I will be back later.

Push-ups. 1 bowl oatmeal, yoghurt, microwave cheese enchilada, salad, ice cream bar, rice, beans, V8 juice, carrot juice, water, coffee 2 cups.

06-04-06 LA CA: 0100 hrs. Finished my chores. Have to get up early and go but still want to write. The IFC show was on tonight. I never watch it but I guess someone does. Patton Oswalt was the guest and Damian Marley was the musical guest. I got this e-mail tonight, I'm leaving in all the writer's typos to "keep it real":

Patton?? Seriously?!?!?!? I love you, Henry, but Patton giving political advice is a bit ridiculous...I love the guy but he is a comedian!! Be careful what your wish for is all that I'm going to say...You hate the Bush regime so bad that you might get what you wish for. Also, I thought that the music choice was bad. Reggae cool,..but not Henry Rollins..Just my opinion... My opinion matters shit...You are the shit

Patton gave political advice? I don't think he did. He didn't tell me how to run for office or how to lie to the American people. You fuckin' conservatives are falling all over yourselves these days. Anyway, I answered the letter:

Your letter didn't make any sense. Patton Oswalt is an American and he can say any fuckin' thing he wants. I do. And so should you. You don't like the music or what the guests are saying on the show then change the fuckin' channel and stop complaining. Definitely don't bring it to me again.

People like this, why do they always find me? Some motherfuckers better brace the fuck up. Get what I wish for? Bring me what I'm wishing for and see what the fuck happens. I am wishing for the President and Dick Cheney to finally tell the truth about Iraq; I am wishing for alternative fuel sources to be taken seriously and pursued—you know, shit like that. I should be careful for wishing for that? I fuckin' hate cowards.

I don't have a single reason to live past the work in front of me. I don't want to die at the moment because that would fuck the film up and they would have to do re-shoots or something. Insurance would cover it and all but they would lose days on the production. Past that and the tour coming up, I don't really care when I die. It's the one thing that allows me to keep moving. I don't care when I go. There's not a fuckin' reason to live past the work and the chance to defy, confront, win or lose. Because I don't have a family or anyone to come home to, I feel like I have won the lottery. It's the one thing I have done right in my life. I have fucked up almost everything I have ever tried. I am not good at any of the things I work at. But I got one thing right. I am alone and have no family ties. I have no kids and there's no woman in my life to weaken my resolve or otherwise distract me. I remember when I went out with women, I liked it too much and the work slipped. I had to make a choice between the happy hang out and the work. I made my choice.

Arms, abs, run. 1 bowl oatmeal, yoghurt, granola, sushi, sesame bars, popcorn, carrot juice, water, coffee 1 cup.

06-05-06 Vancouver Canada: 0056 hrs. In the room. I went long on a write up for one of the radio shows. I pre-recorded a few shows with Engineer X before I came up here. I finalized the notes for this coming Tuesday night's show as well, and sent our web guy all the Dispatches from the last three days too.

The workout was good earlier tonight. I admit I am lightweight on the running front but I am going to step it up. I am doing quick four milers. I will have that up to five this week. It will get upped a bit more by the end of the month and then turn into hill training in July. This is training month three and I am feeling pretty good. I am hitting it hard and all the time. I have never done this much ab. work in my life. Damn, they can take a beating. I am working on my body alright but it's my mind that's not all the way there yet. I want to get back into practice with the guys and hit it some more, then I'll be better mentally. Also, I know this tour is going to hurt and I will need more toughness in my legs. A lot of my fatigue comes from my quads. If I have not trained them properly, they wear out a few songs in and it makes playing hard because I have to use other muscle groups to stabilize my lower half. My body is almost at that "beat it with a stick and it won't hurt" phase. All the ab. and leg work is paying off as well as the hi-rep weight stuff. I need to keep hitting it hard. June is going to be very important for training. Besides the film, all I am thinking about is training and tour.

You have to personalize training and touring. At least I do. When I was younger and had the occasional girlfriend, I would get inspired by her and kind of dedicate the training and touring to her. Affection was a very strengthening and inspiring thing for me in those days. Now it means shit to me. It means not a fucking thing. I am doing this tour for me first and then for Sim Cain, Chris Haskett, Melvin Gibbs and Theo Van Rock. If you train just for yourself, it's harder. It's all you. That's as close to the truth as I get. When it's just me on me, like with the run, the high reps, the stage, it's all about not letting yourself down.

That woman-as-inspiration thing is lame to me at this point in my life. It's been a long time since I thought like that. I meet a lot of soldiers who carry a picture of their wife or girlfriend with them at all times. I can understand that. They are young and it's no big deal PEOPLE ARE ONLY TRYING TO FUCKING KILL THEM EVERY DAY so I can see where they look for anything to give them hope and inspiration. That will never be me. It's all a solo mission until I die. Alone is my truth. I don't force it on anyone—how could I?

I still haven't written anything about the night I spent walking around NYC with the amazing Shirin Neshat, the Iranian artist/activist. The hangout was for the *Into The Night* television show. It was like a month ago or something. I have been working on all kinds of stuff and have forgotten to take the time to write about meeting her. I will hopefully have time today. I will get a lot of work done today. I need to get some sleep. I got three hours last night. Ok, the thing I was going to mention is that I asked her for a reading list of books so I could learn more about Iran and instead of sending me a list, she sent me some books! That's so cool of her. She sent me <u>All The Shah's Men</u> by Stephen Kinzer, <u>Women Without Men</u> by Shahrnush Parsipur and <u>Reading Lolita In Tehran: A Memoir In Books</u> by Azar Nafisi. I brought the first two with me and am a good way into the Kinzer book and it's really interesting. I am learning a lot. I don't have to shoot today so I am going to get a good way into this book and make some notes on the basic history of the country, especially around the time the Shah was deposed. I remember all that. I was going to school with some Iranian fellows at the time.

I wrote to Shirin thanking her. My instinct is to leave people alone but I had to thank her and I was so inspired by all the things she said to me that night. She is an incredible person. I feel so fortunate to have met her.

It's 0134 hrs. I should get off this and get back at that book for a little while and rack. Tonight will be a major shoulder workout. You know that scene in <u>The Deer Hunter</u> where the Green Beret is sitting at the bar and everyone is asking him what it's like in Vietnam and all the soldier says is, "Fuck it." I spend days at a time in that moment. It's good to be dead. Carry on.

Shoulders, run. Yoghurt, granola, rice, shrimp, sesame bars, water, coffee 2 cups.

06-06-06 Vancouver Canada: 0112 hrs. I spent a lot of time tonight working on radio show writing. I wrote about Coltrane. I am out of my league there so I went with how the music makes me feel. I can't write about Jazz with any authority so I have to go with my gut. I am happy with what I wrote though.

Earlier, I went to the gym for my workout and usually there is this trainer guy in there with one of his "clients." The guy talks nonstop. It's hard to concentrate. There's a sign posted that says "no cell phones" and I know he has seen it but his cell phone rings all the time and he talks loud. Whatever. I work out, I leave. So, around 1600 hrs. I'm in there and I just finished doing some barbell rows and I am taking the plates off and one of them hits another one and makes a sound. It's the sound you've heard in a gym a million times. It's not like I was throwing the weights around, two 45 pound plates connected and made a sound. The trainer guy, who's talking to his client who is on a treadmill, stops his conversation and asks me if I can keep the noise down. I answer him back by yelling at him. I told him I know he's seen the sign and so why does he always have his cell phone on?

He says it's turned off and could I keep the noise down. I have to crank it up a notch and I remind him it's a gym and there will be the sound of plates making contact. He stands up slightly and I stand up with him and take a step towards him. He isn't having a good time and his client is looking nervous. The two other guys in the gym are digging it though. He mumbled something about the noise and I told him to have a good workout as loud as I could. I bet I see him in there tonight. I can't wait. I hope he says something to me again.

All day on the news was gay marriage. I guess it's the only way Bush can get people to come out and vote. Republicans might not want to go along with a lot of what he's doing but they'll show up for some homophobia. It's good strategy. I wonder if this is a Rove thing. It's brilliant in a way. The Bush Administration is pulling out all the stops. More and more killing in Iraq. Things are screwed up and our Government will spend who knows how long now on flag burning and homophobia. Don't like gay marriage? Don't marry a gay person. Problem solved. But don't say you're not homophobic if you're against same sex marriage. Hardcore god cultists are so exhausting. It's frustrating to have to share a country with people who don't have the strength to be an American. To be an American, you have to be open-minded. You can't live in the dark ages. This is a great country but so many people just coast on their ignorance, appalling diets and choices and all the rest of us have to pay for their idiotic behavior. I am so tired of America's cultural growth being stuck in some fifties movie.

I was walking down the street earlier today and saw four girls talking in the middle of the sidewalk. One of them dropped a half full bottle of mineral water on the ground. They all looked at it for a second and walked off. There was a trashcan right there but she didn't bother. I watched them walk away and I watched the bottle roll. For a second, I felt like picking up the bottle and giving it back to the girl and telling her to throw it out. Not a good idea. They could say I assaulted them or something. I just left it alone and kept walking. I wondered if I didn't bother to throw it out because I was in Canada. That's not a good excuse at all.

I have film work today. All my scenes are alone. There will be a lot of days like this for me now where it's just me in the woods running around.

I talked to management hours ago and we talked about potentially recording some shows with Live Nation, which is ClearChannel under a different name. They have a thing where they record your show and fans can buy the show on the way out of the gig. I said I was potentially interested. They said the price would be 20 dollars for a single CD. They can go fuck themselves. I told management I would do it for a price of 10 dollars a CD. He said they might not be interested then. Like I said—they know what they can do. We'll see what happens. 20 bucks for a CD, that's why people download and "steal" music, because bands ask that kind of money from their fans. Most of the time, the bands don't even know what the prices are. Most musicians I have met are not greedy people, quite the opposite, actually. I try to sell my stuff as cheaply as I can. It's what you do.

It's late and I am tired from the workout. I still want to get some reading done. I am looking forward to getting to the film set and hitting it. I have a hard week coming up and I am getting nerved up about the two talking shows I am doing in England at week's end. I want to do the shows but the London one is throwing me a little as I have just played there and don't have a lot of new stuff. The agent told me it's a different audience than my regular shows as there's no tube access to this part of London and there's a lot of subscription ticket sales. Paul, the agent, is never wrong on stuff and I trust him. I have been with him a long time. He booked Black Flag, that's how far back we go. I am thinking about the flights, the jet lag and the hustle of getting it all done. It's going to be a long week. I push myself pretty hard. I don't have any reference points though. I don't know what other people are doing. When I tell people what I'm doing, they usually say it's too much. I'm tired. I'm not going to get to that book.

2350 hrs.: We did good work today. I did all my scenes alone. I will be doing a lot of scenes like this all through the film now. The forest we filmed in today was amazing. We were shooting deep inside the forest where it's so dense, it's almost dark even though the sun is out. I felt like I was inside a huge house. The ground was dirt, moss and dead trees. The ground was soft wherever I walked and I could step without making a sound. When everyone was quiet right before a take, the silence was huge. All the trees and moist ground deadens sound and made it somehow more silent than quiet. I had a few moments here and there where I could just sit and take it in. I like the smell of the forest. Reminds me of where I come from. I like being in this film. It's a very good group of people working on this thing.

I like being up here in Canada. I like this room and the time I get on my own. Whenever I do a film on location, it's all I want to do. It is a time I feel free. It is a dodge from other stuff I do and sometimes I don't mind it. I am getting more reclusive as time goes on. It makes more sense to be alone as much as possible. I like to work very hard and I like to work with others who have that same level of intensity, like the people on this film. I would work with Joe the director again on anything he wanted me to pretty much because he is so full-on and intense and driven. I can be around that all day long and it's fine. That kind of human interaction I can hack. You can work hard and do good and not have to get all that personal. Work related and goal oriented relationships are fine. I like working with the band as they are all pros and know what it takes to be good. I like the people I work with like management and the staff at the office. We get it done. Past that, I would rather be on my own most of the time.

I don't understand marriage. I don't understand it when men say they can't stand being away from their wives for more than a day. I hear it all the time. I see couples on airplanes who have to sit apart from each other for an hour and they want to get their seats changed. I guess it's cool to be that into someone but I don't want it for myself. I don't trust it, don't need it and only see it as a liability up the trail.
Yoghurt, granola, salad, vegetables, apple pie, sesame bars, water, coffee 2 cups.

06-07-06 Vancouver Canada: 0127 hrs. I got a letter from a Marine yesterday. He is upset because around him he sees what he calls the bottom 20% of Americans: drunks, useless pieces of shit, criminals, etc. He put a good question to me:

"I wanted to ask you for your opinion; do you still see the value? I don't anymore and I wonder sometimes what is so wonderful about these people that merits me writing letters to a Marine's mom, inventorying his gear, and crossing his name off my roster."

That's some pretty heavy shit. I wonder what our troops think when they are in the chow hall and look up at the TV screen to see some fat fucks in America at a hot dog eating contest stuffing their faces? I wonder what they think as they get wheeled into the hospital to find out if the doctors are going to be able to save that leg while Paris Hilton could sell her piss for a thousand dollars a teaspoon? I wonder if it ever occurs to them that they were sent to Iraq by a sissy rich kid who doesn't know what he's talking about? I wonder if they know they got sold out by a underachiever frat boy who never had to put himself on the line for anything? I think once I got all that, it would be impossible to let it go.

Sometimes I feel like just laughing it off and letting it go wherever it's going to go. It's Republican/Conservative everything in America. Somehow they got the courts, the White House and just about everything else. Look what they've done with it, yet they keep telling you that it's all going so well. If they got 100% of what they wanted, America would be a really freaky place. Sometimes I wonder if I'll have to leave.

They will have take responsibility for what has happened to this country at some point, won't they? Won't there come a time when they will have to admit things didn't go very well? Probably not.

I am glad I am brutal. I am glad I can look at dead bodies and guts and human carnage and not really feel anything. I am glad I can live almost anywhere on almost nothing. I am glad I don't want a wife or a family. I am glad I am alone in the world. I am good to go for what's left of my life. If you don't understand what it's like to have lost, you will never know what it is to be strong.

What the fuck. I just read an e-mail a woman sent me that was

2155 words long. She said that she wanted to say hello to me at some event we were both at but didn't because, " ... *my friends who all have heavy Pisces in their charts were too freaked out by the intense energy in the place to stay.*" The rest of the letter was all about, fuck, I don't know, I couldn't understand it. I just wrote back and thanked her for the letter and told her I didn't know how to respond to a single thing she said. Ok. I'm out. Going back to my All The Shah's Men book. A great read that's teaching me a lot.

2201 hrs. I didn't work on the film today. I read, looked up stuff online and worked out hard. I'm still walking slow from that one.

I didn't go out much today. I am getting wound up about the UK shows. I will have a night in London to get my head around the time change. I will be doing the show on Saturday and then going back to London that night. That's good, I want to get back to get ready for the next show.

I want to do the shows but I haven't done any for a while and I am obsessing about it too much. I get too wound up about stuff. The hotel I will be in has a good gym so I will get in a solid work out on Friday. A Friday night in London will be cool.

The news was depressing today. Ann Coulter is on the loose! Her new book Godless: The Church Of Liberalism is out and she's getting a lot of press. One specific passage in the book was talked about a lot in the press today. I am sure that's just the way she wanted it. She accuses some widows of 9/11 victims of using the deaths of their husbands to get attention and make money. She called them harpies and broads. Here's a quote from her book I saw online today: *"I've never seen people enjoying their husbands' deaths so much."* She was on television today talking about her statement and people were actually applauding. You can get really bent out of shape about all of this but then on the other hand, she's just talking and the people who think she's saying something worthwhile are not the type you could reason with anyway. She's not to be taken seriously and if you do, then you deserve to waste the time you do on it. I have read parts of most all her books. I buy them used online for a couple of bucks. It's funny that she always accuses Liberals of slinging mud but that's all she does really.

I was sitting inside a coffee place hours ago waiting for the pain in my knees to subside and I was hit by a wave of apathy. I don't know if it was apathy as much as the notion that there is nothing you can do about how things are. I have been speaking out against the attack on Iraq since it started and I didn't save any lives. I didn't make a difference. Neither did Ann Coulter, Rush Limbaugh or Air America. Nothing I do with the USO makes a difference. Not one bit of a difference. All the arms and legs still came off, didn't they? All those men and women still came back dead and mutilated. Thousands of innocent Iraqis have died for nothing.

Mark Crispin Miller just released a new book. I am looking forward to reading it. He and I have exchanged a few letters. His last two books ripped Bush to shreds with incredibly well-researched information and well thought-out writing. Mr. Miller is a very intense and clear thinker. I heard him speak on the radio today and he was really great. He's not soft, he's in your face with his point of view. That being said, all his great points didn't change anything really. No one who should read those books ever does. It's usually people like me who already agree and want to know more. Nothing changes. The President still goes out and says really stupid shit and people are just numb to it. You'll never change the minds of the people who still support him and his crisis in Iraq. One man online said that Liberals keep on whining and Conservatives keep on winning. I wonder what the guy thinks he's won? Our country has no money. Millions have no health care. Our public school system is in shambles. It's been all Republican all the time. All of this has been on their watch. How can they look at the last five years and say they've done a good job? If all this shit was happening with a Democrat in office, the Republicans would be having fits. It's all pretty depressing.

I broke through and ran over five miles today. I did it wearing two t-shirts made of rayon, a thermal shirt and a sweatshirt on top. It was very hard going the last two miles. Every time I started to lose concentration, I thought of soldiers in the field and all the gear they wear on their person at all times and then it was hard to feel put out by running on a treadmill in a nice hotel and being a little hot. I am trying to get the body ready for what is to come. I am hoping the running will help. It's been a long time since I have done this much cardio in pre-tour training. I am getting results though. I am feeling good and the ab work I am doing will help as well.

I need to get my head around these talking shows. I think they will go fine but I want the London one to be somewhat different than the one I just did there. The agent says it will be a different audience. I don't know about that. He is always right about stuff but I know what the bottom line with all of this—it's business and the more I work, the more everyone gets paid. I know. I know.

Deadlift, run, leg press, abs. Yoghurt, granola, protein bar salad, sushi, sesame bars, popcorn, water, coffee 2 cups.

06-08-06 En Route to UK: It's almost midnight. Interesting sight below me. The surface of the Earth is covered with ice and snow and the sun was setting, almost below the horizon and just minutes later it's rising. I want to find out what our flight route is.

I am a good way into <u>All The Shah's Men</u>. I have been reading it for a couple of hours now. It's a great read and I am learning a lot about the relationship between Britain and Iran. Seems like not a great deal has changed. It's all about that oil.

I saw on the news that Zarqawi was killed in an air strike. Two 500 pound bombs took out the small building he was in. From what it looked like and from what CNN said, the structure looked fortified. The building was totally destroyed but somehow Zarqawi's face remained quite intact with no burns or disfigurement. I am not trying to be conspiracy theory boy but that's the first thing that struck me. I don't know why anyone would want to cover that up but all the same, it's strange he still has a head.

Flight a little less than halfway over. <u>Big</u> is now on the screen ahead of me. I have a straight shot on the Piccadilly line out of Heathrow to the hotel. I always have a bad time traveling east. In 24.5

hours, I will be in a car heading to the Download Festival. Friday in London I will be a little spaced to say the least.

Deadlift, run, leg press, abs. Yoghurt, granola, protein bar salad, sushi, sesame bars, popcorn, water, coffee 2 cups.

06-09-06 London UK: 1816 hrs. Just back from getting some food and walking around a little. I always try to eat at a place called Wagamama. It's up the street from here. It's one of my favorite places to eat anywhere. I have been there many times.

When I walked out of the Underground up to the street hours ago, it felt like I had just been here yesterday. I knew what I was going to see and I was right. The streets are packed with people. Young, some tourist types but overall, mainly people in their twenties. There's a lot of shops around here so it's always like this. A very short time from now, the bars will start to do a lot of business and the streets will become packed with loud young people. Men in suits, ties partway undone, walking into the middle of the street to hail a cab by basically standing in front of it.

I am pretty tired. I want to stay up later but I have to be in a car and on the road to the show at 0900 tomorrow so I don't want to stay up too late.

This isn't really a tough part of town but it does have a lot of loud and aggro people on the street at night. The streets around here smell really bad.

Deadlift, run, leg press, abs. Yoghurt, granola, protein bar, salad, sushi, sesame bars, popcorn, water, coffee 2 cups.

06-10-06 London UK: 0745 hrs. I have been up for quite some time. I took a walk into Soho. I saw lots of broken glass bags of garbage outside of bars and men cleaning up in front of some of the places. There's a lot of strip bars around here. The smell of garbage, urine and vomit is intense in some parts. I hardly saw anyone on the streets. I saw a few white guys, hard looking men carrying plastic bags with who knows what in them. A couple of black men started talking to me. One wanted to shake hands and get the conversation going, a hit up for change or something. Others, mostly Rastas, gave me the nod and asked if I was alright. Drugs? I'm a pilgrim, man. It has always struck me how industrious some homeless people are, especially early in the morning. Hustling their gear, getting their day started. They don't have the luxury of sleeping in. In so many cities I have seen men pushing their shopping carts with the rising sun reflecting off their faces.

As I walked toward Soho, with the sun in my face, I thought about a recording of Dylan Thomas reading his poem *Quite Early One Morning* that my mother had when I was growing up. I don't think the poem takes place in the summer but nonetheless, I was thinking of it.

Soho at this hour of the morning is quiet with hardly any cars or people around. Neon signs turned off, men sweeping trash and cigarettes into the street. It makes me think of how people choose to pass time on this planet. For all those people who were outside my window until at least 0430 hrs. it was a night out, it was something to do. It would never occur to me to spend a night like that.

It's these small moments that make travel worth it for me. I have no idea how the shows will go. I don't know what today will bring. Thinking of tonight's show last night made what little sleep I got not very good. I was somewhat relieved this morning just knowing I will be getting on the road to the show soon enough. Like a condemned man who gets confirmation of the time of his execution. I don't know why I feel this way before some shows. I am looking forward to getting out there, I just wish I was going right now.

I see that I have spent a good deal of my life in this compressed state of unease. I have small pockets of relief now and then. Like the ride back to London after the show is done will be pretty good. Perhaps Wagamama will still be open when I get back down here and I can get some chow and some writing done in my room.

It sounds lame but I always like to listen to some of the classics when I am in London: Buzzcocks, Damned, UK Subs, Ruts. Just knowing that so many amazing shows happened in this town all those years ago makes listening to those records here all the more cool.

I am sure it's not good for me to be this stressed all the time but it's one way to be sure that the performance will be as good as it can be. I can't ever allow myself to become lax on the job. It's how I protect the work. Always value it and undervalue myself is how I try to do it. I treat my body as the tool with which I get the work done. As far as enjoying things, I guess I do but I get the work done and that's the priority.

2241 hrs. We got back from Download hours ago. I caught a ride from the hotel up to the show with a guy Road Manager Mike hired to take me up there. Mike met us at some airport en route. I am forgetting the name of it now but I'll ask RMM when I see him tomorrow. Anyway, we got in and through all the lines of cars and whatnot about an hour before I was supposed to go on. I sat in a trailer and got the ideas for the set together and waited for RMM to take me to the stage. He eventually did and I went on right on time at 1350.

It was like last year when I did the show but this time to about three times the amount of people. Last year, I feared getting bottled or heckled right offstage but everyone was cool to me and the same happened today. It was a huge tent and the place was packed all the way to the back. The audience was amazing. They just hung in there with me for the whole time.

I hopefully imparted the one thing I wanted to get across to them. It was important to me to at least remind them that this was their time, this was their crowd and to recognize it and not let this time go wasted or unnoticed. I told them about the first times I was out seeing bands and what it meant to me and how it made me who I am now and that it was at the age they are now where the shows were hugely influential on the rest of my life. This of course, is true. It's also true that everyone takes shows or anything they do in their own way but it is important at some point in your young life to say, "This is me. This is what I am all about." It seemed to get across to them.

It is important to see that time of your life as a time of self-definition and revelation at that exact moment and not later on, looking back at it in retrospect. Fuck retrospect. Sometimes you have to make

A Dull Roar

history as you breathe and know it. It's those early shows that were most important for me, seeing bands play and experiencing the music as a young person. I wish at that time someone had said to me something like what I said to them today.

It's hard for me, at this age, to look at all those young people and not feel a great deal of affection. I will never meet 99% of them but if you have been there, you can tell when someone else is at that point and I only want to tell them the best things I know. One of the things I enjoy about being older is I can actually say something of small worth to a younger person now and then.

Anyway, on a scale of one to ten, the audience, the thousands of them that were there, were an eleven at least. I am so happy to have been in front of them today. Just thinking about it gets me slightly out of the depressed state I am in at the moment.

Depression is nothing new. Like a lot of people, I have dealt with depression for as long as I can remember. It's one of the first things I am aware of being aware of. I remember it from when I was very young. Dread and depression have been with me for my whole life. Sometimes it's not so bad but sometimes it makes all things difficult to do and I have to fight through it. It's hard on tour with shows every night. Jet lag brings it on so there's always a bit of it when I make trips like this. I have never been good at getting over jet lag. Going east is the hardest. I racked for a couple of hours when we got back here from Download, I was so tired I knew I wasn't going to be able to get anything done. It's usually the hardest sleep to pull myself out of but I came out fast when it hit me that I was wasting a Saturday night.

Depression hits me all the time when I am outside of America. When I feel this way I think of the city I came from, Washington DC, and I listen to music from there and it makes things a little better. It was the thought of DC that wrenched me out of the sleep I was in. I felt like I couldn't get enough air and I sat up wishing I could be walking down the streets of my old neighborhood right at that moment. It hits me like that. I'll be on an airplane and my mind goes right to those streets. Whenever I can, I take pictures of those streets, I have hundreds of them on my laptop. I look at them and it evens me out some.

2 protein bars, 1 cup of yoghurt, miso ramen, water, coffee 2 cups.

06-11-06 London UK: 0120 hrs. Just back from walking around Piccadilly Circus. It's packed with people out there. It's a place where you can meet someone you know, someone who knows you, or a fist in the face very easily. There's a lot of loud drunk people out there. As I walked through the people, I heard different languages, smelled sweat, perfume, flowers, alcohol, tobacco. People were sitting all around the Eros statue. The traffic was thick, mostly taxis, buses and limos. There were a lot of beautiful women out there tonight. London is full of them. I stood out there and looked at people for quite awhile. No one bothered me besides the men who were handing out flyers for nearby clubs. One man came up to me and asked, "Clubbing tonight, sir?" and then looked at my clothes, withdrew the flyer and moved on. I have my usual low-security prison convict look going. The all gray, utilitarian, institutionalized look. I have never gotten the clothing thing together. When I see men walking around with shopping bags from clothing stores on their arms, it looks weak to me. I am sure that's lame but that's me.

I just looked out the window. It's 0201 hrs. and a lot of people are at a bus stop across the street. I watched people there last night too. For the next two hours or so, that bus stop will be full of people until the sun comes up. As I was looking out the window, it occurred to me that people's lives can be summed up with a few words, or a few things. You can put a policeman's badge on the table and that one object will sum up, at least some part, of his life. It hit me how many times I have stayed in this hotel and looked out on this street and perhaps it's one of things that sums up my life. A trail of rented rooms and airplane boarding passes. Movement and temporary dwellings.

The hotel room is the model of perfection to me. I only get out of it what I put into it. I walk in and set up my computer and music access, which has been greatly improved by the advent of the iPod and small speaker set ups for them. I organize my stuff as I set up camp. Sometimes I bring coffee, filter and cup if I know there will be a kettle for boiling water. In the UK, there's almost always a kettle. I also have a small portable one to take along. It's a simple and small environment that I inhabit temporarily and with only a few items. Sometimes when I look around the room and see the few things I have with me, I wonder if this isn't the best way to be. Living out of a small dwelling as a base and then going out from there to small rooms all over. I think I have said this before—if I won the lottery and had a lot of money, I would live in hotels most of the time. I think it would be great to live in different places all the time and not really have any one place you call "home." One of the best things about being on this film in Vancouver is the fact that I'm in a hotel room. To live in Vancouver and then be able to leave with two bags and be gone is a great thing. I have reference items like books and records but I don't notice if I don't see them for long periods of time. It's great to be in London and not have to think about a car or "stuff." I like anything that minimizes space and weight. That's why the iPod and the laptop have been great things for me. I have all the music I'll ever really need on the iPod and the laptop holds lots of articles and information. Why leave the road at all, ever?

Run. Miso ramen, egg salad sandwich, granola bars, water, coffee 2 cups.

06-12-06 Vancouver Canada: 2255 hrs. I'm back. Took awhile. Road Manager Mike and I got on a Piccadilly Line train to Heathrow around 0850 hrs. We were making good progress until right before the Acton Town station. The train came to a stop there and we waited to hear what was going on. Finally a man came on the sound system and said there was a breakdown with the computers and all the trains on this line had been stopped and he didn't know what was happening. It's not like we could get off the train, we were in the middle of nowhere. Finally, the train limped to the Acton Town platform and we got off the train. The station was full of people trying to figure out how to get to their destination. RMM and I walked a few blocks away to see if we could get a cab to the airport. We were lucky and managed to get one. We got to the airport and since we were on different airlines, we parted ways and dashed to check in.

I got checked in alright and was at the gate for boarding. There was a bunch of people in front of the boarding area. The agent at the doorway said the air-conditioning unit had stopped inside and it was already full of people and very hot so we were going to have to wait out here. We eventually boarded the flight one hour and some minutes later than the original boarding time. That's nothing new at Heathrow. I don't remember any flight leaving on time out of there. That wait combined with the one on the train was a bit draining. We left the lobby of the hotel around 0845 hrs. and the plane took off at 1330 hrs. Yeah.

I got back here, put my bags down and caught up on some news. It's all bad. The Gitmo suicides are being spun all kinds of ways. Ann Coulter continues to get high profile exposure from the dumbass stuff she said about the Jersey Girls and there were usually adults on Larry King defending her. It's a whacky place, America.

I felt dead on my feet but I was determined to hit the gym and I did. Good work out. For the running part of the work out, I did about three miles of quarter mile runs as fast as the treadmill would go. I wanted to shock my body out of what it was used to as far as running. I don't know much about physical fitness but I know my body responds to change ups in the routine and I know that you can almost get out of shape by not changing things now and then. Those sprints were good.

I got back to the room and went out for some chow. I found a Thai place I had not been in before. It was pretty good. At least there weren't many people in it and it was relatively quiet. People are loud in this neighborhood. This is a place where people go to eat, drink and hang out so it's loud. It's not a violent neighborhood, just loud and crowded. One thing I have noticed is that when I am sitting in a restaurant, it seems loud but there's hardly anyone in the place.

A Dull Roar

People are just loud in general when they're around here.

I went from the Thai place to a Starbucks and got a coffee and sat outside at a table. Again, there were some people at other tables and it was as if they were yelling at the top of their lungs at each other. It's strange around here. I drank the coffee and plugged in the headphones. I really like the crowd control aspect of the iPod. You don't have to listen to people talking when you don't want to. I make a point to always have an iPod with me wherever I go now. I listened to some good music and imagined I was in DC at night, on the Avenue, in my old neighborhood. I live in my head and have a fairly strong imagination that serves me well in these situations. In a few minutes, I am no longer in Vancouver and I am back east.

I don't acknowledge any place as home. Home, to me, is a destabilizing concept. For me, anything that can be thought of as "stable" can always be taken away as anything else can, but it will hurt more. I don't even use the word home very often. I don't believe in it. It's just another thing I would come to depend on and I hate anything that I depend on as I feel it holds power over me. I figure if someone finds out you like, want or need anything too much, they'll find a way to take it away from you or otherwise ruin it. So, I have taught myself not to attach and only value things that are pretty hard to ruin. That's why I like seasons of the year. There's not a lot some motherfucker can do to the month of October. You can legislate or try to block it but it's still coming after September.

Still, if there was any place I would consider "home" it would be my old neighborhood in DC. I like to walk around the streets there. I don't need much from the place. I have a good time on my own just walking around. It's hard to roll the streets up and fuck me out of the chance to walk around. So, I like to walk around alone on the streets of where I lived before I moved to California. The move to LA from DC was the major corner I turned in my life. I have never liked LA and don't have any good memories of the place. LA has a violence I don't understand the way I understand East Coast violence. There's good parts to the place and I have had a lot of good luck there but it's not my kind of place and all these years later, it's still not. Ever since the day I left for LA to be in Black Flag, I think of DC all the time and value the times I have to be back there. It's always good to see Ian MacKaye. It's always good to check in with Ian because he's the most solid person I have ever met. I always have all this stupid bullshit I put myself through—the fucked up way I am living my life by field stripping and destroying time as it goes by. Most of the time, I don't want to be alive but I stick it out so it's good to check in with Ian because he's so zero bullshit, it gives me some perspective.

In LA I stay to myself because it makes it easier to do time there. Being around people only makes it more difficult to be there. I get the work done and try to not interact with anyone I am not working with. When I am in DC and on my own, it's a better version of alone. When I walk around there, I am actually happy. It's a strange feeling for me but it's how I feel. I feel happy just walking past places I used to work at or places I knew from when I was young. The way the air smells at night, the trees, the moisture in the air—it's all I need. I wouldn't mind being there right now. When I am there, I am reminded of the simplicity of my life in those days and sometimes I really miss that. No matter how simple your life is now, it is not as simple and to the point as it was when you were younger. You can't help but drag more stuff with you as the years go on. Experience has a price tag.

Chest, abs, run. Airplane food, noodles and fish, water, coffee 2 cups.

06-13-06 Vancouver Canada: 2326 hrs. They didn't need me on the set today so I kept myself busy doing other things. I interviewed David Johansen of the New York Dolls for Interview Magazine at 1530 hrs. today. He was great. I have met him a couple of times now. Once when I was on his radio show and then again when he and the band came out to LA and played on the IFC show. He doesn't disappoint in person. I love his voice, it's huge, like a bullfrog talking to you. Today, we talked about the new album, One Day It Will Please Us To Remember Even This, which I have heard some of and really like. The most interesting part of the conversation was when we talked about

Arthur Kane, the New York Dolls original bass player. If you saw the recent documentary on the Dolls, <u>New York Doll</u>, you saw how much Arthur needed to re-connect with Johansen. It meant so much to him to be in the band again and to be with David onstage. Within weeks of the band making their reunion appearance at the Meltdown Festival, Arthur Kane died. David wondered if Arthur was fighting back his illness to get to that last shot and then when he got it, he checked out.

On the news I watched that Teflon fat fuck Karl Rove speak in New Hampshire. He was ripping on the Dems expressing anger over the handling of the failed liberation of Iraq. *"They may be with you for the first shots but they're not going to be with you for the tough battles."* He talks like he was just there getting shot at. I guess he was striking back at Murtha and Kerry, those two pussies who were in Vietnam but don't know about war like Karl Rove does—a real fuckin' man. It's amazing how he refuses to take on the real issue and twists the logic so if you are against the invasion and occupation of Iraq, you are seen as anti-American, anti-troop and pro-terrorist. Yes, it's great that Saddam Hussein is not around anymore to kill his own people, you baby Huey bastard, but it's not worth almost 2500 dead, 18000+ injured and who knows how many trillions of dollars. Compassion for the Iraqis was never the real reason for going in. That some people still defend this administration is incredible, there are some stupid motherfuckers out there.

Apparently, the letter I wrote to Ann "The Man" Coulter that aired on the IFC show is now making the rounds on the internet. I heard that Arianna Huffington dug it. I am getting a lot of letters about it. Ann's got those runaway bride eyes now. She really looks bizarre on TV these days. She appears on all kinds of shows. She's got fans. There's people who probably only read three books a year and hers is one of them. I think Rush Limbaugh wrote the foreword to her new book. Must be cool to have such a high-profile drug addict as one of your fans. I think I saw her on CNN twice last week. I am sure she's on Fox almost every day. She says all the stuff those foaming maniacs like to hear. I love it when I get hate mail from people who watch Fox and think Bush is a great President. I always write them back and tell them the truth—that they're fuckin' morons. There's no reasoning with them and there's no need to be cool. That makes things really simple, doesn't it?

It's frustrating that these people rarely go through any of the pain that they heap on others. That's the part that really gets to me. The hypocritical double standard and the fact that so many people are alright with that. That Rove dodged the bullet with the indictments surprised me about as much as it did him. I don't think any of those bitches will go to jail. Bush won't be impeached and history will probably remember him as one of the good guys. Bush, Rove, Cheney, Rumsfeld, Wolfowitz never went to war, yet they have so much to say about bravery and sacrifice and people eat it up. I can't take it when I see someone in the Army applauding Bush. Any man in the Military is ten times the man George Bush is. Bush is not fit to fetch their water. They should at least trade salaries.

I got in a good workout today. I have been running a little better the last few days. Today was a six-miler and it felt good. I have been using the iPod for runs, mainly to drown out all the people who use this gym to watch television, talk and have conversations on their cell phones. It's hard to concentrate on the run when someone is having a conversation next to me. Before I used the iPod and had to listen to someone's bullshit conversation while I was trying not to puke, I would chant "Allahu Akbar" and that would always make them stop. I like the iPod better. Today was <u>Houses Of The Holy</u>. I used Slayer's <u>God Hates Us All</u> for yesterday's 440 runs.

Tonight, after I ate, I took a break from writing and sat at the coffee place and watched people walk by. A lot of couples and homeless people. It's a strange combination. I don't know much about what happens in the regular world, I don't know what is the thing to wear or what to listen to so it's always interesting to look at people and see what is "happening." One of the things that's interesting is the clothes some people wear that are already kind of fucked up looking.

You can buy clothes with frayed edges and tears in them for a lot of money. I watched one guy walk by with his hot girlfriend. For almost half a block, he adjusted his ear plugs so they would hang behind his ears. If I went out on a date and the female was adjusting her ear plugs, I would just tell her to put them in her ears, turn up the music and fuck off. People are strange to me.

The nights here have been great. I walk around, eat some food and find some place to sit for a little while. Not many people talk to me. One guy came up to me tonight and asked me if I was me and the fellow at the grocery store thanked me for the music. People here are very friendly and polite. It's easy to get along here so far.

Arms, run. Yoghurt, granola, salmon teriyaki, sushi, sesame bars, popcorn, carrot juice, coffee 2 cups.

06-14-06 Vancouver Canada: 2338 hrs. Today, no workout. I ran and lifted three days in a row so today I let the body rest but it was really hard to resist going to the gym. I will hit it hard when I get off work tomorrow night. In the morning, I head to the set to rehearse a fight scene that we'll be shooting Friday. I am glad we're getting some time to work on that scene. I have done a few fight scenes and it's always better to rehearse them. I remember one where the other actor and myself ended up injuring each other pretty hard even though we had worked on it. I don't know how it will go tomorrow but I'm sure it will be a lot of work. I don't mind the physical work. I'll take it over dialog any time. I don't have a lot of dialog left in the film now. It's mostly fighting and running.

I have been thinking about taking a trip to DC when I get this film done. I will have a few days off in July before band practice. I could get out of LA for a few days on July 5th after I do the radio show. Trips like this are the things I use to keep myself motivated. It's that carrot at the end of the stick. It's not like I am hating where I am or what I'm doing but the idea of walking around on those streets and looking at the trees is a good tool to keep the morale up. I have found that it's good to put small things like that a few miles ahead of you on the trail so you have something to look forward to.

Henry Rollins

Going back to DC is like returning to a reference point. It's a true north. When I am there, I know where I am. I spend so much time getting to the next place to get to the next place that I get somewhat lost in my own shuffle. It's good to have a day or two where I have no assignment other than to walk around. When I am there, that's what I do for the most part. I just walk around streets I walked decades before. Sometimes I retrace old routes I used to walk to different jobs and actually go into the place just to see what it feels like so many years later. What's great for me about some of these routes is that not a lot has changed. I guess it's a way of checking in with myself.

I try not to attach to anything or anyone. During the first year I started living all over the place, I learned that the less you attach yourself to, the better. I think it was Nietzsche who had a one liner about that. I am sure I'm paraphrasing but I think it went along the lines of: that which you possess is that which possesses you. I think there's a lot to that. I don't want to miss a person or a thing. It is a bad battle strategy. Anything that could be deleterious to morale out here has to go. However, as much as I hate to admit it, I do miss walking around on those streets enough to go all the way out there just to do it for a few days.

One of the hardest parts about a visit to DC is when it's time to leave. Something I had been looking forward to is over and it's hard to take. There are a few recurring moments that almost always happen and are always painful: One is when I walk out the door of my friend Ian's house for the last time of the visit. Another, which is worse, is the cab ride back to Dulles Airport. There is an extreme sadness that hits me hard as the cab leaves the neighborhood. A sadness so profound, it almost negates any good memories I have accrued over the time of the visit. I feel like my life is draining out of my shoes. It's enough to make me think twice about going out there in the first place.

The exact opposite is true of the ride into town. Just seeing the trees on the GW Parkway as we head to Key Bridge makes me truly happy, something that doesn't happen to me very often. I have taken that ride many times over the last quarter of a century. I wonder if I lived there, would all the things I feel about the place abate as the surroundings would become familiar? Would it turn into just another place to exist? Would it make me want to go somewhere else?

To a certain extent, I try to keep myself out of comfort zones. I say a certain extent because if I wanted to push myself harder, I would spend more time around people. That's very difficult for me to do. Being alone is much more comfortable and most of the time, if I have an option, that's where I go. It's one of the reasons I try not to go to DC all that often. I don't want to give myself too much of what I want. It's like when you feed a dog all it wants to eat. The dog will make itself sick. If I am in surroundings that are too pleasing too often I fear what could happen to me. I am barely hanging onto where I am as it is and since one of my main motivations is desperation I fear getting all I want. I truly do.

Desperation keeps me lean and mean and leaning into the wind. Failure is a great factor in my life. I have to factor in a certain degree of failure into all things I do because I am not good at anything. Desperation, failure and dissatisfaction are huge parts of my equation. I would rather almost get it or fail miserably most of the time. Success would fuck me up. Periods of sustained happiness would be my downfall. Well now!

Yoghurt, granola, minestrone soup, ginger cookies, water, carrot juice, coffee 2 cups.

06-15-06 Vancouver Canada: 2241 hrs. Live and learn. I thought I was in pretty good shape. Wrong. We worked on a fight scene today. A few stunt guys and I blocked out the entire scene and ran through it a bunch of times at different speeds. At the end, we were all out of breath and had dirt all over us. It's going to look good. But damn, those guys are in some serious shape. I'm going to have to change up my training or something. It's good to do that anyway but I need to step it up somehow. I got back here and had to have a little lie down before I went to the gym. I did some shoulders and abs and then a fast four mile run that felt pretty good. I have to be up at 0400 hrs. and I think it's going to be a long day getting that fight scene together. Who knows, it might just come together, we nail the master, get all the close ups and we're done. I don't know but I have a feeling it's going to be a long day. Not very good hate mail today. You motherfuckers have to step up your game too.

Shoulders, abs., run. Yoghurt, granola, veggie burger patty, sesame bars, water, carrot juice, coffee 1 cup.

06-16-06 Vancouver Canada: 2322 hrs. Today was long and I'm glad it's over. We did good work but it was a long day. I left at 0645 hrs. and came back at 2222 hrs. I am pretty baked and my body took some hits. Both knees got smashed up pretty good and I cracked my elbow on something and at one point the actor I was fighting with gave me a pretty good right to the jaw. He didn't mean it, of course. I spent a lot of time hanging upside down from a harness. The upside down part isn't all that bad. The harness though, that's not so great 6 hours in. We got it done and our director is happy with the work. So, I am pulling my weight and working for a living. It's never old to me, earning my keep and making my way in the world. It was a priority very early on. I would have been happy to be in the working world by 14 or so, no problem. I would have much rather had a job and a room in an apartment by 14 like I had when I was out of high school. I was done with the idea of home very early. It's probably one of the reasons I am like I am.

I only slept about three hours last night but felt pretty good today. I dozed off for about ten minutes after lunch and that did me good. I don't think I can stay up too much later now and that's too bad as Friday night is my favorite time of the week.

I just looked at my calendar and I have been up here on and off for almost a month. I thought it was more like two weeks. When I am working like this, I don't notice the time go by.

I hacked those fight scenes much better today even though we hit it for hours. I guess it took my body a little time to get used to the different kind of activity. I am glad to be back in the room and on my own.

Yoghurt, granola, scrambled eggs, 2 muffins, tofu and vegetables, sesame bars, water, coffee 1 cup.

06-17-06 Vancouver Canada: 2311 hrs. I slept pretty hard after all yesterday's festivities. I didn't sleep much the night before and that probably had something to do with it as well.

Today I mainly worked on notes for the radio show. I try to put 1000 words a day into one project or another. So far I am past 2000. I have been behind with the film and jet lag. A week ago, I was in London. This last week has been a blur. Sometimes that's how I like it. Just one thing after another and you just run at it and try to keep up.

I didn't get out much today. I went to the grocery store and knew it was going to be one of those days where I wouldn't be good around people so I got some food and ate in my room. Some days, I'm not good to go around people and I try to keep myself out of general population. I am living in a loud and busy neighborhood. This is where people come to eat, buy clothes, drink and be seen so on the weekends it's very populated.

In the late afternoon I went to the gym and did part two of my shoulder workout, ran a lot of fast quarter milers and did abdominal work. The running hurt but I got through it.

Dashboard Confessional played on the IFC show tonight. The hotel doesn't get IFC but I know they must have played because the angry letters are now coming in. I don't have anything against the band at all but they really weren't my choice to be on the show. They were on a list of bands for the show and I kind of waved them through. Basically, I wasn't watching the ball. Like I said, I have nothing against the band but they're not my idea of a good band for the show and they are very popular and don't need our little show for promotion. I knew I was going to get some static about their appearance and now I am. Hopefully not too much. I know it must be confusing to people who watch the show with any regularity. Perhaps after this broadcast, they won't be watching all that regularly any more. I can blame no one but myself on that one. A sample:

"Dashboard Confessional is probably the number one cookie cutter MTV pop punk trend following band out on the market. As a fan of just about everything Rollins has done up to this point, I feel the need to let him know this. His show has lost all artistic merit in my book. I would never of pictured him as a guest host on TRL, but now... So thanks for letting me down Hank." --JD

It's a waste of time to blame anyone but yourself when something bad happens. Most of the time, if you were more on the ball, you wouldn't be in that situation. That's at least true for me. I have no one to blame for any bad thing that comes my way for the most part.

I got a letter yesterday from one of the old gang from the Black Flag days. He was writing about our leader, Greg Ginn. Black Flag was Greg's band and all the songs that everyone likes, chances are, he's the one who wrote them. He was an amazing guitar player and song-writer. I don't know if he plays now or what he's up to. Anyway, this old associate wrote me about GG. Rarely do I hear from one of the old boys when the topic of GG isn't raised. There's little doubt that any-one who had anything to do with the band or who had close ties to the record label was left unaffected by him.

Greg doesn't like me. That's clear. If he ever talks about me in interviews, he rips me. I am used to it. It's a Saturday night and GG doesn't like me. I got it and I'm still here nonetheless. I don't lose sleep over it but one thing that did cause pain is the thing that was raised by yesterday's brief correspondence and it's a testament to how much those times meant to all of us and how much they are still a part of our lives now.

I remarked how it was sad how the whole thing shook out at the end. A letter came back agreeing and adding that people from those days still write him and tell him how much it all meant to them and how hurt, bitter and generally confused they are about how every-thing ended. Apparently GG doesn't really like any of us, so, we're united in that sense. We're like some survivor's group at this point.

It took me a while to isolate what hurt me most and longest but I finally figured it out. It was, for me at least, that GG made if difficult, if not impossible, to come away from our years on the road with Black Flag with any sense of pride. Pride is a sentiment that I usually try to stay away from because I think it can hang you up as much as it can do anything good. That being said, the players in that particular band took it all very seriously. We toured hard, practiced hard and gave it all we could. I am not saying GG didn't. He did. He worked as hard or harder than any of us on our best days. It's just that GG wasn't cut out for leadership. He never gave us any encouragement. Even the smallest compliment from him would have gone so far. We killed it every night onstage for that guy.

Perhaps he didn't understand or see the need to boost morale but in any case he made it a very hard and confusing environment to work in. I don't know a single member of that band who hasn't said something to this effect to me over the years. I am not saying we were all good and he was all bad and I am not ripping on the guy like he does to me. He gave me the opportunity of a lifetime and it's the reason I am where I am now. But I would be lying if I said there wasn't a lot of pain in the rearview when it comes to those times.

It sticks in the throat to have given so much and feel like it meant nothing at the end. As it is now, I keep all Black Flag records, flyers and anything else having to do with the band separate from everything else. I never look at any of it except when I have to, like when we released the revised edition of Get In The Van. When people tell me they like the band, I am always polite and say thanks but it means nothing to me because it feels like they are talking about some band that has nothing to do with me. When someone says the band changed their lives or something, like I said, I am polite as it changed my life too but I always either try to change the subject or say a quick thank you so we can be done or I tell them that the band and all those great songs were GG's, which is the truth.

The time I spent in Black Flag is one of the reasons I identify so heavily with the Military. I had a lot of that discipline and sensibility drilled into me from a very early age and it has served me well. With music, film, and I'm sure a ton of other occupations, being professional is an absolute must. I am in the entertainment and service industry side of things so it's what I know and I can tell you, a sense of duty and professionalism is huge in the environments I work in. I thrive on it. I identify with Marines more than they'll ever know.

I understand how they feel when I hear injured men tell me they want nothing more than to go back to Iraq and get back to work. That pride and love of duty is the cause of one the major disconnects people in America have with the mentality of the soldiers. If you tell them the Invasion of Iraq was wrong, they don't always understand that you're not being critical of them personally. As soon as those boots hit the ground there, it's all about pride, attitude and guts. The right and wrong elements are immediately off the table. I understand. All I'm saying is I wish I could feel a little better about those years because believe me, we all gave and we gave all. So, not the best memories but I just stow it and keep moving down the trail. I don't see any other way.

It's been a good night. It's well past midnight now and I have been in my room, listening to music, writing this and stuff for the IFC show and I've been drinking heavily. There is a really good market next door to the hotel and they have fresh carrot juice, so it's been an evening of mineral water with lime, carrot juice and coffee. Outside my window, several floors below, people are still yelling. They serve alcohol in Canada and a lot of Canadians have been tipped off about this and are doing a lot of independent research.

Shoulders, abs., run. Yoghurt, granola, clam chowder, rice crackers, sesame bars, water, coffee 2 cups.

06-18-06 Vancouver Canada: 2341 hrs. I spent most of the day writing stuff for upcoming radio shows. I didn't go out except to go to the grocery store. I didn't feel like dealing with all the noise outside, which was considerable. I think it was World Cup related. Lots of people with flags cheering and walking around, that has to be it. I ran 7 miles today. Felt good when I did it but I am feeling it in the knees now. Tomorrow is a day off from running. I am trying to run six days a week. I am hoping to get a ten miler done before I wrap out of here.

One of the actresses on the film and her husband very kindly invited me to their room for dinner and I went. They are cool. The food was good, too. So, that was alright. I got back from that awhile ago. I walked around outside a little after noticing the crowds of people were gone.

I got a letter from Ian. He said Fugazi bassist Joe Lally's solo album is all done. I heard the demos for it several weeks ago and thought it was really great. I can't wait to hear the final version. All kinds of DC players are on it. Fugazi types and Wino from the Obsessed are on it for sure. I don't know who else. Ian also said that progress on the new Evens album is slow but moving forward. He's been in one studio or another between the two projects. I am so glad The Evens are getting another record together.

I stayed away from the news for the last couple of days. Now and then, I have to give myself a break from the constant bad news and all the people saying that things are going well in Iraq. It's such crap. It's depressing to know that the bad guys like Rove, Cheney and the rest will get a pass and never have to deal with what they did. It really has nothing to do with Bush anymore, he doesn't make any of the policy. He just staggers through his dumbass, embarrassing speeches and does what he's told. Never changes the message so the douche bags can say he's staying "on message" and he never says anything of any importance. Now and then, I need a break from the cowardice and the lies and the millions of people who think we're doing so well.

I feel good though. I feel good that I am alone and have a job. I am glad I am working hard on set every day I am there and putting in time at the gym to be ready for the tour. I am glad I still take all this stuff as seriously as I do. When you no longer fear it and want to serve it, you should go.

I want to get out there and see what the band can do in the world. At practice it sounds really good. I think so at least. I sometimes wonder if it's just me wanting it to be good though. If it's sounding and feeling so good, then why did it not feel good at the end of the 1997 tour and make me conclude that we had finished our work? Are we in denial? Is it like when you go out to dinner with the woman you stopped dating a year before and you're reminded of all the reasons you broke up except this time I'm not remembering why we broke up? I am hoping that it's all real and will prove itself onstage. It will prove itself onstage one way or the other. I'll just have to wait and see what way that is. It could be great or it could be a month long disaster.

Run. Yoghurt, granola, fish, pasta, popcorn, vanilla ice cream, sesame bars, water, coffee 2 cups.

06-19-06 Vancouver Canada: 2247 hrs. I will be up at 0400 hrs. for an 0530 hrs. pick up. It will be a long day. I did a lot of writing for the radio and IFC shows today. I gave my body a rest from the gym and will hit it tomorrow. The gym, along with the fight scenes I have to do tomorrow, will give me a good workout. I did not shoot today. I would have rather been at the set working but that's the breaks. I never get bored on this set. There have been films I have done that were really hard to get through. This one is not one of them.

I spent time today working on annotating songs for a radio show I want to do on July 4th of all DC area bands. I figure it's a big holiday and there will be a lot of activity in the nation's Capitol so I might as well pay tribute to that. Also, it's just me being selfish and wanting to write about music from the city I come from.

Nothing happened today. I spent some time thinking about why I do all the things I do at the rate I do them. I came to the conclusion that I know myself well enough to know that I am lazy and unproductive and am working against those truths. It's like mowing a lawn. You don't mow it just once. I have to keep hammering away at my complacency and mediocre expectations of myself. I use this self-contempt to move me to action. I learn lessons all the time and try to retain them. For instance, yesterday I finally ran 7 miles, I probably had that run in me for some time but my inherent lack of willpower kept me from getting there. I have to demand more of myself now. I

A Dull Roar

see that there's not a lot of time left where I will be able to get around and do things how I do them now.

I do my best to stay busy because I have found it keeps depression at a distance. Depression is a fairly constant factor in my life. It's with me more often than not and I have learned how to deal with it. Immersion in work, or what I can convince myself is work, is one of the ways I distract myself. Work is a way I distance myself from myself. I self-medicate with work. Took me awhile to figure that out but I understand it now. The harder I work, the more I am involved within it and the less I am thinking about myself. That's probably cowardly but that's how I deal with it. It's either that or inaction. At the end of the day, I am not really inspired or driven or even all that ambitious as much as just trying to stay upright, fed and fighting.

I am looking forward to working tomorrow. I like the chance to prove myself in this film. I worked my ass off getting that fight scene to be full-on the other day.

Clam chowder, sesame bars, rice crackers, cookies, popcorn, water, V8 juice, coffee 1 cup.

06-20-06 Vancouver Canada: 2247 hrs. I am sorry but I can't write here tonight. I did over 15 hours on the film today, which was difficult and compounded by the fact that I didn't sleep last night so I am really not good for much except falling over. We did a lot of cool stuff today. It's great working outdoors all day but I have noticed that it's harder than working inside. I bet there's something to that. People should probably spend more time outside.

Scrambled eggs, sesame bars, pasta, fish, water, coffee ? cups.

06-21-06 Vancouver Canada: 2325 hrs. I slept last night but didn't sleep all that well. I woke up after about 4 hours and stressed out about stuff and then fell out for a few more hours and then went to the set.

I waited for hours to work and then they said I was cut for the day and they'll throw today's work in with tomorrow's stuff. I got back here and ran five miles and then did a leg workout. That trainer I yelled at the other day was in the gym when I walked in. He glared at me and I just stared back at him.

There was a great moment during the run that happened about three miles in. I have been running a lot and it's been hard on my knees and they are hurting more and more as the weeks go on. At about the three mile mark, my knees were really hurting and I started losing concentration. This is a moment when my inherent mediocrity tries to take over and I have to fight it with the desire to better myself. That my legs wanted to fold after only three miles made me mad. I thought of all those nights coming up and how fucking hard it's going to be and all those moments partway through the set when my legs will be shot and I will be in a lot of pain and the level of anger I got to just thinking about it gave me the strength to press on. A lot of times when I am feeling tired while running I just think of the fact that we're opening for X and how much I want to feed them their guts every night. I like them but any band I open for I want to destroy. It's the only way. It gives purpose to training and everything in my life.

I came back in here, changed and hobbled to the market and bought some food. I ate the food and have been working on writing for the IFC show. I am behind and I am trying to catch up. I need to send in one more thing. I'll get that done tomorrow hopefully and be done. They all need to be in the teleprompter by Saturday.

I have to be up in four hours to go back to the set so I have to try and get some sleep. It's been hard lately. I am starting to stress about the tour. At this time I am not able to keep all the stuff I have to do compartmentalized and it's all running together. I have to keep hammering away. In a week from Saturday, I will be done with the IFC show for the year and I will be wrapped out of the film and able to zero in on just the tour.

We have been doing good work on the film. Yesterday was hard but we got some really good shots done. I've had a great time working on this film.

Run, legs. Scrambled eggs, fish, clam chowder, sesame bars, minestrone soup, rice crackers, protein drink, water, coffee 2 cups.

A Dull Roar

06–22–06 Vancouver Canada: 2348 hrs. I didn't sleep last night for longer than an hour. I don't know why I couldn't sleep. I got out of bed around 0530 hrs. and wrote up the last of the IFC stuff and sent it in. I did a 12-hour day on the film.

I think I have overdone it on the running. It's hard not to run every day. I really like it but I have developed a great case of shin splints on my left leg that hurts like a bastard. I can take a lot of pain and am used to my body letting me down but this pain is extraordinary. It makes me yell out loud. So, I will have to cool it on the running for some time. I'll hit the bike to keep myself breathing hard.

Of course today, with my knee ringing with pain, I had to do a lot of uphill running. I had arrows shot at me and an axe hit a tree next to my face. It was all really cool but hurt like a bastard to get up those hills quickly and not limp. Sometimes our director would ask if I had another one in me and I would tell him that I was good to do another 100 takes. It's true. There's no way I'm not going to kill in every scene for our director Joe. When I was doing the actual running and whatever else, there was no pain. It was after the take where the pain was substantial. It's alright though, I got the shots he wanted and we got through the day. Even if I didn't like him as much as I do, I would always give the director what the director wants. Whenever I am on a film, I always strive to make sure the director and producer know they got the right person for the job. Can't let them down.

I have done quite a lot of films for someone who isn't an actor. On a few occasions, I have seen an actor dial in the performance or be too cool to really give all and it's absolute torture to be trapped in a film with them. That's what has made this film so great to work on—everyone is so full on and trying to get the best takes possible, from the cast to the crew. It's been great. If I could be in more working environments like this on films, I would go after more parts. I hate auditions. I hate hanging out in waiting rooms with people as we line up to go in and read lines to a casting agent. That being said, if work like this was guaranteed on the other end, I would put myself through that agony more often.

Henry Rollins

I have to get up in a few hours. Since I didn't really sleep last night, I am going to try for at least 5-6 hours tonight. I have a lot of work to do until next Friday when I wrap out of this film.

Deadlift, abs. Scrambled eggs, sesame bars, minestrone soup, rice crackers, water, coffee 2 cups.

06-23-06 Vancouver Canada: 2117 hrs. Back in my room. I was on from 0715 hrs. until about 1600 hrs. Not so bad. I got back here and worked out as soon as I could scrape myself off the couch.

We didn't do a lot today, just some insert shots and small scenes. It has been great shooting in this park all these days. We usually shoot in deep forest where the trees are massive and covered in moss. The ground is usually soft and has a strange bounce to it because it's mainly comprised of dead trees and leaves. It's cool and moist inside the forest but there's a lot of mosquitoes and that can get to you. The way the light filters in and reflects off all the different textures of green is amazing. I have not seen more than a minute of the film on a video monitor but what I saw looked great with all the natural lighting.

There's no drama on this film that I know of. I have done films in the cesspool of LA and there's always some fucking drama going on between some of the actors or with the director or producer. It's such bullshit. I've seen all kinds of stupid shit like the males hitting on the females, people coming to work high, people coming in really late. There's none of that kind of thing on this film that I know of. I think if there were something like that going on, I would have heard about it by now.

It's a Friday night, my favorite night of the week and I am trying to enjoy it but it's hard as I have to be up in a few hours and have a long day ahead of me. I have an 0300 hrs. wake up and an 0430 ride to the airport. I get to LA at 0950 hrs. or so and go right to the studio. I have some teleprompter stuff at the top of the day, then Stephen Gaghan comes in for interview at 1300 hrs. then there's more teleprompter and then, hopefully, I am out the door around 1730 – 1800 hrs.

I will do my laundry, prep for Sunday's work and then, wait a minute, my schedule, is not showing any work on Sunday. Damn, could it be I have no work on Sunday? Perhaps I could convince Engineer X to come to the radio station and we could tape a show for this coming Tuesday and not have to use a re-run. I'll write management and see what the deal is on that. I could get some work done at the office if that Sunday is indeed an off day.

Nice news report today of a 4-foot alligator lunging at a man in Pottstown, Pennsylvania early this morning as he was retrieving a newspaper he misthrew. I like that. I like the idea of alligators in PA. Unfortunately, alligators don't live that far north in America but it sure would be cool if they did. This morning on the way to work, a large black bear ran across the road to our left. I like the idea of having to be careful being outside your house because there are bears around.

Chest, abs. Scrambled eggs, sesame bars, rice crackers, V8 juice, carrot juice, water, coffee 2 cups.

06-24-06 LA CA: 2230 hrs. I will have to catch up here later. I am not all that tired, more fried/wired from the day. I think now that this day is done, I can get the other ones knocked out alright.

I had the perfect seat on the plane next to the kid who didn't want to sit still for a second of the flight. I know how it is and liked him alright but he made it hard to sleep so it didn't happen. I got to the studio and had a little while before I had to do anything.

I did some teleprompter reads and then Stephen Gaghan came in for his interview. Really cool guy and easily one of the most fascinating people I've ever met. A good part of the interview was talking about his film Syrianna. The stories he told about traveling the world with ex-CIA man Robert Baer as he gathered research for the film were completely nuts. I mean, completely. The whole room was riveted on his every word. That's the part I want to write more about when I am more awake and don't have this schedule breathing down my neck. Put it this way, it's enough for a one-hour special just on him and the film. He's completely humble about it all but the people he met and the things he heard are jaw drop material. It was really intense talking to someone who is that brilliant. He was extremely articulate. It was a highpoint for sure.

The rest of the day was mechanics. We did good work but it's all kind of foolproof as it's teleprompter reads and if you get it wrong, you just do it again.

I have really damaged my left knee. It has to be from the running. It's nonstop pain. It's ok if I take my weight off it but when I am walking around, damn. It's going to make training and the shows a bit more challenging than it already is.

I managed to get to the grocery store. I figured I should get some food in here and some to take back to Canada. At check out, there was this female who always goes out of her way to say something kind of, fuck, I don't know how to describe it, I guess she doesn't like me so she gives me this wise ass bullshit. Last night a man rang me out and she bagged up the items and asked me, "Need help carrying that to your car?" I had not seen her in months, I didn't think she even worked there anymore and then when she said that, I remembered her. Of course I didn't say anything, I just looked down, took my stuff and left. Over and over again, I have come to the conclusion that for the most part, people are better when they're on the page or the screen. In real life, a lot of the time, they're just alligator food.

Protein bar, bagel, cream cheese, pasta, rice bowl, cup of yoghurt, water, coffee 2 cups.

06-25-06 LA CA: 0657 hrs. I have a couple of hours before I have to be responsible for anything. I was really hoping there would be a CD I purchased recently waiting for me at the office when I went in there last night. I just found a copy of the 12 Hits From Hell album by The Misfits and I wanted to load it into my iPod so I could take some notes on it for an upcoming radio show. I figured I could make good use of the downtime at the hotel this coming week. It wasn't there though.

I didn't rack out as soon as I wanted to last night. I have been so tired at lights out, I don't remember much of what has happened before but thinking about it now, it was closer to 0030 hrs. when I fell out. I was up at 0450 hrs. and figured I should get up and get it going as this will probably be the schedule for the rest of the week and this is a good chance to get as used to it as I'm going to get.

My call time is not so bad. I should try to get some things done around here or the office before I head down there. I could go to the office, do some cleaning and get some work done for upcoming radio shows.

2242 hrs.: A good day today. Again, I am behind, have to be up early as hell and have a long day. Perhaps I can catch up on the plane. Interviewed Johnny Knoxville today. Really great but I knew it was going to be a good one. I have always thought that guy had a very cool thing. The kind of thing that you can't take lessons for. You just have it. Whatever it is, he's got a few truckloads. I will recount a bit about the interview tomorrow or perhaps there will be some time when I get up to Canada.

I have to watch <u>Factotum</u> now. It's based on the Bukowski book of the same name. Matt Dillon is in it and I am interviewing him tomorrow and then bailing out to the airport. I am going to try and get up again at around the same time I did this morning.

Oatmeal, bagels, cream cheese, salmon, potato and tomato salad, water, coffee 2 cups.

06-26-06 Vancouver Canada: 2225 hrs. I got in here a little while ago and want to rack out as soon as I can. I am setting the alarm clock for 0400 hrs. and will be sticking to that all week.

I interviewed Matt Dillon today. Our producer on the film, Jeff, has worked with him before and told me last week that I would enjoy the interview with Matt. He said that Matt is a sharp guy who is very articulate. Jeff was right, Matt was a great interview. I was struck by his sincerity and his humility. He was really cool and we did a good interview.

Mostly, we talked about his new film, <u>Factotum</u>, which is based on the Bukowski book of the same name. I think they probably drew from other books of his as well. I thought Matt did a good job as he didn't try to imitate Bukowski, the way Philip Seymour Hoffman got into Truman Capote, but achieved great Bukowski-ness nonetheless.

The Dillon interview and a few other things were all we had to do today. The show's producers couldn't get a 4th guest in time for the tapings, so instead of wrapping today, it drags out even further until July 5th when I think we bring in Kevin Smith of <u>Clerks</u> fame. I was really hoping that by this coming Friday I was going to be done with the IFC show and the film so I could concentrate on the band tour. I'll get through it.

I have to get up early so I should stop here. I don't feel like stopping but I want to put in a good day for Joe tomorrow. I think I get off work a little early and will try to get some more written then.

Oatmeal, yoghurt, bagels, cream cheese, fish, vegetables, water, coffee 1 cup.

06-27-06 Vancouver Canada: 0503 hrs. I got up around 0350. I couldn't believe how fast the time went sleeping. I woke up once around 0200 hrs. from a bad dream that I can't remember. I have a lot of those. I have these dreams where it seems I sabotage everything in them so nothing goes right. In a dream I'll be standing somewhere and immediately jump onto the side of a train that's heading into a wall. I'll meet a woman and notice that I've handcuffed myself. Dreams like this are a constant with me. They are the only dreams I really remember these days. It's probably just acting out some kind of self-hatred or something.

I am watching CNN out of the corner of my eye and the reporter is standing in front of a building in Baghdad that I remember seeing when I was there. I don't know if I'll ever get back there but that trip will stand out as one of the stranger ones I've experienced. It's lame to brag about it or try to impress people with it but it was one hell of a week, that's for sure. It was one of those times that I will always tie in with other times in my life. Like when I first toured with Black Flag, the big tour in 1982. These times in my life have become reference points.

I have not heard from the USO in some time. I wonder if I have become undesirable to them. I have nothing to indicate that. Perhaps they are busy with other stuff. It would be good to get back out there with them after the tour is over, if they'll have me.

Usually, the earlier I get up, the less depressed I am. Writing also helps. Ok, I have to get ready to hit it. I have a 0555 hrs. pick up.

2030 hrs. I just got a call from the set and my call time has been moved ahead again. It's now 0815 hrs. Those poor bastards are still there. I got there a little after 0600 and the crew was already there so they are heading into hour 15 or something. That isn't uncommon, especially on the last few days of the film and it has to get done so it gets done. I was told that on Friday, I might be working through the night into Saturday and might not be able to make the morning flight out of town. I told them to book whatever they wanted, we get the film done and then we'll worry about flights. Everyone on this show works really hard.

I did some quick scenes and some press and then I was out of there. My whole day on set was about 6 hours. I came back here with the intention of writing and working on a radio show I am doing about The Misfits where I want to break down the 12 Hits From Hell album and compare the tracks to the original mixes. The 12 Hits promo CD is hard to find and I wanted to put it on the radio so perhaps some interested parties will now have access to it if they weren't able to find it on the internet, where it's actually not all that hard to find and download. I have a copy of the CD and I thought it would be cool to do at least part of the show on this very great record. Anyway, I sat down to a-b the mixes and started falling asleep at the desk so I thought I would have a little lie down and woke up about 4 hours later. So much for the idea that I am only going to sleep from 2300 – 0400 hrs. all week and somehow that will be enough.

I am doing damage control on my body as best I can at night after getting back from the set. I am training hard for the tour, doing the film, the IFC show and the radio show. It's all good stuff but it's taking its toll on me. I don't want to wear myself down before the tour. I will work hard in July to maintain muscle mass and watch protein levels and also work on getting restorative sleep regularly.

The days before the band shows up in LA for practice is now filling up with things. I have tour press to do, and I just signed on to be part of an audio book version of Max Brooks' book <u>World War Z</u>. I was told Alan Alda and Carl Reiner are attached to the project. Brad Pitt just nailed down the film rights, beating out DiCaprio for them. Could be a good bit of work. They need it done really soon so when I get out of this film, I'll start getting my head around the script for that and go in and get it done.

Keep it interesting, I say. I try to keep my life interesting. My reason for this is not admirable though. It would be easy to write up some cool bullshit about living every day to the fullest. I think that's a good idea although I don't think I get anywhere close to doing that on any regular basis. I try and make my life "interesting" or at least busy because it keeps my mind off myself. The less I think about myself, the better I feel.

Events are more eventful than I am, so I go towards that. A lot of the work I do is a solitary pursuit but it takes a lot of concentration to complete the task and in that, I get away from myself for hours at a time. It's chicken in a lot of ways but that's how I get by. There's a lot of things I have seen and been through that I would like to forget or have deleted from the hard drive so, a lot of the time, my mind isn't a place I like to spend a lot of time in.

It's one of the things that makes human interaction beyond a certain point very difficult. I can talk to people and I can listen when they talk to me but I don't want to know anyone all that well and I don't want anyone to know me all that well. It's just not interesting to me in the least. In the past perhaps but not anymore.

I would rather work and get things done. None of what I do is of any importance but it gets me through the hours. I feel worthy when I am throwing myself into something that will be a trying experience. Like the band tour coming up. Just thinking about it makes my stomach shrink. That's when I know it's the right thing to do. The challenge of it, the risk of it going badly unless I really give it all I have, that's the thing that keeps it real. It keeps me real.

The last few days, I have not been looking forward to the gym like I usually do because of my left knee being so cranked. I am kinda addicted to running. I would do it every day if I could. Not being able to do it for the past several days has done some damage to my morale so I have to train though that. As I was suiting up for the gym I was thinking that I'll just do a lot of other hard exercise and get it done and that will get the morale up. I went heavy on arms and abs this evening and feel better about the knee being blown out.

I thought about going out earlier to hang out at the coffee place across the street to get out of the room for awhile. I looked out the window and saw all the people on the sidewalk in front of the place and figured I'd be better off here. People—when in doubt, avoid.

Arms, abs. Yoghurt, granola, fruit, muffins, minestrone soup, rice crackers, sesame bars, water, carrot juice, coffee 1 cup.

06-28-06 Vancouver Canada: 0559 hrs. I have been up since 0350 hrs. I fell out a little past 2300 hrs. last night. I slept solid until I woke up and thought about the tour and then my knee started ringing and I couldn't sleep any more. The internet system is down at the hotel which keeps me away from some stuff I wanted to look up. Perhaps I am online too much. It's a perfect place for someone like me.

The news has pictures of the DC area flooding. Wheaton MD flooded. I have not thought of Wheaton for I don't know how many years. I don't remember what connection I had with the place.

More soldier death. More Iraqi civilian death. Watching the news every day and hearing adults rationalize the bullshit they have steered America into ruins my day. The crawl at the bottom of the CNN screen reported a man in Oklahoma committed suicide at a party. The bullet he shot himself with went through his head and into the chest of a 16 year-old girl and killed her.

In a couple of days, it will be two years since my friend's mother passed away. I don't know if the family is going to do anything special on the day to remember her. Last year they did and I was there for it. Ginger. I think about her all the time. I knew her since I was very young. I wish I could be there on the 30th but I will be here working.

2008 hrs. I wasn't in there too long today. We're shooting in a different location now. We're out of the woods and doing interior shots. I have two more days on this. Time has gone very quickly. I left for the first day of this film about 37 days ago. One of the reasons the time passes quickly is because I'm not attached to anyone. Attachments to people and places makes it hard to be away. I'm glad I don't miss anyone living. I miss some people who are gone but there's nothing I can do about their status so I can't spend too much time on those thoughts. Some of the only things I have gotten right in my life is that I never married, am not a parent and am still single.

I just watched Jerry Falwell on CNN doing a lecture at Freedom College, at least that's what it said on the podium he was standing behind. He was doing his usual bullshit on the war on homosexuality and out of wedlock birth. I used to get mad at people like him but now I don't. Perhaps it's time for these people to mobilize and take it to the street so they can feel the backlash. They are sheltered by the weakness of their minds. A guy like Falwell doesn't run into the real world very often and he isn't a realist. None of those guys are. They are just amateur tyrants, cowards without the spine to come in the front door with their prejudice. Falwell and his people should get out of America and move to Iraq. Perhaps they could set up a church in Iraq and convert Shia and Sunni Muslims to Christianity.

I saw most of that Scorsese doc on Dylan tonight. Now that was inspiring. The doc had footage of Pete Seeger singing during the heat of the Civil Rights Movement and Dylan singing about Medgar Evers—talk about guts. How could you come down from the intensity of times like those? I don't think I have ever seen Dylan at his present age in an interview situation. It was interesting to hear what he had to say. It was interesting just to watch his face move. Talk about cutting through the bullshit. The song *Masters Of War* has not lost one second of speed since it was written. How old is that song? 40 years at least. Those times were so wide open and full of potential they make the times we're in now seem like nothing more than machine moves and business transactions.

When people are getting slaughtered every day in Iraq and you have to wade through the non-event of Starr Jones leaving *The View* to get information, I think that it's time to really let people start feeling the impact of their ignorance and cowardice. The weight of cowardice. America elected Bush. In some ways, we deserve what we're getting. The people who still support him deserve all the heartache and thin wallet time they get. Fuck it. I'm done with it. If you brought him to the dance, then dance with him. That so many Americans will be stupid enough to elect another Republican president, which I think is a very good possibility, in 2008 makes me think that perhaps it is time to let it go to the dogs.

Here's some fucked up alternative solutions I came up with, they won't work but what the hell, they're just concepts maaaaan!:

Gay marriage. Fuck it. Let marriage be between a man and a woman. Let the homophobes have their lame, god-soaked ritual. Gay people should come up with something else. If they want to make the union official, they should make up a new name for it, make it really cool and just leave marriage to "straight" people, homophobes and Christian activists. It will be a victory to all those who are tired of arguing with adults with the intellect of children. Closed-minded homophobes will never be changed. Look at all the people who listen to Pat Robertson and think he's great. Look at all the people who applaud the President as he staggers through one of his embarrassing speeches. By dropping the same sex marriage issue, then Jerry Falwell and pieces of shit like him have less to talk about and will have to go fuck off where they came from.

Intelligent Design. Fuck it. Teach it in schools along with the Theory of Evolution. Let the students decide. It will be a perfect way to illustrate natural selection. The stupid ones will go with ID and the smart ones will go with Darwin. The stupid ones will be able to fill all those jobs vacated by the illegal immigrants after they get run out of America by some taxpayer brown shirt hit squad. They will eat shitty fast food, smoke and drink. They will be too illiterate and ignorant to make good choices and will destroy themselves. God will not save them. Wait, even better, in all states that vote overwhelmingly Republican, don't even bother with Darwinian Theory at all! Just give those young and impressionable minds Intelligent Design, Irreducible Complexity and Abstinence Only sex ed. and watch the whacky shenanigans begin. In a few generations, you'll have enough soldiers to fight the War On Terror in China! There you go, problem solved.

Shoulders, Eggs, tomatoes, yoghurt, granola, minestrone soup, rice crackers, sesame bars, water, carrot juice, coffee 1 cup.

06-29-06 Vancouver Canada: 2142 hrs. Got back here a little while ago. Today was really cool. We blew up two people. It was great. I had a three count to get around a corner before a cannon of fake blood and guts was set to come my way. On "two" I was supposed to be getting the hell out of the way. I was moving a little slow off my mark and barely got around the corner of an RV when the cannon went off and a wall of red blew past me and exploded against the wall.

Tomorrow, I go in around 1500 hrs. to start my day. It will be about half way through the shoot day and I think this one will be going very long. I have an 0500 hrs. lobby call for the ride to the airport and have been advised that I might very well be working right up until then. It's the last shoot day and everything that's not done has to get done. My last scenes will be hard to do, these are the scenes where I will use that body cast they made of me weeks ago.

My knee was hammering me today and I think it will be hard to train through it in time for tour. It's not improving at all.

I got back here some hours ago and fell out on the couch for about 20 minutes and tried to get myself to the gym but I don't have it in me. I will hit it before I go to work tomorrow. That will keep me on schedule as I wasn't going to be able to work out tomorrow.

Saturday I will arrive back in LA and get some office work done. I will finish all the work for the radio show on Tuesday so it's out of the way. I have press and studio stuff all next week, right through the holiday.

A Dull Roar

I have to use the weekend to get some solid sleep. I really have to watch the quality and level of nutrition in these last few weeks before we go out. I'm in pretty good shape but can do better. I will do a lot of calisthenics in July and as many push-ups as my right wrist can stand.

It's not all that late but I don't think I can stay up any longer. I have been feeling tired and strange for weeks now. This film was a good bit of work but it's been a lot of work and I'm glad that it's coming to an end so I can get onto the next thing.

I still have to do all the tour press. I am sure I will be doing some while on tour but I have a lot to do before and it starts in a few days. Next week will be full of work, even though it's a "holiday." I don't take holidays so it's all the same to me. I hate doing press. I can do it, I just don't like doing it. Most of the time, the journalists are cool to me and I am always cool back. I have no reason to be otherwise but I'd rather not do another interview again as long as I live. Music press is full of wise guys so I have be ready to take the beating from men who write about those who do. I'm sure the questions will be why this line-up at this time, etc. There's nothing you can do but answer the questions as best you can. Damn, I'm beat.

Eggs, tomatoes, granola, tuna fish sandwich, tamale pie, salad, water, coffee 1 cup.

06-30-06 Vancouver Canada: 0533 hrs. I tried to keep sleeping but I couldn't. Have been up since 0430 hrs or so. I am thinking of my friend Ginger who passed away two years ago today. This time two years ago, I was on a flight from DC to LA to start work on a film. I wanted to stay in DC on that day but I had to start on the film. There's nothing to do about her passing away. I cannot change the facts but all the same, I sure miss her.

Desperation and depression are huge motivators in my life. I wake up most of the time with a sense of dread. I will be sleeping and a thought goes off like a bomb in my head and my stomach will contract and I have to get up and do something. That's how I've been waking up lately. I have been thinking a lot about the tour, getting nervous about it. I just want to get it going. I have to be patient.

For me, stress has always been a good thing. It keeps me sharp and motivated. I have no back up besides my bank account so I have to work all the time to make sure I survive America. America is not my friend. I love America and there's no place I'd rather be but when push comes to shove, or even way before that—you're on your own in America. If you're not aware of that, in denial or unprepared for that truth, you are in for a rough ride.

I have felt this way for as long as I can remember. It started with feeling I was on my own during my childhood years. I was never the woe is me type. I just saw it as fact that I was going to have to look out for myself. My parents were not any kind of support system whatsoever and the sooner I could get by my own, the better. When I hear about people moving back in with their parents I just don't understand why they would want to or how they could do that. I would rather live on the street.

I live in the Conservative shadow. They want people to be self-reliant but don't care that there's a lot of people who never get a chance to acquire the skills to be self-reliant. In fact, it seems like it's the last thing Conservatives want, it would be too much competition, the economy would shift. I guess I don't live in the example of conservatism. I live in the knowledge of it being the way it is in America. I have prepared for and dealt with the wrath that it exacts upon me. They are greedy. They have other words to describe it though.

I have not given up fighting back but I have come to the conclusion that if anything is to change for the better in America, Americans will have to do it themselves with little or no help from the government. It will all come out of our pockets. Perhaps the Bush legacy will ultimately be that he brought America together by abandoning it. If you look at New Orleans it's easy to see by now that those people are on their own unless other Americans step in to help. Government will not help.

My constant sense of dread and desperation keeps me on my own for the most part.

A Dull Roar

0951 hrs. Ian and I shot a few e-mails back and forth. I told him I was thinking about him and his family today. He wrote back. It's always so great to hear from him. He's one of the people I put the brakes on for. I wish I could hang out with him in DC for a day before the tour starts but I don't think I'll have the time to get out there. I've been thinking about it though.

I wish I could be at the set and working on the film. I want to cross the finish line and get onto the next thing.

I was hoping that by late tonight I was going to be done with the film and the IFC show. The IFC show's producers were unable to get a 4th guest for last week's taping so I have to go in on July 5th and interview Kevin Smith. I think it will be a good interview. I am a fan of his. I saw him do a monologue at the Spirit Awards earlier this year and he was really funny. It's a drag though to still be on this show when I should be onto the next thing. I will see a screening of Clerks II on Monday and then interview him about it.

I think we did good work on the IFC show this year. I don't get along all that well with the producers of the show so it's a struggle. They are good people but we don't get along. It got better as the season went on but it's still not a great working environment. The writing on the show is good. Their stuff is way better than mine, that's for sure. Anyway, we did good work and hopefully people will dig it. The producers and staff of the show work their asses off and I respect that very much. I don't expect the show will be picked up for a 3rd season but it was a good bit of work anyway. It was cool being asked to do a second season. I have never been asked back for anything. Like with my record contracts, the label always dropped me as soon as they were able to. Record labels have all lost money on me so I understand.
Rice, shrimp, protein bar, water, coffee 2 cups.

JULY 2006

07-01-06 Vancouver Canada / LA CA: 0537 hrs. At the airport, waiting on my flight. Wrapped out of the film around 0315 hrs. this morning. I was the last shot. Pretty great, me lying on a cement floor with a tube on my neck spraying at least a gallon of fake blood on the floor. Should look good. I was head to toe in that stuff. It showers off easily enough but it's a drag to have on you all day. It was good to get pulled out of that bloody shirt for the last time.

That was a 13 hour day. I have not slept yet and can't wait to get on the plane so I can try to get a couple of hours of sleep. I think the other actors are staying for the wrap party tonight. Everyone was cool but I don't want to stay. I like that they're all sleeping and I'm out of here. By the time they wake up, I am long gone. I couldn't see staying longer for any reason.

I am very sore and very tired. Hopefully I will get some sleep on the plane and some more at the house and then get around to some work. It's Saturday, that's so great. I am glad I will be getting some use out of the day in LA. There was nothing more for me to do in Vancouver. It was a good time and I am glad I did it. The best part was that Joe, our director, was satisfied with the work I did. It meant a lot to me that he hired me with no audition. I wanted to make sure he got all the shots he wanted. It's daylight and there are sparrows flying around in the airport. I am barely able to keep my eyes open.

2111 hrs. Today has been a blur and I want to note it before I forget it altogether. I got in around 1100 hrs. Had a very interesting conversation with the driver who told me about the time he was one of a caravan of stretch limos taking some Tajik execs and their families all over So. Cal. to shop and how they ran up quite the bill. He said Unocal picked up the bill.

When I got back to my place, I dropped my bags and reckoned that I should keep moving. I went to the grocery store and then to the office and then back here. I cleaned and did work on the radio show and then started to feel pretty bad. A combination of no sleep and deeper exhaustion. I became unable to look at the computer screen and my knee started pounding so I figured I would put my head down for a little while. I tossed and turned for a few hours and woke up or at least got tired of the bad dreams I was having around 2032 hrs. The place is hot. Summer is definitely here.

I ate a salad and drank some carrot juice and am evening out a little. I am glad I went the extra distance to get back here when I did. I am glad I didn't stay for the wrap party. I like all of those people but I don't like myself in those kind of situations. I don't like what comes out of my mouth and I always regret it. I always fail when I try to be normal and hang out with people. I could do it but it would take a lot of training. I would never really just be there in the moment but rather would be acting like someone at a party having a good time. You know those shallow, self-aware people who are so hard to be around once you have them figured out? That's me. So, it's best for me to be alone as much as possible. It's how I'll end up at the end of all this anyway so I might as well cut out the middleman. I don't ever want to hang out in a room full of people no matter how cool they are.

I am pretty beat and I have to turn that around now. I have to get more sleep this week and in the weeks upcoming. I can't be in negative or static mode in my training for the tour. Doing the film as well as the training for tour has toughened me up but at the same time wiped me out to a certain degree. So, I have to recover and build on the work I have put in on the body in the last three months.

I had a good time working on Wrong Turn 2. One of the best things in life is working amongst motivated, talented and intense people. You learn a lot and you get to give all you have to something and that's the best. This was a great team of people to spend five weeks with. There was only one time where I got a little pissed off and that was a time when we were about to start a very intense scene and the actor I am doing the scene with, who is standing less than a foot away from me, is texting someone on his phone. Right before the next take, the actor is on his phone, talking away. The director took the phone away from the actor and work resumed. That was lame but I have worked on films where most of the cast were like that. To get them to get to their marks, they had to almost be pried from their phones. It's hard to get it done, no matter how good or bad or heavy or light the material is, when people are half-assed about it.

One of the best things about working on the film was the director Joe Lynch, who I can't say enough good things about. Joe is so full-on and intense. When you are really geared up for a scene he's right with you. For some of those scenes I was getting myself in quite a state, it's the only way you're going to get it across.

There were some great moments last night. I was fit into a vest made of small squares of sheet ply that they fashioned from that body cast they made of me weeks ago. I was shot with a stunt arrow. At one point I had an air tube and a blood tube snaked up my leg into my shirt so an arrow on a hinge could be sprung on command and blood could come from the wound. After that, I had tubes glued to fingers so when I was struggling with a razor wire bolo that was thrown around my neck blood could come out. It was an interesting night. I am glad I am getting to see some of this stuff. Sometimes when I am in the middle of something like this, I remember working in Washington DC and that I'm doing pretty good out in the world, finding my way and making it all work out somehow.

1 bowl oatmeal, protein bar, 2 cups yoghurt, shrimp, spinach, carrot juice, water, coffee 1 cup.

07-02-06 LA CA: 1314 hrs. On the back porch in my small patch of shade. I have spent a lot of time in this chair. Yesterday while in traffic to and from the grocery store, I contemplated the heat I was baking in. It was hot as hell yesterday. When things are hot and moist, I think of things blooming, the fragrance of flowers and vegetation being held in the water that's in the air. It is not comfortable weather. Clothes irritate and one becomes aware of the smell of everything—including oneself. There's drawbacks surely but heat and moisture are life. Out here in this hot and dry landscape of desert, concrete, stucco, crime lights and air pollution, the summer is death. It is dry, barren and smashed flat. During the day, there is no smell in the air besides car exhaust. The heat is a steady, standing wave of opposition to everything living. One endures and survives.

I have read and written a lot in this chair. One of the recurring thoughts I have had in this chair is of the opening moments of Bulgakov's The Master And Margarita when Homeless and Berlioz are visited by the Devil. Summers ago, I sat here on the weekends and read the plays of Alfred Jarry. I want to get back to reading more fiction but I feel kind of irresponsible when I do. I feel like I should be reading history since American soldiers are in the middle of such an awful situation. I feel like I am making light of their situation by not reading something that pertains to the reason they are out there getting shot at. I do miss reading literature. I should throw some in. Perhaps I'll start tonight.

I have been reading some interesting articles online and trying to understand why some people, who are obviously intelligent, support Bush and the invasion of Iraq but put down Gore and his eco-awareness pursuits. They go at him and his film An Inconvenient Truth like he was advocating child molestation. I guess they think he's getting in the way of their profits. It seems to me that Conservatives are basically at odds with Democracy. To them, government gets in the way of business. Regulations and other limits that make them conform to things like laws and amendments are a pain in the ass. I understand. I can see a situation where an oil company wouldn't be into a guy like Gore talking about the need for alternative energy supplies. I wouldn't expect them to fund the research beyond just looking politically correct. It's like Philip-Morris telling people that smoking can lead to health risks, they'll say it but they don't do much about it. Solutions and progress hold nothing for these people. Solutions would fuck them out of a job.

The oil companies must laugh at all these people and their hybrid cars and talk of ethanol. It's such small stuff compared to their profit margin and sheer tonnage of merchandise they're moving.

If you're a Conservative, government is nothing but that which gets in the way of your progress. If they could privatize education then they could exclude even more people from the opportunity of a better life. If you have a guarantee of many people with a life of crime ahead of them and another group never getting past minimum wage, then you can really rock. You won't have to share, won't have to make room, won't have to get along. It makes a lot of sense, if you're a fuck-er. I can't see any of these people ever changing their minds. They think that big business will save us all. It will save them mostly but it will save millions of people just enough to get by and live a life of always keeping the wolf from the door and those who can't get by, they just get crushed. I think the current administration wants parts of the American population to magically disappear, move away or just die. Katrina: The Perfect Storm!

Bush must be one of the best things that ever happened to Conservatives. He's getting government out of the way so they can get the business of business moving. I can see why they hate Liberals and Democrats so much. What's amazing to me is that they have been so successful at getting people who won't benefit from their plans to vote for them. Those who will never reap the rewards of business and the bottom line vote for the same people who fuck them over. The Republicans are the party of the "War on Terror" but hardly any of them served in the Military. When I hear politicians and Fox News pundits ripping on Veteran Democrats it really gets me going. To hear Geraldo Rivera say that he's seen more combat than John Murtha, damn man, that really makes me want to pound that sissy. You can't buy into what these cowards are putting across though. It's like get-ting mad that your favorite professional wrestler lost his match. It's just talk, they know what they're doing, they know how to get people going.

Chest, abs. 1 bowl oatmeal, protein bar, 1 cup yoghurt, minestrone soup, protein drink, rice crackers, carrot juice, water, coffee 1 cup.

07-03-06 LA CA: 1917 hrs. I have been up and at it since 0700 hrs. I finally got some real sleep last night. I don't remember what time I fell out but I got at least 7 hours of sleep, which I definitely needed.

I did an interview at 1000 hrs. and then at 1215 hrs. I met up with Joe Lynch, the WT2 director, and we went to a screening of Clerks II that I needed to see for when I interview Kevin Smith on Wednesday. It was pretty good. There were moments where the film seemed to go all over the place and I didn't understand what film he was trying to make. I wonder if he might be a better writer than director at this time. There were a lot of good moments though.

Now I am waiting on Heidi and my stomach is getting wound up. We're going to go to the Hollywood Forever Cemetery for a screening of the new Ramones live film called It's Alive. It's the footage from the It's Alive Ramones album that was recorded at the Rainbow Theater 12-31-77. It's a great live album. I have had it since it came out in the summer of 1979. All these years later, we find out that the show was shot on film and it's only now being released. The film footage was apparently locked up in a divorce settlement with the man that shot the footage, Nick Abson, and sat in storage for almost three decades. This will be the first showing of the film. The reason my stomach is all knotted up is because Linda Ramone asked me to introduce the film tonight.

It's not like I don't have enough things to say about the band or the album, which I have listened to many times over the years, it's just that I don't want to stand out there and talk about the film and get heckled for being in the way of the film. But of course I said yes. I am always happy to help Linda out and do anything I can on the behalf of The Ramones. It's an honor that she thought of me at all.

2255 hrs. I am back from the Ramones film. The whole evening went really well. We drove over to the cemetery and went in the side gate, were given our passes and parked. I don't remember how we got backstage or whatever you call it, the holding area but we did and I did photos with Linda Ramone, Steve Jones, Joe Sib and some other people. I thanked Linda for letting me do the introduction and she said I was her only choice which made me feel good. Soon enough, it was time for us all to walk over to the podium where we would be doing the announcements and stuff. As I stood there, people started to notice me and came over and asked to do photos. It's never a problem to do this so I did a bunch of photos and signed a bunch of things. People were extremely friendly to me and it restored my faith in the human race for awhile.

Joe Sib went on the stage and told the crowd that I was about to hit stage and people cheered. That was a relief. A minute later, I was on and talking to a field of people. I told them about the first time I saw The Ramones. We had all piled into Ian MacKaye's car and went to the show. I was right up front. The show and the band changed my life. Then I listed some facts about the film and said how cool it was that we were the first audience to see it. I talked about how the nagra audio synch for all the footage was stolen so they had to hand synch all the footage to the multi track audio. That's a lot of work. I don't remember what else I said besides how excited I was to see the film. Then I said thanks and walked off and people cheered and some people yelled. When I hear someone yell from the audience I always figure it's going to be something mean but people were yelling stuff like "I love you Henry!" which is very nice to hear. I don't know why, but I really like that kind of thing.

So, I was standing there with everyone else, waiting for the film to start when more people came over and asked to do photos with me. It's intense the way some girls are these days, you do a photo with them and they just grab you and jam their breasts into you.

The film. Damn, what a great piece of work. It's almost beyond description how perfect and how powerful The Ramones were. Especially this line-up with Tommy Ramone on drums. It's all the members together that made them great for sure but it's Tommy's drumming that really nailed the pocket of the band. I was almost in tears while watching the film it moved me so much. Especially seeing the close-ups of Johnny. To me, he is Rock and Roll. The way he murdered that Mosrite guitar, his facial expression, his attack. He was the man.

The Ramones will always be some of the most charismatic players ever. Watching them tonight was to witness undisputed legends.

I was having a great time singing along and rockin' out, when right during the first verse of some song a girl walks up and asks if I have a marker. I told her no. She comes back again right at the beginning of *Sheena Is A Punk Rocker* (my favorite Ramones song, I was fully rockin' at this point) and asks if I can sign something and I told her after the song was over. She got on her cell phone and walked away. I guess this event wasn't as important to some people as it was to me. I don't understand how you can be standing in front of a massive screen watching The Ramones play and have anything else on your mind.

There were a couple of other interesting moments besides the film: One of the old Ramones crew guys came up and told me that Vincent Gallo had requested copies of my IFC show because he was considering coming on the show. Like it's his decision. I told the fellow that it's really not for Gallo to invite himself and that I wouldn't want him on the show anyway. There's nothing I want to know about that particular Bush conservative besides when he'll be shipping out to Iraq to fight the "War on Terror." Also, Alan Arkush, the director of Rock 'n' Roll High School, introduced himself and we spoke for a moment. He was really cool and it was an honor to meet him.

Partway through Rock 'n' Roll High School which came on after the live film, Heidi and I took off. We tried to find Linda to thank her and all but we couldn't find her. I wonder if she was tripping on seeing all that footage of Johnny that she had never seen before. I hope it didn't upset her.

I'm very tired now.

Arms, abs. 1 bowl oatmeal, 1 cup yoghurt, minestrone soup, protein drink, rice crackers, 1 ice cream bar, carrot juice, water, coffee 1 cup.

07-04-06 LA CA: 1209 hrs. Heidi wrote me and said that Linda liked what I said last night. That's a relief. I would hate to let her down. It's quite a big deal when someone trusts you to do something, like Joe giving me a part in the film with no audition. That was huge. I never take any of that stuff with anything less that grim seriousness. That's what had me so wound up last night. I didn't want to let Linda down.

I went to the grocery store a little while ago. It's the way I check in with humanity on weekends and holidays. It's one of the only places I go in LA. I can count the places I go with any regularity on one hand I bet. I am not adventurous and am trying to cope with LA by dealing with as little of it as possible. It gets worse as I get older. It's strange to have lived for so long in a place I don't like very much.

The drive to and from the store was a Didionesque experience. There weren't many people on the road but as always, there's the three second lag at the green light. I think the heat gets to people. It just stuns them. It was a little past 1100 hrs. and already it was at desert hate temperature. Yes, I said desert hate. This weather hates people, it hates all living things.

The heat takes its toll on people here. Some of the homeless men I see on Sunset Blvd. are so tanned they look like smoked meat. They are often shirtless and somehow look to be in pretty decent shape. Not many calories uploaded in a day and all that walking would do it. Sometimes I see them in hooded sweatshirts and sweat pants, sitting in a parking lot just baking away. I can't understand how they can deal with the heat that must be building up under those layers.

The lack of traffic brings out the loneliness of this town. Garbage blows down the streets, you can see the dried remains of who knows what all over the sidewalks. Sunset Blvd. has some of the saddest men walking around on it. Men my age with their sleeves cut off to show off their tattoos, dyed hair, sunglasses, just trying to hang in there. There's nothing to hang in there for or with in this town. There's no code here. Not much sense of community here. Just a bunch of people from other states who came out here to realize the dream.

Last night was encouraging. I met a lot of young people, a lot of them had Ramones shirts on. They were all very friendly and seemed quite undead. People here aren't bad and I'm not in a position to judge but Los Angeles is hard on people and I think after awhile, it wears them down and hammers them until they are dwellers, a different version of being alive than other places I've been.

2154 hrs. What a rip off. No radio show tonight. They had some holiday programming so there were no shows tonight. I found out as I was getting ready to go down to the station. I had such a good show planned too.

Earlier today I had a long conversation with Janeane Garofalo. I think she somehow has talked me into painting her apartment. I don't know how she did that. She's a very funny person. It's nice to hear a woman say, "Conservative douche bag" the way she does. At one point, she asked me if I was handy. I said probably not. She then asked if I could paint. I said I wasn't artistically inclined. She said that was fine and she needed someone to paint her apartment and since I like NYC, then it should be no problem. She said I could have all the seltzer water, coffee and sandwiches I wanted. We talked about the book Shah Of Shahs by Kapuscinski and started recommending book titles to each other. She recommended some fiction titles to me after I told her that I wasn't reading fiction these days because it makes me feel like I am taking my eye off the ball. She gave a convincing argument as to why I have to get some fiction/literature back into my reading diet. I have been staying away from fiction for awhile since I've been reading all these history and social commentary books and I really miss fiction. Anyway, she made me laugh my ass off for a long time.

Talking to Janeane made me temporarily forget my disappointment over finding out there would be no radio show tonight. I was doing my show during some holiday in 2004 when the station was in the middle of a U2 marathon and my show got in the way. People were so mad when we cut off a U2 song to start my show. I got incredibly heartfelt hate mail from people. It was hilarious. Angry Catholics. Achtung Catholics: I jack off all the time and I'm not going to hell because there is no hell and when I see priests and cardinals walking around in their lame outfits, I know that you are pathetic. That you protect so many child molesters is beyond me. Your last pope absolutely knew what was happening and didn't do anything about it and that makes him a criminal. Congratulations. You deserve U2.

One of the best things about doing the radio show is my Tuesday night burrito and taco I get to eat. I really look forward to that meal. I went for it tonight even though there was no show. I saw a homeless guy hanging outside the place so I bought him two chicken tacos and a coke. I gave it to him and he hesitantly thanked me. Maybe he thought I was nuts.

1 bowl oatmeal, 1 cup yoghurt, protein drink, rice crackers, veg. burrito, taco, carrot juice, water, coffee 1 cup.

07-05-06 LA CA: 2138 hrs. Wrapped out of the IFC show. I interviewed Kevin Smith about his new film Clerks II.

Kevin Smith's films are cool but very unadorned, there's not a lot of coverage on scenes. Where some directors are all over the shot covering it from all kinds of angles, Kevin hits it with a wide shot, not many cut aways and then onto the next scene. For me, it keeps me more in the story but puts a lot of pressure on the actors to keep the scene happening and that's where I think there are weak points in his films. When we were talking about that, I brought up Woody Allen and those lock off shots he does where the actors are left to act for minutes on end. He said he rehearses the actors for a few weeks before shooting starts and then he basically leaves them to it. In Allen's films, it really works but in Smith's films, it's sometimes the thing that makes them weak. I enjoyed Clerks II for the most part but there were moments where it seemed that the actors didn't know if the scene was over or what was going on and things became somewhat static. Any problem I had with the film was remedied by the great performance of Rosario Dawson, who was fantastic all the way through.

After Kevin left, I did some intros and outros and that was the end of my work for the show. I don't know if there will be another season and if one is offered, I don't know if I will take it. I'll have to give it some thought.

I put in a good shoulder workout tonight and will do more shoulders tomorrow night. I have been keeping the television off and getting my news online or on the radio for the last few days. I want to get off the television news thing and get more reading done. At this point, the incoming information is fairly flat. More dead in Iraq. Ken Lay washes out at 64 and will do no time. One of the fellows on the set today suggested that perhaps they should throw Kenny Boy's corpse in a prison cell for 20 years. I like that. But what I like even better is my idea: I think Ken Lay's wife should go and do her dead husband's time because she knew what he was doing and she could have done something, so she's as bad as he is. Interesting how the White House Press Secretary, Tony Douche Bag Snow, is trying to distance the President from his dead pal Kenny Boy. These people are all so horrible. What will it take to get the country back from these tyrants? I don't know but I am happy to keep bringing my knife to the gun fight.

Now that the film and the television show are wrapped out, I can get to work focusing on the tour. I have been training for weeks and for the most part, I am ready. I have done some damage to my left knee that will take some time to train out of but it's better than it was last week when it was waking me up all the time. Now the pain only wakes me up about once a night. I don't know why it chooses to start hurting like a bastard at night.

I am looking forward to getting on the road and getting these shows going. We will be playing the set in front of people at the practice place on July 25, two nights before the tour starts. I want to do one show before we go out there in front of a paying audience so we can see if there's any parts of the set that need work. I just hope no one in the band is dragging ass when they get here. Everyone seems into it but I don't want to see anything less than full on kill. I know they all know what's at stake, I just hope it means a lot to them.

I am pushing muscle groups hard at the moment, getting myself tempered for the shows. I like that I am sore all the time. It's the best way to feel. When nothing hurts, I feel vulnerable. I only feel strong when I am under pressure or stressed or over worked. That's when it's real. Anything else is just waiting around to be run over. I have been at great levels of exhaustion for weeks now. I have been racking out at night with no memory of turning the lights out, what time I stopped working or what I was thinking before I fell out. I think that is good. It's going to take that kind of training and conditioning to get through this tour. I need to get a few of the shows under my belt to see what I need to change or improve as the tour goes on. It will be interesting to see how close the training I did comes to giving me what I need out there. I also plan on training hard early in the day while on tour to keep muscle groups strong so I'm not in recovery mode too close to show time.

I like this way of living. That's why I liked being on the film, dedication to a single objective. The tour is even more of a single minded pursuit than the film work because it's the same thing every night. It's the most intense commitment I have ever made. Every night—the set. That's all. No one to call. Nothing to do but execute the maximum delivery of the music. I am not religious but I bet this way of thinking has some similarities. I like to think of it more as a warrior mentality. The discipline this requires forces me to be better than I am. I am not all that good at anything I do but what I aspire to and what I aspire to be is good.

It is 2236 hrs. and I can barely keep my eyes open and have to stop now.

Shoulders Pt. 1. 1 bowl oatmeal, 1 cup yoghurt, protein drink, bagels, cream cheese, pizza, rice crackers, carrot juice, water, coffee 1 cup.

07-06-06 LA CA: 1953 hrs. At the house, just finished working on some upcoming radio broadcasts. I probably put too much time into that show but it feels like good work. I got some work done at the office today. I was glad to get out of bed early this morning. It was another night of waking up full of dread and depression. A lot of my time is spent all nerved up. I always think everything is going to run out or quit or die or give up. I jump at the next thing like an animal that hasn't eaten in days.

Kevin Smith said something to me yesterday that I have been tripping on. We were talking about how much we like George Carlin. He worked with him in <u>Dogma</u> and I met him briefly at MTV years ago. Anyway, Kevin was saying that George is somewhat apolitical. He reckons it's all going to hell in a hand basket so fuck it. He said that's why he thinks Carlin didn't deal on Ann Coulter when they were on Leno together recently. Kevin reckons Carlin doesn't give a fuck about what she does or thinks. That's kind of cool.

There are different ways of dealing with the present state of the world. In a way, just saying "fuck it" is like cutting out the middleman and getting to the beating that is most likely coming our way. I think Conservatism works well because it appeals to fear and greed. It justifies a lot of what some people would call cruel and selfish. Like that great monologue Michael Douglas delivers in <u>Wall Street</u>. That is the modern Conservative. I figure these people will eventually get all the things they want because they have fear and ignorance working in their favor. To be one of these guys takes little study or knowledge and no virtue, just get all you can and fuck the rest if they weren't man enough to take it back.

It's boring to think about it all. The only choice I have is to be unburdened by fear as much as possible and move forward for as long as I can. Nothing else interests me. I don't want to settle down. If I stopped moving, it wouldn't be settling down as much as it would be falling back behind the tree line and not coming back out. Who cares? There's millions of people in the world and they're all going to die like the ones who came before them. I don't feel special and a lot of the time, I don't give a fuck if I die the next day. I am not a tough guy. I just don't care about dying, don't care about a normal life. I know I can't hack it in the real world. You have to have your senses beaten out of you to hack it out there. To work some fucked job for years and be dead on your feet beats the daylights out of you to the point where it's all the same. That's why they make cheap beer. That's definitely riding the Fuck It Express. I can't do that but I sure can't see going through life married and harnessed. I'd rather be harnessed to my own fucked up obsession. I am incompetent and frustrated all the time so what I think it's all about is mostly bitter, rage-based and self-serving.

When I sit here alone in this house, I feel like I am doing the world a favor. When I am out in the world I feel like a weapon in the hands of a cornered coward.

Shoulders Pt. 2. 1 bowl oatmeal, 1 cup yoghurt, protein drink, sushi, carrot juice, diet coke, water, coffee 1 cup.

07-07-06 LA CA: 2340 hrs. I have done little else than work on the radio show since 0830 hrs. I have a few shows that I will be able to do live and then about 6 that will be pre-taped. I want to make them as good as I can so I went at it all day and I think I got a lot done.

I can feel a good long spell of depression coming on. I can always tell. It's always near the full moon. The farther away from the full moon it starts, the worse it's going to be. I have at least a good 3 - 5 days coming up. I don't mind it. It's just a part of my life now. I don't medicate, I just weather it. I reckon it makes me better at knowing myself. I think some drugs are ok but for the most part, I think they keep you from your true self.

A lot of things keep you from your true self, I think that's one of the reasons people go for some things like jobs they don't like but are secure. The low risk factor has a price to be paid. Some people have to get married no matter what. It's the thing they aspire to more than anything. Have to make that connection. Can't go through this life alone. Have to make more and fill the house with more eaters. Have to pack the time with going to soccer games and moving slowly through airports. It's a way of sidestepping a lot of life's banal day-to-day horror. I understand but don't want any part of it. I want to be strange and on the outside. For me, it's more true than more conventional paths.

Solitude and isolation used to be hard when I was younger but I worked at it and pushed through. Being self-sufficient and a loner are things I have worked at and aspired to for a good part of my life. Only

Henry Rollins **169**

in the last several years have I achieved the level I wanted to take it to. I can't say I'm proud of myself but I know I've come a long way from where I started. Now the time passes and it's nothing to spend days with little or no contact with anyone. When the phone rings here, I wince. There's only a few people I want to talk to with any regularity. Infrequency is the key.

We've hit an interesting time with the Invasion of Iraq. As far as I'm concerned, anyone who signs up with the Military now knows they are going to Iraq. They have seen the stats, they have had ample opportunity to research what an IED can do. They have seen the number of injured and the steadily increasing death toll. So, they know. Right. From now on, there's really nothing to say to them. There's no money to pay for their rehabilitation when they get back. There's no "winning" in Iraq. There is doing your time there, rotation after rotation—nothing different than rotating the chambers of a revolver and putting it to your head at this point.

The powers that be are eventually going to get all they want. They're almost there. They'll ban gay marriage in all the states and Christian douche bags will think they have some kind of power. It will soon be time to give up on the idea that virtue and good can triumph over bad. I wonder if they will have to take responsibility for what they've turned the country into and deal with the backlash.

I've lost my emotional involvement with all of it at this point. I don't get mad anymore. I just calmly call it what it is and do what is required and if I'm required to say things that some people will find offensive and upsetting, that's entirely fine. It's a wonderful thing to offend and upset them. If it involves alienating people, my only regret is that I was unable to alienate them at an earlier date. I have no desire to change anyone's mind. If you're a homophobic conservative douche bag, that's your problem but know that I am also your problem. Of course, I'd rather not get into it with anyone. I would rather not be touched, talked to or bothered and I do all I can to keep it that way. Like a snake in the wild.

Push-ups. 1 bowl oatmeal, 1 cup yoghurt, protein drink, salmon, spinach, tomato soup, rice crackers, V8 juice, carrot juice, water, coffee 1 cup.

A Dull Roar

07-08-06 LA CA: 2213 hrs. I have written almost 5000 words today. How the hell did I do that? I have been at it on and off for about 14 hours, that's how. There's my Saturday shot in the face, stabbed three times and left to exsanguinate on the street unnoticed.

I left the house briefly to go to the office to look for some work materials and then was back at the keyboard the rest of the time pretty much. Perhaps I'm entering into the Thomas Wolfe period of my life. All I know is I can do 12 hours of writing standing on my head. I have been working on my stamina for many months now. It took a long time to be able to stay with it that long but I am getting my head around it.

My temper goes up and down in waves. I try and regulate it and most of the time I can but sometimes I let it get the better of me. Every once in awhile I get a letter from some conservative douche bag who wants to engage and they never expect the short reply that I give them, like how they are douche bags and should go play in Baghdad or admit they're just pussies. It manages to get them mad. But they are conservative douche bags and what they think of me isn't really going to keep me up at night. How anyone can get behind Rush Limbaugh is beyond me. People are strange. Most of the time, I leave them alone. I just got a letter from a conservative douche bag that I answered and we'll see if he/she gets back to me.

It's too bad that it's too late for a lot of things. It's too bad that in such a short amount of time so much has gone wrong in America. There are some things that have been destroyed that are never coming back. All the deaths that have occurred in Iraq and the fact that Democracy is all but dead. It was such a great concept. America was such a great place. Now it's an ok place full of really good people who are getting screwed by out of shape white males like Karl Rove who do really fucked up shit Monday through Friday but always get to church on time. Their supporters, like the douche bag who will no doubt be writing me back very soon, are rabid and dangerous. If these people were shot in the street like mad dogs America would be a better place. The people who should be assassinated won't be because the people who should do it won't. So, instead of progress, you have a great nation lead by douche bags who are supported by raving psychopaths. If there weren't young men and women dying for all this, it would be a lot of fun to bait these douche bags all the time but there's a country to save and a future to realize somehow, so one has to keep one's poise. Most of the time it is possible.

I hope the workout and all the work I have done today will allow me to sleep. It's not hard to get to sleep these days, it's hard to stay passed out though.

A couple of hours ago the phone rang for the second time in about four days. It was Ian. So great to hear from him. He and Amy are working very hard on the new Evens record which they are recording at Dischord House on a Tascam 8 track. He says there's ten songs done and they are going to take it to Inner Ear soon and mix it. I can't wait to hear the new stuff. I saw them play two or three new songs last summer and they were great. He said all those songs were recorded. Then he told me about a book he has been reading that's been blowing him away called Punk Rock: An Oral History. All the stuff he was telling me from it I had never heard before like who had been in what band, how the Damned formed, etc. He said the book is amazing. I ordered a copy. He also said that Joe Lally's solo album is all done and mastered. Joe was the bass player in Fugazi and there's a lot of DC types playing on the record like members of Fugazi and Wino from The Obsessed. It's going to be a great year for Dischord.

I'll write more in the morning. The workout got to me and I'm fading now. That was a good long pull of work today.

Here's an insert for you. My "correspondence" with the conservative douche bag with no name and apparently, no spell check. Took the douche bag days to get back to me. Must have been busy wiping the pavement off his knuckles.

Douche bag makes contact!

Can you tell me some of the lies that Henry lists about Bush, He said something on Google.tv about Iraq is a disaster, Corporations getting money, etc. It would help me -- TG, http://truthguys. blogspot.com

My reply!

TG? Is that your name? You can come straight to me, douche bag. What the fuck do you want to know? Drop me a line you fuckin pussy. -- Henry Rollins

And then the retort!

Hey Tatoo boy, what happened to the left being understanding and inclusive.... hahahah. No really I just want to know exactly what rights Bush has taken away, and have you called Billy Boy Clinton to thank him for screwing up Iraq, North Korea and lack of action in the middle east. Bush is going down in history as the guy that cleaned up 8 years of Clinton and Gore the bore Do Nothing that has brought us to your crap you talk about. oh no, I am a Conservative moving to LA with $200 million to fund movies people want to see for a change.... Liberal- Marxists be afraid be very afraid. TG is TruthGuys moron.

Whoa! This is the "opposition"? If I were the Bush Administration, I would be so embarrassed to have this lunatic on my team. He's has $200 mil. and he can't even spell? I'm no Marxist but I am a little afraid. No I'm not!

Deadlift, shrugs, abs, push-ups. 1 bowl oatmeal, 1 cup yoghurt, protein drink, salmon, spinach, tomato soup, rice crackers, minestrone soup, V8 juice, carrot juice, water, coffee 1 cup.

07-09-06 LA CA: 2238 hrs. I figured what the hell, it's the end of the week and I have been a good boy so I'll go get some frozen yoghurt at this place over the hill. I parked near and walked over. I looked through the window there was about 7 people in line. I knew I couldn't stand in there that long. I really wanted that yoghurt but in the end I got back in the car and headed back here. Sometimes I can deal with people and sometimes I can't. I guess it's summer time so a lot of people are out late. It's also pretty hot out too.

I worked all day on radio show writing for upcoming broadcasts. I think I got in a few thousand words. It's not the easiest writing but once I get about three hours in, I am able to go all day pretty much. I went to the grocery store around 1530 hrs. The man at the check out at the grocery store asked me if I had served in the Military. I told him no. He said I looked like a guy he served with. That was all the conversation I had today. The phone didn't ring and that was good. It rang three times yesterday. One hang up, one person asking for Jeff or Chet or someone and Ian.

I don't like where I am at the moment. When I don't like the place I am mentally or geographically in, I go other places in my mind and operate from that space. For the last hour or so, I have been back in my old apartment I used to live in 25 years ago right before I joined Black Flag. It's dark except for the desk lamp and the room is very hot. I lived right by the front door. My friend John had the bedroom. I had the stranger hours so I took the front. I would come back from work and sit there in my underwear and sweat. Some nights it was almost impossible to sleep because of the heat and humidity. Anyway, I have been there for awhile now. It's one of the ways I take a break from myself.

Sometimes I can't stand being here. Can't stand being alive. I don't want to kill myself but sometimes I have to take it minute by minute. It's one of the reasons I live alone and keep to myself as much as I can. I got through the weekend by writing about music. I didn't watch any television. I am tired of television. I am sick of the cowardice of CNN and Fox and the rest of them. They're all cowards to me now. It's better with the television off and the music on anyway. I have the new <u>Harpers</u> magazine and will try to get some of that read this week. Past that, I am sick of what's happening out there and I know I am powerless to stop young men from getting killed in Iraq and powerless to stop pretty much anything else in the world. At some point you have to reconcile the fact that the human race is bent on destroying itself and the planet along with it and enjoy what you have and the time you have left.

I am sitting in this house but it's not home. When I visit DC, I don't consider it home either. No place I ever lived with either of my parents I ever considered home. It was their place and I was merely a tenant who didn't pay rent. Never felt home anywhere. It's one of the reasons I like hotel rooms. It's the eye of a storm. It's an agreed upon territory. I have rented that space for a limited time and in that time, it's relatively secure. There's only one door and it's triple locked. You could bar all the windows in this place and I'll still wake up all the time. It's not home. Nowhere will ever be home to me. I don't want it, need it or trust it. The dark rooms in my mind are home. My thoughts are home. They are mine and no one can take them. As I get older, the more I enjoy my thoughts and memories and my imagination. A lot of times I like the idea of things more than the things themselves. I like to think of people more than see them. I like people in books and on records way more than in person. I have a lot of books and records and they sit very quietly. That's the best deal. I have to be up in a few hours. If tomorrow wasn't Monday and I didn't have to deal with real world matters, I would sit here for at least another two hours and write about how beauty, sadness and solitude enhance each other.

Chest, push-ups. 1 bowl oatmeal, 1 cup yoghurt, protein drink, tomato soup, salmon, spinach, rice crackers, V8 juice, carrot juice, water, coffee 1 cup.

07-10-06 LA CA: 2318 hrs. I worked all day at the office and finished up three radio shows which I will hopefully pre-tape tomorrow. They're good shows, too. That was my weekend. I turned in part of the manuscript of this book to Carol and will hopefully hand in more tomorrow.

I got back here and sat down and went right back to the writing. I did more work on the radio show that I put together about the Misfits. I worked out hard and brought in my notebook because I was thinking about stuff and wanted to make notes on the ideas between sets. I wrote about how I trust people's hatred more than their love. I would not go out of my way to be hated but I trust people's brutality more than the "better" aspects of their nature.

The house is hot. I never use the air-conditioning. I would rather sweat and let it work me. My shirt is sticking to me. I gave myself a hair cut tonight. I'll chop it severely once more before we leave and that should hold it for awhile.

I am almost there mentally and physically. Almost ready for the tour. I am lean and training hard. My threshold of pain is up and I hate myself. Have to have the self-hatred. Keeps me true to the songs, to the writing. It's the only way I can see clearly. I have to see all the awfulness. If there is some good in there, I am not interested in it. I am not looking to be a good person. I am trying to be real and keep seeing it for what it is. What I see is isolation and short instances of relief wedged in between the bricks of dread and anxiety. I seek to confront. Not that I want to vanquish and be victorious but it's because I think it's one of the only times it gets real. It's because it's always a fine time to die and now that I no longer care how long I live, it allows me to go right into the thick of it without hesitation. There is nowhere else to go as far as I can see.

Sometimes these are truths I put aside when I have to be around people. Like when I was working on the film. I didn't think like this when I was on the set. I only thought of the shot and the work and I tried my best to listen carefully to the director so I could give him exactly what he wanted. When I was alone in my room and on the street I went back to toughening myself by analyzing my failures and pointing out my shortcomings. Disappointment moves me forward. Perhaps this sounds negative. I don't agree. I think not facing the monster is negative. I think living a lie is negative. Like so many of those fake Christians who say one thing and do another; like many of those conservative douche bags who live on the lives of others. There's nothing worse than a coward.

Arms, abs. Oatmeal, protein drink, ice cream bar, protein bar, minestrone soup, rice crackers, carrot juice, V8 juice, water, coffee 1 cup.

07-11-06 LA CA: 2251 hrs. Back from the radio show. It was great to be on the air again. I think it was a good show. I hope they liked it. I am very tired and can't stay awake too long. I just can't keep my eyes open. I went hard today. I had an interview for a BBC documentary and that took a long time and then I worked on two manuscripts until show time. That is very draining for me. Looking at the computer screen and typing in corrections wears me out after a few hours. I went to the studio early to do some pre-tapes for upcoming radio shows and then did the shows. I was in there for over four hours and that too was a drain. Being around people takes its toll.

I got the arrival information from Road Manager Mike and the band lads won't be in until next week. I will have part of the weekend to get some writing and editing done. Part of my Saturday, actually a good part of it, will be boned by having to go to Comicon to do some kind of appearance on Saturday. I don't want to go but the IFC types want me down there for some reason. My manager urged me to do it. He said they don't ask much of me, etc. I don't know what I will do there except feel foolish and lose a lot of time I could have spent working. If you're not careful, people will keep you from the work. People will make you mediocre if you hang out with them. They will make you run-of-the-mill if you stick around.

Oatmeal. Shrimp and rice, burrito, fish tacos, chips, water, diet coke, carrot juice, coffee 1 cup.

07-12-06 LA CA: 2151 hrs. I am back at the house and have already worked out and eaten. I worked on radio stuff for a little longer than I should have. I have to read over the nine page script for <u>World War Z</u> tomorrow. That was that voice over thing that was offered to me last month and it came through and I hit it tomorrow at 1500 hrs. I don't know anything about the book or the series. All I know is it's work and I'll take the work. I will almost always take the work. I trust employment. It is one of my favorite things.

Over the last two days I have become more and more wound up about the tour. I hope we will be ready. The last practices sounded good. We have one more week of practice and then we hit it. I hope these guys' heads are in the game. I know they are good musicians and all but I am concerned that they be focused on the objective. I am probably too intense on all this stuff but still I worry. The last two days it has gotten me up early in the morning. I want to get this first practice happening. I want to see what the mood is. All I know is I have been training for this since April and hope they have been doing something as far as working towards these shows. I am sure the shows will be fine but I will be monitoring everyone and everything every fucking day. If I come to the conclusion that it's 99% or less then I am out. I would rather not do music at all than do it half way. I hope the band wants to kill.

I have been getting my work done for the most part but it's been hard the last few days. Depression weighs me down and makes everything a little harder to do. It's hard to deal with people when I am depressed. I know that I am in a bad mood so I am really careful to be cool around the few people I have to deal with.

I try and interact with as few people as possible. I have to work at it. As the years go on, it gets harder and harder to deal with people. I don't know what the end result of this will be. Do you eventually just live in a small room and not see anyone? That's like the hotel experience for me. That time in Vancouver was great as far as being on my own. When I wasn't working on the film, I spent all my time by myself. I guess that's why the time flew by. It's easy for me to do time like that. I don't live as much as exist. I do time. I think living is different than what I do. Living, the way I see people around me do, seems far more engaged than how I am getting through. When I was in Vancouver, I would walk around and see couples and groups of people and never once was it something I wanted. Even when I would see a guy with a good looking woman, and there were a lot of good looking women there, I never wanted to be the guy. I honestly can't remember when I wanted to be. I went out on a few dates in LA awhile ago. Dinner and goodnight. They were very nice women but about ten minutes in, I couldn't wait for it to be over. It wasn't anything they did. I just didn't care about anything we were talking about, didn't want to know more, didn't want to say anything that I was not prepared to see posted online and overall just wanted to be somewhere else. I tried it a few times to see if anything would change and it never did. I just didn't give a fuck about the situation outside of wanting it to be over. When it was it was a relief. The best part of the night was driving back to my place alone. The whole time I knew it was no good but I gave the normal hustle a try anyway.

I don't hate people. I don't feel that I'm better than anyone. I can see the sincerity in everyone I meet. People are painful. It's painful to know them. I can only take so much of it before I become sick with it. The few people I see on a regular basis are good to see now and then but I don't think I could sustain seeing anyone all the time in a non-work situation. It's not that I don't like them. I do. Very much. They can have anything of mine right now and keep it. It's still hard to be around people. One person I can deal with is Road Manager Mike, we've toured together for about 8 years. This will be our last tour together. He's moving on. Nothing lasts forever of course but damn, I sure will miss him. He's one of the finest people I have ever met. We had some great times out there.

Now all I want to do is kill these shows. I want to train and play and write and read and kill it. The shows are worth living for. I like the simplicity of that. That's about all the life I can handle. Train and hit it. It's great to live in an environment where the phone doesn't ring very often and there's not many people to deal with.

Shoulders pt. 1. Oatmeal, yoghurt, protein drink, spinach, salmon, frozen yoghurt, water, carrot juice, coffee 2 cups.

07-13-06 LA CA: 1840 hrs. I am back from the office and the voice over thing I had to do. Three hours of press and so far, they have been very cool. Not fucking with me yet. It can't last much longer.

The voice over was good work. It was a good piece of writing. It's basically a monologue of a man recounting his time body guarding the rich and famous in the time when zombies were waging war with the living. World War Z by Max Brooks. I didn't know that Max is the son of Mel. That's pretty cool. In any case, I read well and the producer said I nailed it and that I finished really quickly. I have worked in this studio before. The last time I was in there I did some short stories of Elmore Leonard for an audio book. They sent me a couple of them when they came out. I sent one to Ian. I have never played the thing, I just shelved it. That's what I do with almost all of that stuff. Most of the time I buy it online and just put it on a shelf. Of all the films I have ever done, I have only seen two of them all the way through. The others, I just shelf 'em. The last thing I want to look at is myself on a screen. Editing the talking DVDs is agony. Thankfully, management is a good editor and does about 99% of it.

2021 hrs. Post workout. Another good shoulder workout. It's good to break it up into two nights. As I hit the sets, I played songs from the set we'll be playing. I sang along between sets to stay in the music that we'll be living every night. I will be listening to the set all the way until the first band practice next week. I am not worrying about the set as much as I was yesterday. I think it made me feel better to sing the songs out loud and know that I am actively working on them. I always benefit when I am active and getting on top of anything that is bugging me. I am always better when I confront, when I run at it, into it. It's better to be conflict than to be in conflict. Better to be war than to be in war.

2325 hrs. I just got off the phone with Janeane Garofalo. We spoke for awhile. She wants me to call into Air America tomorrow to be on the show she does with Sam Seder. I think it's going to be her last day or close to it. We went over the whole idea again that I am going to paint her apartment when I get a chance. She told me that I am going to paint her apartment unless I hear otherwise. I have a feeling I won't be hearing otherwise any time soon. She is a very funny woman. I don't really know her, we have just spoken on the phone a few times but I really enjoyed the conversations. We are both loner types so it's interesting to exchange insights.

I am feeling a little better than I was yesterday. I am feeling better because I don't have to go to Comic-Con until next weekend. Yes, I have to go to that thing in a week from this coming Saturday to do something related to the IFC show. I don't know exactly what it will be. Some kind of appearance. I said yes because management told me to do it. He said that IFC doesn't ask all that much of me so I should do it. It is true that they don't ask much of me. It's more a matter that I will be there for two hours with men in Darth Vader outfits and I really don't see what it's going to do for the show.

I am tired and falling off so I have to rack out for a few hours. I will check back in post press tomorrow.

Gotta Get Outta This Town Dept.: This came in via the press gal: Johnny Cash, amazingly, is doing a new music video. The song is called *God's Gonna Cut You Down*. They are looking for a "select list of famous faces" to be in the video because I guess Mr. Cash isn't in any condition to hit his marks. "Participants are asked to dress in black and are allowed to participate in the video in any way they choose. They can "sing a verse, recite a verse or just stand there and be counted or simply say something about what Johnny Cash meant to them. The select who have either already finished their footage or are scheduled to perform include: Sharon Stone, Kanye West, Justin Timberlake, Patti Smith, Red Hot Chili Peppers' Flea, Whoopi, Dennis Hopper, David Blaine, Diddy, Jon Bon Jovi, Robert Downey Jr., Tim Robbins, Shelby Lynne, Lisa Marie Presley, Graham Nash, The Gorillaz, Scissor Sister, Tony Hawk, Rob Thomas and Kris Kristofferson."

I passed. I respect Johnny Cash and love his music as much as the next person but there's some things you don't need to be a part of. I would LOVE to see what Sean "We invented the re-mix" Combs has to say about Johnny Cash. What a town. Got a match?

Shoulders Pt. 2. Oatmeal, rice bowl, granola, salmon, spinach, tomato soup, rice crackers, yoghurt, carrot juice, water, coffee 1 cup.

07-14-06 LA CA: 2014 hrs. Just getting the engines started for the weekend work-a-thon. I did press for almost four straight hours today. They were all cool again, which is surprising to me still. I went on air with Janeane and Sam Seder on Air America. I guess I did alright. I always feel like my mind moves a little slower when I am on that station. I called and left a message with Janeane thanking her for letting me be on the show.

I have not had a chance to watch any news today. I don't want to turn on the television and just sit there watching but I want to get an update on what's happening in Lebanon and Israel. Until one side is destroyed completely, it will never end. It's not the kind of conflict America has ever been in. It's not over oil or Communism, it's not a revolution and it will only end when there's no one alive to fight anymore.

Earlier today I got a call from one of the producers from the IFC show saying that the show was just confirmed for another season. He said they want to make it their signature series like they did this year. That's all very good news. I told the producer that was great but we all needed to sit down and have a long talk about the show and if we want to carry on. He said there wasn't much choice and I said there sure was. Try to make me do another season if I don't want to. He said he wasn't expecting me to say these things. I told him that everything's ok but that we all need to have a meeting and that we could do that when management gets back in town. We left it there.

I think it's great that we have been given another season. It's one hell of an endorsement. IFC has been very good to me. But still, we have to sit down and have a talk about things. We need to have a lot less stress and more flexibility in that show. There were some very strained moments on the set. It's not that any one of the producers are bad people. They are really good and they work their asses off but all the same, we need to iron some things out so we can work better together. Not a lot of big stuff but if another season will be like the last one, I will seriously have to consider not doing it. It's not worth the aggravation.

My instinct is to always work. Work no matter the conditions and work no matter how I'm feeling. Don't pass up work. Most likely I'll take the work even if those guys stress me out as much as they did this year with lame bullshit because I need the work.

There is a three-ring binder on the floor next to me. It holds the first draft of the April, May and June entries of this book. The pages have been gone through by Carol and as always, she has found a more than humbling amount of mistakes and just awful sentences, which she points out. Each page will take several minutes each to correct. There are 114 of them. I have been here so many times before. I will set a goal of 25 pages and see how far I get. I don't want to spend the weekend doing this. I wanted some time to think about other stuff and try and battle out of this tunnel of depression and anxiety I am in. I am going to work on some radio notes for a little while and then see how it feels working on the manuscript.

Calisthenics. Oatmeal, yoghurt, corn chips, hummus, spinach, salmon, frozen yoghurt, carrot juice, water, coffee 1 cup.

07-15-06 LA CA: 2208 hrs. I'm in a fuck it mood. I am not watching or reading anything on what's happening between Lebanon and Israel. I am sure a lot of innocent people are dying. I am sure each side is blaming the other. Anything else I need to know? No. Fuck it.

Today I worked on the manuscript and made a lot of corrections. I try so hard to be clear when I write. I don't want to obscure the idea. Unfortunately, to accomplish that seemingly simple task is most often beyond me. I have always struggled with writing. It's never been anything less than frustrating with results that fall below standard. When I read a great feature article in a magazine or a writer like Kapuscinski, I wonder how they are able to write with such purpose and clarity. It's obviously beyond me but I work at it.

It's very hot where I'm sitting. I have all the doors closed and I never use the AC. My shirt is sticking to me and every few minutes I break for a set of push-ups or chin-ups. I will be doing this all night long. This place has been hot all day. I keep it this way because, and here's the lamest reason but it's the truth, because the oppressive heat reminds me of DC. I really wanted to go there for a couple of days before this tour started but one thing lead to another and there was no way I was getting out there. I wouldn't have had a good time anyway. All I would have done was thought of the tour and that I had to get back to LA where band practice was going to start soon. That would have been lurking in every thought I had while there. So, in order to at least get a little of it, I have turned my house into a Nazi hit box from Hell.

The tour has me now. I'm already on it. Fuck it. I feel a little deader than a few days ago. That's good. I dead-up all the way until the tour starts and then when we go out, it's just the show, recover, train, recover, the show, etc.

Besides my knee blowing out on me and not being able to get a few more runs in, I feel pretty good. I have to beat a little more sense out of me. That will happen at band practice. The final caning before we go out there.

I don't know what the tour and the band means to the others. It's all life and death to me. It's just fuck it let's go. It is darkness and humiliation. Failure and dust. All the training I have done for this tour won't make a bit of difference. Something else will blow out. Something will bring crushing disappointment. That is what comes along with this line-up for me. I remember so much misery on the 1997 tour, it was one of the worst years of my life.

I have been listening to our music for the last two hours. I have been playing the song *Also Ran* over and over. I like that song. Come In And Burn has some of my favorite lyrics I have ever done. People didn't like that one! Press folks were oh so mean to me. At least they left the band alone. Fuck it.

I got more e-mail from the conservative douche bag who has been writing me his insane bullshit. His thing now is that there's WMDs in Iraq. I'll wait for Rumsfeld to tell me all about it. Fuck it.

I looked at some who-gives-a-fuck online news a moment ago and read that an Italian magazine published a photo of Princess Diana right after her car wrecked and her sons are bent out of shape about it. I went and looked for the picture and found it. If it's real, it's a sad photograph. Other sites say it's not real. I always thought she was pretty cool, especially when she dumped that silly husband of hers. What a sack of weak genes that guy is. All those corny British news-papers are inflamed and not running the photo. They are writing ever so mean things about the Italian magazine publisher. His response was great. He basically told the British tabloids that they really have no solid ground in saying something shouldn't be printed. If it were my magazine, I would never print the picture but he's right in what he said to the Sun and Mirror. Fuck it.

Now I'm "happy." I am resolved. I am alone in this hot room. This is the truth of my life right here right now.

Also Ran

Now that I'm at the end of the line
I stand at the edge of myself and look down
Yes, I know that the best is behind me and my future is hard
and real
The road is rough, the days are tough and the nights burn my
skin
Here I am setting up for the long one
The last time digging in
>Now I see why people throw themselves away
>Now I see why people live alone
All the ones I know who fell off, dreams cut short, and debts
all paid off
Some might say you're gone but you'll always be here with me
So easy to let yourself fall through the cracks and not look
back
So hard to take it when you find that no one really cares
>Now I see why people throw themselves away
>Now I see why people live alone
>Now I see why some people see blue skies when
>others see grey
>Looking up from the bottom I see the stars in the sky
>I am therefore I go
The cheering crowd has seen the winners
Packed up and gone home
Power is as strength won't do
The truth will never be told
First to start and the last to quit
The loser runs longest but unknown
Here I am setting up for the last time
I am nothing but my will

Calisthenics. Yoghurt, corn chips, hummus, tomato soup, spinach, salmon, bananas, carrot juice, water, coffee 2 cups.

07-16-06 LA CA: 2200 hrs. I didn't do a whole lot today besides work on upcoming radio shows and proofread. I ran some errands and worked out very hard. Oh yeah, I tried something today and it worked out great. I cranked up my stereo and played a CD of songs we're going to play in the set and sang along like it was a show. I even got a mic to hold onto. I stood in my living room and went for it flat out.

I practiced *On My Way To The Cage* three times back to back and was soaked by the time I got through it. It was great and I was able to work on some sticking points I had with the tune. By the second time I was going through the song, I was completely in it. After that I hammered away at *Burned Beyond Recognition* and that was good too.

Chris and I e-mailed back and forth about songs and what would work well together. I am liking that combination of *Cage* and *BBR* as the first two songs in the set. That would be really intense.

It's Sunday night. I am in my room. Tired of working in the front room so am back here. I was hoping to get some reading done but the weekend was taken up with radio show writing and proofreading. I plan on taking some books on tour. Having a lot of people on the bus tends to make me stay in my bunk because there's not a great deal of room to hang out anywhere else. In there I get a lot of reading done. The bus bunk is one of my favorite places to read.

I am an obsessive person and I live in a small world. I talked to two people on the phone this weekend. One was a police fund drive solicitor and the other was someone I don't know very well at all who wanted to loan me a Czech film called <u>Closely Watched Trains</u>. The other calls were hang ups. Past that, I said thanks to the guy who bagged my food at the grocery store and talked a little when I bought a pound of coffee at the Peet's on Ventura. I consider that a good weekend. This isn't a town I am able to go out and walk around in. It's not laid out that way. New York City is a city I like to be out in. Los Angeles is a city I try to stay out of even when I'm in it. Also, the bottom line is that people are painful and I've had my fair share and I am cool to stay in here.

This week will be flat out. Tomorrow is the last day before the band gets here. Tuesday, Slayer is taping for the TV show downtown, the band arrives and I have the radio show. I am ready for the show but it's going to be a lot of hustle tomorrow making sure everything is squared away for the band's arrival. I cleaned up everything on Saturday so the band members who are staying with me should be good to go. I have done some packing. I have a few days before I have to get that tightened up. I won't be taking much and will be doing laundry in sinks at venues and wearing it dry. I am going to be up early and at the office as soon as possible.

Chest, abs. Yoghurt, protein drink, granola, rice milk, bananas, spinach, salmon, carrot juice, water, coffee 1 cup.

07-17-06 LA CA: 2340 hrs. Just finished working out. It's very hot in LA right now. By the afternoon, you would think you're in Texas or Arizona. I don't remember if it was this hot last year. The news said that today California hit an all time high in power usage and Governor Assengrabber asked that people conserve electricity as best they can. I rarely use the air conditioner. I'd rather just swelter.

I did use the air conditioner for a few hours today because I had a film crew in my office who were doing a documentary on the artist Shepard Fairey. Shepard is perhaps best known for his Andre the Giant posters he has slapped up all over. There's a good chance you've seen the poster of Andre's face with the word "OBEY" beneath. Shepard's new book Supply And Demand, an overview of his work, is fantastic and worth checking out. There were a few people he asked to be interviewed for the project and I was one of them. He designed the poster for our upcoming tour, the poster for the IFC show and he designed the set for the intro for the IFC show as well. He's a very interesting guy so it was cool to talk about him. I am a fan. Recently, he did a very limited edition of portraits of the members of Roxy Music. There are 50 sets in all. Steve Jones bought 25 of them for gifts. I think he was the one who requested that Shepard do them. I bought a set and so did management. They look great.

That took up a big part of the day and after that I started working on corrections of this manuscript. I did that on and off for the rest of the day and then took it back here and kept on working. There were so many mistakes and poorly written sentences, it took about three hours more work to get done with my 25 page goal. I am in day #04 of editing the first draft. I will be working on this every day until mid-September.

An interesting phone call today: I spoke to Joel Webber at Men's

<u>Quarterly Magazine</u> about a travel story I will hopefully be doing for the magazine in September. If all goes to plan, I will be heading off to Burma to explore and write about the country. We have been working on this on and off for a few months now. Burma might be tricky to get in and out of. Should at least be interesting. Could be the last thing I do. That's fine. I hope it happens.

I have one book on Burma. I will take it with me on tour and start educating myself on the country and its history. This is the kind of thing I live for. Keep moving and keep it interesting. I hope to be traveling hard in the last few months of the year. I will have to be back in LA in mid-November for office work but I will get out again in mid-December and go from Russia into China on the Trans-Mongolian Express. It will be cold and bleak. Good to go.

Tomorrow will be busy. After the band arrives, I go downtown to watch Slayer tape and then I have to jam over to the radio station, tape three shows for broadcast in August and then go live at 2000 hrs. Wednesday, band practice starts. We are out of here soon and we'll see what all this training and anticipation amounts to.

Arms. Yoghurt, bananas, spinach, salmon, hummus, corn chips, tomato soup, rice crackers, carrot juice, water, coffee 1 cup.

07-18-06 LA CA: 2430 hrs. I won't be able to put much down here. I am roasted. Today was long like I knew it would be. Band came in and I took them to the grocery store, took Melvin to his hotel and then went back to the office and picked up Chris. We went downtown and saw Slayer tape for the IFC show. I want to write more about that experience but it will have to wait. We took off out of there and into the hell traffic of LA. I dropped Chris off at my place and jammed down to the radio station to pre-tape three shows for August. Went from there to get some food, ate quickly and then we were on the air. I just got back and filed my radio notes, sent in the Dispatches thing and entered the songs I played into an index I keep. Now I am very tired and really want to clock out. The house is hot and sleep will be hard tonight. Tomorrow is the first day of band practice and I can't wait to get in there with the guys finally. More later.

Oatmeal, protein bar, protein drink, hummus, corn chips, burrito, taco, carrot juice, water, coffee 1 cup.

07-19-06 LA CA: 2156 hrs. Good band practice today. Everyone showed up to hit it and I think we are going to really kill it tomorrow. We played a lot of songs. We didn't get to every song we're playing on this tour but we got close. We didn't play *Icon* or *Also Ran*. There may have been another we missed but we'll get to them tomorrow. We played parts of *Shine* over and over, making sure we were all on the same page in the middle section. *Almost Real* sounded the best it's sounded so far. I finally got my head around the low down section that was giving me trouble at the NYC practices.

I got another lesson in pain today. If you do it right, there's nothing like the first day of band practice. All the old injuries come back to visit. The knees hurt, back, etc. It's great in my opinion. Pain is just an invitation to excel. You're lucky to have the pain, it's the calling card of excellence. I was happy for the pain, it was giving me all the information I needed as to what areas I need to work on the most.

I am back from dropping everyone off at all their respective locations and I still have to work out. I am determined to get through a night of shoulders. I think it's good for the body to understand that a lot will be asked of it. I have contempt for my body. The aging process is such a crushing disappointment to me. I work harder and harder and as the years go by I can feel my body failing and not giving me the return I demand of it. So, I get mad at it and put it through more work. It's a separation of mind and body. My mind says my body is its tool, and it is, but it no longer stands up to the strength of the idea. There's no way the idea can change. I cannot lessen the intensity of what the performance should be. I just have to suck it up and take the pain. I can do that. That's one thing I am good at. I can take the fucking pain.

The upside of the last few months of training is that I could feel it today. My back is strong and all the abdominal work I have been doing paid off. Overall, I had a lot of energy and we played a lot more than what will be asked of us nightly on this tour. I will play as hard as I can every night and then recover with equal attention. I will train hard in the day, get some sleep to recover and treat the set that night as the cardio workout that gets me in better shape for the shows that are to come. Every day will optimize and condition me for the next one. Bottom line is that I am in good shape for this tour because I did the right thing. I gave myself enough time to beat myself into shape without going past peak. At least I hope I have not over trained, it's easy to do that.

2302 hrs. Done with shoulders and food. I will be falling behind on inputting corrections to the manuscript because there's no way I am getting any work on that done tonight. I want to go over some lyrics and make some notes.

My voice was pretty good today. A couple of songs felt a little rough on it but all in all, it held up pretty well. If I can get some sleep tonight, it will be better tomorrow.

In the next few days, I have to consolidate my thoughts and get ready to not think of much more than the shows. I like to work this way. It's what I did to be effective in the film I just finished. It was the world I lived in for weeks. The tour, the songs, the band and crew— they will make up the world I live in until September. It's the best way for me to really nail it. I like that discipline, that tightening of the focus that borders on obsession. Maybe what some see as obsessive I call focus. Doesn't matter. Getting it done matters.

Band practice, shoulders pt. 1, oatmeal, protein bar, protein drink, hummus, corn chips, carrot juice, salmon, spinach, tomato soup, rice crackers, yoghurt, water, coffee 1 cup.

07-20-06 LA CA: 2206 hrs. Today was a good day at band practice. We sounded really good and way more on top of things in general. We made a set of 16 songs and played them straight through to hear how they go together and especially for timing purposes as we only have one hour onstage on this tour. What we thought would be an hour actually timed out to be about 73 minutes so we'll have to do some adjustments there. We'll have time for 13 to 15 songs depending on what we play. Songs like *Liar* and *Almost Real* are about 7-8 minutes each. Others are a lot less. It will depend on how it feels. I think it's a better idea to play more songs than less. *Shame* is a bit long compared to other songs. A few shows in, an hour is going to feel pretty light-weight. We are going to work on *Liar* more tomorrow and start working on *Step Back*, which I had not heard in a long time and really liked when I listened to it the other night.

I am practicing in 4 t-shirts that are too small and a thermal long sleeve shirt that is also too small. It is hot and restricts breathing. I have to fight to get the songs out. It's worth it. I soaked through all of them when we blasted through that set.

An hour isn't a long time onstage but at least we'll make it a really good hour.

After a trip to Guitar Center to get some gear we all went to a Thai restaurant and ate. It's hard to describe how great it is to be with these guys again. They are some of my favorite people in the world and I truly value their friendship. I don't hang out with people and do my best to stay to myself as much as I can but it's always great to spend time with these guys even when we're not working. After dinner, I dropped everyone off at their respective places and Chris and I came back to the house. He's staying in the guest room. I looked over the early morning agony I will be enduring a few hours from now. I have about 2.5 hours of phone press starting at 0550 hrs. It's for the IFC show.

On Saturday morning, I will be heading to the airport to fly to San Diego to do two hours at Comicon. I don't know how to spell it. It's that comic book convention they have every year. I don't know anything about comic books but IFC has a booth there and they want me to sit and sign pictures of my face for two hours. That will easily break the viewership of the show wide open, I'm sure. I will then fly back to LA and get in around 1700 hrs. The whole thing will take about ten hours. When asked to do this I said no, that I had band practice and I really had to apply myself there. Then management said I should do it, that it's close to the time when they will be making up their minds about a possible third season of the show, etc. And stupidly, I caved in. So, it's my fault. I should have stayed true to my unit and the tour but instead I sold out and caved in. So, any lack of sleep and difficulty I will endure on that day is all mine. There's a lot of people involved with the IFC show. There's not one person at IFC that I have met and don't like. They are really cool. All of them are smart, switched on and for some reason they like me. I wouldn't mind doing this completely pointless exercise on Saturday if the band wasn't in town and we weren't getting ready to go out on a tour we all have been working so hard towards. The band all understand and say they can play without me and get things done. Perhaps I can go right from the airport to band practice and hit it with them until they are worn out. I'll ask them what they want to do about Saturday when we get together tomorrow.

Band practice, protein drink, hummus, corn chips, carrot juice, noodles, vegetables, yoghurt, water, diet coke, coffee 1 cup.

07-21-06 LA CA: 2227 hrs. Today was productive but very long. I had a lot of phone interviews to do early this morning. I got up around 0530 hrs. and started in soon after.

0600 – 0610: KPRI San Diego CA Host: Madison

0610 – 0620: KBKS Seattle WA Host: Jackie & Bender

0620 - 0630: WZGC Atlanta GA Host: Barnes & Firfer

0630 – 0640: WARW Washington DC Host: Stevens and Medley

0640 – 0650: WNNX Atlanta GA Host: Tucker, Leslie & Jimmy

0650 – 0700: KQRX Odessa Midland TX Host: Kevin Porter

0700 – 0710: KLAC Los Angeles CA TX Host: Mancow

0710 – 0720: KRAB Bakersfield CA TX Host: Meathead, Desi & Rocky Nash

0720 – 0730: Red Bar Radio Chicago IL TX Host: Mike D

0730 – 0740: WBZA Rochester NY TX Host: Kimberly & Beck

0740 – 0750: KOZN Phoenix AZ TX Host: Colin Boyd

0750 – 0800: MTV

Thinking about it now, I don't remember much of it. I sure don't remember the MTV one happening at all. They were all very friendly and asked about the IFC show and the upcoming tour. I tried to get some sleep afterwards but I couldn't do it.

Heidi called and said the shipment of the 2nd pressing of <u>Fanatic!</u> had just arrived and told me to come to the office and deal with it. I went down there and the driver, Sim and I pushed the pallet of books up the driveway. I came back here after they were stowed and had enough time to grab my gear and Chris and then we picked up Sim and Melvin and went to band practice.

The set we did yesterday timed out at almost the exact same time as before, 73 min. We took out *Shame* and put in *Liar* to check out how that sounded. Both songs are the same length. Basically it's looking like a 13 –15 song set as I thought yesterday. We did all the songs in the set and then went onto other songs. Between listening and playing, we got through a lot but it took a long time. Post set, we did *Shame, Almost Real, Shine, Alien Blueprint, All I Want, Fool* and a couple of others that I can't remember. We went back and did *Liar* again and it sounded better. We still need to work on the outro a little but I think it's ready for show time.

Today I wore three t-shirts, a long sleeved thermal shirt and a sweatshirt. I didn't take any of it off. The AC was off and it made me have to work really hard to get through the songs and keep moving the whole time. I am trying to make it as hard on myself as I can so the shows feel easy in comparison. I did notice that my wind was good today and I think all this training has not been in vain. I am light but tight and it feels like a good weight to play at. All the muscle I have on me makes sense. I think all the medium weight reps were the right idea as well as all that abdominal work. Diet is good and strict. I have lost my appetite for things I shouldn't eat.

I am trying to empty out my mind and just think about the shows and the pain and the lyrics and all that but it's hard. I am distracted by the press I have to do for the tour as well as this trip I have to make to San Diego in a few hours. That's going to put a dent in practice but I think we'll be alright. The guys will just go to practice a little later (which I am sure is fine with them) and I will join them around 1700 hrs. and we'll do some work. I will be fried but I'll still get in there. I just walked in from the garage a little while ago after working out. There was no way I was going to miss the work out. Anything I can do to strengthen my resolve is a plus.

We were in there for a long time today. It's not always great when you practice that long but we definitely need it and it did us good. Being in a band all these years has taught me a lot. I use a lot of discipline to get it done. None of the things I do seem too extreme to me. If anything, I easily could have done more to prepare for this tour.

Shoulders pt. 2. Band practice. Rice milk, granola, protein drink, bananas, hummus, corn chips, carrot juice, salmon, spinach, water, diet coke, coffee 1 cup.

07-22-06 LA CA: 2212 hrs. At the office. I felt like working here tonight. I like the lighting better and I like working here on weekend nights. This place feels like work more than the house does. I am trying to stay awake and keep my thoughts from straying.

The Comic Con, or "The Con" as it was referred to when I was there several hours ago was really cool. The event sells about 100,000 tickets. It was packed in the Convention Hall and, as the day went on, it got louder and the temperature rose steadily. I thought there was going to be more costumed people walking around but there wasn't. Perhaps there's more of that kind of thing later in the day. There were some interesting outfits walking around but not in the numbers I thought there would be. It was mostly just people in t-shirts and jeans, checking everything out. There was a lot to check out, too. Every square inch is taken up by displays, cut-outs, screens and people.

I landed around 0854 hrs. I got in the car and it took almost an hour to get through all the lines of cars to the VIP drop off area. I went into the green room and asked the woman at the front if she could call someone from IFC and tell them that I was there. She did and they sent up a guy to take me to the IFC booth. As we wove through the people and displays, I heard a voice over the PA say something like, "Henry Rollins was just seen walking past the ... " I couldn't make

A Dull Roar

out the rest. People started turning around and looking at me. Soon enough, we were at the IFC area. There were screens with my TV show playing. There were posters of my face all over the place and a long line of people waiting for the 1100 - 1300 hrs. signing. It was about 1022 hrs. and there was no way I was going to have that many people wait in a line that long just to meet me. I asked if we could just start the thing now and they said that was fine. So, I found a spot to stand and we got it going.

It was like an in-store or a USO meet and greet. I stood in one spot until 1300 hrs. and didn't move until I left the building. It was intense. My throat was giving me grief because I went for it hard the day before and didn't sleep much last night. I could feel it start swelling so I did my best to talk under the noise. The people I met were incredibly varied: Army, Air Force, Navy, punks, dads with their kids, young people who seemed incredibly shy and could barely say their names out loud when they wanted the poster I was signing personalized and older adults who told me about the times they saw Black Flag. I got a lot of questions about what I thought about "The Con" and if I was staying to check things out. A lot of people told me how much my books meant to them and how different ones helped them out at different times. A lot of people said they had already got their tickets to see us on the X tour and couldn't wait. All in all, they were a really cool bunch of people.

The comic book, fantasy and Sci-fi world never struck me as escapist as much as it seemed a place for people to get some solace and be allowed to wander in their imagination. They don't strike me as the kind of people who always fit in, throw the ball really well or get the girl. I guess it's that Geek thing. I always thought that was more interesting than the jock and tough guy thing. At least the comic book and Sci-fi fans seemed like they read and valued intellect. At one point I signed a poster for a young guy who is probably going to have a hard time getting a date to the prom. Several minutes after he had left, he came back and stood around until I was done and as I was walking out he started following me and the security I had all around me started trying to deflect him. I couldn't hear what he was saying at first. I stopped and told the security people it was cool and they backed off. The kid said someone had stolen his poster and could I sign another? He had one with him and I signed it. I was glad I was able to do that and that moment is now my favorite part of the whole day and made the whole trip worthwhile. The kid got a signed poster even after his other one got ripped off. That's cool.

There were moments during the signing that were really strange. I would look past the person I was talking to and there would be a half circle of people taking photos of us. Other times I would look up to see people taking pictures mixed in with press people taking pictures and filming.

So like I said, I walked out of there with the security guys and some IFC people and back out into the humid furnace of San Diego. The car took a long time getting to the pick-up spot because of all the cars, cops and people. I got to the airport and barely made the flight to LA just like I barely made the one to San Diego. The trip was not all that well planned and while I was getting searched for the 2nd time I was in a pretty bad mood but I got better.

I went from the airport right to band practice. The guys had been in there for some time working on things. We played *Step Back* for the first time and it sounded good immediately. We worked on *Civilized, Almost Real* and *Black And White*. They were pretty tired from the hours of practice before I arrived and my throat was killing me so we called it a day about an hour in.

I dropped everyone off, went back to the house and then went to the office. I am too tired to work out. I'll head back to the house soon. I had some things that I wanted to write down here about an editorial I read in the July 20th Washington Times called *Vacationing In Beirut*. The writer basically says that travelers to Lebanon had been warned repeatedly by the Government that it's an unstable region and that rescuing them drains Military manpower and resources from other places. He calls them "whiners" that aren't taking responsibility for their actions. The writer also notes a 1956 law that authorizes the State Department to charge evacuees for their rescue and that the law was re-approved again a few years ago, with House Minority Leader Nancy Pelosi voting in favor of it. My sentiment is that it would have never once occurred to me that America would rescue me from anything happening anywhere in the world, including America. There's no wool covering my eyes. The only money for me when I am old is what I earn and save myself right now. I understand with not a speck of doubt that I am on my own in America and on my own outside of America. America doesn't have my back. Only I have my back and my back is only covered by what I own and have saved. That's how it is and even more so now with the current Administration. The Conservative douche bag spoke the truth in the op-ed.

The Constitution is not there for you. Forget about it. Public education is not going to be improved because there are a lot of people in powerful places who want it just the way it is. It's better for making the Army or crime an option for the disadvantaged. It keeps everyone in their place. You give more people a better education and you will have less crime in this country and more people competing for better jobs and that would throw a monkey wrench into the workings of the power structure.

Millions of Americans are homophobic and if they could vote on the topic of whether same sex marriage should be outlawed there would be an overwhelming majority of people coming out against it. If I were gay I would just say fuck it. Fuck these people. I would just stop talking to most straight people, not bother to fight for marriage rights and leave that to the god-loving Christians. I would tune the fuck out. It's not worth it to get the approval of these shit heads in the first place. Gay folks should have their own weddings at people's houses and make it a cool and memorable event, put rings on each other's fingers and be done with it. Fuck getting married in churches. Make churches for straight people and homophobes. Let them have it. There's nothing happening in churches that you can't do somewhere else. The homophobic Christians don't want gays to have the same benefits or rights because to them, gays are horrible and their demands for equality are illegitimate. I hate to sound defeatist but I don't see these people ever changing their minds. Perhaps it's just a matter of time until the stronghold these people have goes the way of the whites-only water fountain. This is where my disconnect with America is: I don't think things like this will ever change. I want to be wrong of course. I have come to the conclusion that you're on your own in America. Get that through your head and you're good to go. That's what the op-ed piece made me think about.

Band practice. Rice milk, granola, banana, hummus, corn chips, carrot juice, water, coffee 1 cup.

07-23-06 LA CA: 2335 hrs. Damn I am tired. I don't know what happened. It's not all that late and I am on empty. I think I didn't get enough food in today. That has to be it. I played hard earlier. We laid into the set and I went for it as hard as I will be at any other time and then we worked on *Step Back* but weren't sure of the length of a few sections so we left it there and will pick it up tomorrow.

I took Melvin back to the hotel and as we were pulling up, who did we see checking in but Mr. Theo Van Rock. He came outside and we all hung out for a moment. This was the first time the five us have all been together since 1997. He's looking good and ready to rock. So now we're all back together and I think we're ready. Today's run through of the songs satisfied me.

I got back here and headed into the garage to work out. I did a bunch of deadlifts off a platform and a lot of abdominal work and then sat down here and felt like I was going to keel over. It has to be the lack of food. I blew it today on nutrition. Not a good idea this close to the tour.

I am ready. Voice feels good, set feels good and I think the guys are all there. There's a lot riding on this and I want it to kill every night. I was wondering about everyone's commitment level until tonight. This is nothing new. I always figure no one is as extreme on anything as I am. Sometimes certain members of this band can be somewhat low key and you could think they are a little not on the mark but it's just how they are and it took me a little while to remem-

A Dull Roar

ber that. They are in fact all there and into this. Watching Sim play though the last part of *Starve* is one of the most amazing moments of the set. I had forgotten how he just explodes at the ride out.

I had a great conversation with Janeane Garofalo earlier today. I am not one for talking on the phone but I always enjoy talking to her. I like her sense of humor and her smarts and her speed. Today we talked about how lame it is that we have lost the word "fag" to the world of PC. It's such a great word and has great versatility but it's no good if someone thinks you're a homophobe, that's not something I would like anyone to think about me. But saying, "Would you fags hurry up?!" is the only way to really get that across. I said we should fight to get it back. We also talked about how we're getting "gay" back to a certain degree. I told her about the shirt I saw at Comic-Con Saturday that said, "Homophobia Is Gay." Then we talked about how wonderful it is to be able to say "douche bag" on FM radio. I told her that I try to never say the word "Conservative" without saying "douche bag" immediately afterwards. At this point, it's the only way to say the word at all, the other two words have to be in tow. I recommended she check out Camus' <u>Resistance, Rebellion And Death</u>. She left a message later on telling me she indeed did and was digging it immensely. That's cool. I am too tired to write anything else.

Deadlifts, abs. Band practice. Rice milk, granola, banana, protein drink, hummus, corn chips, carrot juice, water, diet Coke, coffee 1 cup.

07-24-06 LA CA: 2257 hrs. We played the set in front of a small invited crowd tonight. It was people from management's office, my office, Indie 103 and others the band members invited. The set sounded solid. Last night it was 60 min. 05 sec. and tonight it was 60 min. and 3 sec. We went from song to song with very little talking or tuning. I think we can pull this set off and stay in the time limit. The set isn't written in stone so we'll be rotating songs in and out all tour I reckon. I hope so. There's a few songs I really want to play that aren't in the set as yet. We'll get to them. As soon as the set was over, I went right to Theo and asked what he thought. He said it was good and we were ready to go. It was a relief hearing that from him. I feel the same

Henry Rollins
199

way. I think we're all there.

Nothing else really happening around here besides the drill of me driving to the office, hotel, band practice and house every day with a car load of band members. I am writing this in between sets of bench press and ab crunches. I was determined to workout tonight even though I am feeling tired. I don't want to start losing weight to the heat.

Last night, I was too tired to do anything after I was done writing here but I managed to get some pages of Camus' Resistance, Rebellion And Death read. I had not read from that book in several months and talking to Janeane about it made me think I had better get back to it. I re-read some pages and looked at the stuff I had underlined. Camus fascinates me. There are passages in this book that speak as loudly now as they did during WWII. I don't think people in power positions change much. What could possibly change all that much besides the technology? All tyrants say they love the people they hold power over and want nothing more than peace and prosperity for all. Slobodan said it, Bush says it, they all say it. And the people they oppress and intimidate into silence are always in the same position: They are morally grounded and actually believe in Freedom and Democracy but anyone who questions the President's naked agenda of death and greed gets hunted down and charged as traitors, or for giving comfort to the enemy. None of this shit ever changes and the endings are always the same: There is a lot of suffering and after a long time, the truth comes out and people are better off than they were before. It's going to take a long time before America's better after the Bush disaster but somehow, I think America will be ok. The people here are good, poorly represented but good. That being said, it's still going to be hard for anyone who is stupid enough or delusional enough to think that America will be there for them. It's beyond everyone pulling themselves up by their own bootstraps and all that happy bullshit. It's now to the point where if you're not ready to survive America, you're a goner. America is not your friend, it's the place that gave you the line of credit and its business. Sometimes when I try to come back into the country from Canada, I get the third degree from some border dick. So, I'm supposed to stay in Canada? Hey, maybe I should. Maybe I will. I could live there just fine. I would only miss my old neighborhood and some people who lived there. Past that, I don't miss anything really. I miss some dead people but they're dead. So am I. It's the only way to go.

The depression has not been all that bad today. It was pretty bad before the band got here. All the anticipation and everything. Also, the IFC show has been green lit for a third season. I don't know if I want to do it. I will have to do some thinking about it. I know they want to do a press release and all but I want to sit down with all the parties and talk. When I was at Comic-Con the other day, the IFC press lady said congratulations on the third season and I didn't say anything in return. I didn't know what to say. It's a good show and everyone involved is really cool but there needs to be some discussion about a lot of aspects of the show and what the producers think are good ideas. When I hear the ideas they have for musical guests for example, it shows me how distant we are from each other. I am afraid that to make the show all it can be, I would have to be there almost every day and involved in the planning and writing. I don't mind the work but it can't take up that much of my time. It's not worth it to me. I will have to figure out what to do about all that. It makes for a lot of 0430 hrs. staring into darkness sessions for me. The workouts and the band practices have helped me with the stress and the depression. I just have to keep remembering to stay dead. When I am dead, I see clearly. I don't get all bent out of shape. Before I play, I know it's going to hurt so I get revved up and throw myself into it. I greet the pain. The pain isn't used to someone coming up to embrace it. I think I throw it off a little. It hurt to play tonight. The first 5 songs were really hard but I was good to go. I think I'm going to get through the shows fine. I am looking forward to the on tour workouts and the time to read and write and be alone.

Chest, abs. Band practice, yoghurt, 2 protein drink, 1 protein bar, hummus, corn chips, carrot juice, water, coffee 1 cup.

07-25-06 LA CA: 2350 hrs. It's late. I got back from the radio show awhile ago. I went from the station to the office to work on the show notes to get them off to our site guy Tony so he could post them ASAP. It was a good show tonight, it went very quickly. We got a lot of music played. I try and talk as little as possible in order to get as much music on the air as possible in the two hours I have. I played two great Be Bop tracks, Don Cherry's *There Is A Bomb* and Eric Dolphy's *17 West.*

Today was the last day of practice. Road Manager Mike was there as well as Darrell, who did front of house sound on all the tours I did with Mother Superior. He's going to do monitors and deal with stage stuff along with a fellow named John who I only met yesterday. We went through songs we hadn't paid any attention to in a few days: *Also Ran, Shine, Almost Real, Shame, Alien Blueprint, Step Back* and maybe one other. We laid off the other songs we had made into a set to not burn them out. So, practice didn't go all that long.

I went from practice to the office to the house to the radio station and started setting up for the show. The day was a bit of a blur. I don't have a lot to say but I am feeling pretty good because I think the band is all there and all the hard work has paid off. I think everyone in the band is excited about the tour. All these people are great, have a great work ethic and everything but I was wondering what all this meant to them and I think it's safe to say that everyone is full on into this.

Now I want to get a few shows done and get my head around what it's really going to be like out there. It was good to do that set last night. I went for it flat out and felt good afterwards. I will have to up that bar and keep pushing myself as the tour goes on. I will have to really watch my diet. I am lighter than when I was working on the film. I am going to start upping my protein intake a bit and see if that helps.

Sleep has been difficult the last few nights with the anxiety and the heat. My room gets a bit cool around 0600 hrs. for a little while but then heats right back up again.

Band practice, yoghurt, granola, rice milk, protein drink, hummus, corn chips, 1 veg. burrito, 2 tacos, carrot juice, water, coffee half cup.

07-26-06 LA CA: 2311 hrs. This is the last night before the tour begins. I have been training for four months for this tour. I have been thinking about it every day with everything from enthusiasm to dread. I have trained hard and tried to eat right.

I feel apprehensive about the shows but at the same time I think we have really pulled it together and taken it seriously. I know I have. I feel relief that we are finally getting out there. Now I have a place to go with all my anger and overall fucked up-ness. The shows are going to hurt. The pain puts me at an altitude I can't get to off the road. The pain I endure to play as hard as the music demands, the promise of it every night, I either rise to it or get crushed by it. I feel stronger when my pain threshold is up. I have been working out to toughen my body as well as my mind. The show is George Foreman. I am Ali. I am going to take a beating but I will prevail. That's how this music is. It is a fight. It is conflict. It is confrontation.

I go into this tour as a member of the band but at the same time, totally on my own. It has always been this way. This is Road Manager Mike's last tour with me. I don't know what he's going to do next. I am glad he came out for this one. Of course I wish it wasn't the last time we were going out there together but I am so glad he will be there.

I will be spending as much time as I can on my own. I have been thinking about how to stay fit on this tour and I had a great idea I want to try tomorrow night. I will play the set and then get in a workout while X plays. I will be tired but perhaps I'll have enough steam to hit some of the lighter workouts afterwards. That would be ultimate. I could completely wear myself out, get some work done and then rack out. It would be great not to be staying up late and taking advantage of the early stage time to recover voice and body. I am in pretty good shape at the moment. If I do it right, I very well could be in better shape a week from now. I notice I have lost a little weight since the film, probably from this last week of practice. I can't wait to hit this. In 24 hours, I'll know some things I don't know now.

Shoulders pt. 1. Yoghurt, granola, rice milk, protein drink, salmon, spinach, rice/shrimp bowl, carrot juice, water, coffee 1 cup.

Henry Rollins

07-27-06 Cabazon CA: 1842 hrs. On the bus. Soundcheck is done. We played *On My Way To The Cage, Also Ran* and *All I Want.* They sounded good to me. It's great to hear these songs through a real PA. I think we're going to be alright.

We left around 1115 hrs. We were supposed to leave around 1030 hrs. but somehow I screwed up the call time and was late.

Something interesting about the bus that I should note here. A couple of months ago at the Bonnaroo Festival in Tennessee, a tour bus was leaving the festival grounds when a young man threw himself in front of the bus in a suicide attempt. The bus was going fast and hit the man squarely and killed him. That's the bus we are on. The front end is messed up and the door doesn't close easily. The man was near 300 pounds I am told. We don't have internet access at the moment so I can't get any further information on the event but I will when I can.

Here's what I found:

MANCHESTER, Tenn. (AP) — A man was killed when he was hit by a tour bus carrying bluegrass artist Ricky Skaggs after a performance at the Bonnaroo music festival has been identified. Joshua Overall, 21 of Hamilton, Ohio, was hit by the bus as it traveled south on Interstate 24 at 7:50 p.m. about a mile from the exit for the festival, said Melissa McDonald, spokeswoman for the Tennessee Department of Safety. "The young man just walked out into traffic," she said. "There was no fault on the part of the bus driver. It was unavoidable." The bus was estimated to be traveling around 55 miles per hour before the accident. No charges will be filed against the driver, McDonald said.

I am not as stressed out as I was yesterday because we're here and about to do it and all the training and focus is paying off. I felt good at soundcheck. This band has a lot of bad memories for me. Not the people, the shows. I remember some shows where I was having such throat problems that touring was relentless depression. I have been trying to forget that part. Just because it was bad for me back then doesn't mean it has to be bad now. I should try and lie down for a little while. I'll check in here again after the show.

2333 hrs. First show done. I think we played really well. I went out in back of the venue half an hour before the show and did the 2nd half of the warm up. I take an hour to get my body ready for the stage. I get the heart rate up and eliminate all the thoughts that are not about the set. It's very effective. The last half an hour I spent jumping around with Slayer playing in my headphones. That was really good.

As soon as we hit stage, I knew we were going to be fine. I looked at Sim and he looked so serious, so ready to unleash it, I knew it was going to be good. We went right into *On My Way To The Cage* and it fucking killed. It was the first time I have done the first show of a tour and was able to feel the results of all the training. Where I'm usually out of breath, I wasn't. Where my legs are usually getting a little shot, they weren't. Tonight I felt as I do about five shows in. We have a day off after the first three shows. I will be in the pocket by then. The set is 13 songs and it went quickly. We finished with *Liar* and it sounded really good. The stand out of the set for me was *Volume 4*. All in all, a good first night. All the practice paid off. It definitely wasn't amateur hour up there.

I worked out in the parking lot earlier today. The first of a lot of good tour workouts I hope. I hit shoulders hard and did a lot of sit-ups and push-ups. After I finished that, I sat and read from <u>Resistance, Rebellion And Death</u>. It's a great book and much better the second time around. I am going to try and read a lot on this tour. It was great being on my own this afternoon. The venue looks out at a beautiful mountain range. I believe I am near the place where I spoke at the hotel in La Quinta.

I am sitting in the back of the bus with headphones on. I don't want to hear anyone's voice. I don't want to hang out with the band. I don't have a problem with them, I just want to be on my own and have this time to myself. Tonight was the night I had been working towards for months. All the training and all the dread and anxiety that I have been dealing with have lead up to this night. It's a reason for living. I don't know how it is for the others in the band, but for me, this is basically all I care about. I don't have family and I don't give a fuck about keeping in touch with anyone or loving or being loved. This is it for me. The challenge of all this. Delivering while knowing that I am dealing in diminishing returns. I am getting older and it's much harder to play so I am basically going out swinging as hard as I can as I go down. That's how I see it. This isn't good times for me. None of this is a good time. It's a real time. It's the real deal up there. It's real pain and a real test. That's what I am good for. Nothing else captivates me as much as this.

Shoulders pt. 2. Show. 2 protein bars, yoghurt, 2 protein drinks, salmon, vegetables, rice, lime popsicles, water, coffee 1 cup.

07-28-06 San Francisco CA: 1708 hrs. Downstairs at the venue. Staying quiet. Voice a little tender from last night. I felt it at soundcheck a little earlier so I want to conserve it as best I can. I should be alright.

I'm not going to try and workout here. There's no space at the venue and the sidewalk outside the Warfield is mostly homeless folks and it's not the most stable environment to have stuff out on the street.

2335 hrs. Sitting in the back of the bus. It was a good show tonight. Again, the training and work I did preparing for this has paid off. I have my head around the set now and have some control with it now. In a few shows, I'll be able to start beating on it. It's beating on me at the moment but I'm holding my own. I'll own it soon. As soon as the show is over, I want to be out of there and as far away as I can get. It is difficult to deal with people after shows. Sometimes there's people on the guest list to see after the show. I like them but before shows I can't deal with anyone and afterwards, most of the time, I just don't have anything to say. I had a name on the guest list tonight. I talked to her briefly before the show on the phone but didn't see her or her husband afterwards. They had after show passes but I don't know what happened to them. Perhaps they didn't come to the show. I have known her so many years, she's one of the best people I know. Her husband is great and their daughters are just incredible. I wrote her an e-mail and told her I hoped she had a good time and to get back to me about what happened to them post show.

For me, the optimum is to not know anyone anywhere, come into a city, play the show, meet the people at the bus afterwards and then leave. Other members in the band have their cell phones ringing all the time, I don't get it. I'm not trying to put them down but I don't understand how you can possibly think you're going to be any good at this night to night if you're talking to all these people and fluttering around. On the 1997 tour, it seemed like the show that night was getting in the way of one member of the band's social life. There's a little bit of that now. People don't change that much. It pisses me off a little but that's life. He's a good guy and is kicking ass up there. For myself, I have my own trip with all this. Every night is a pass across the whetstone. I am the tip of the spear. That's it. I am not a chatty effervescent person. I am here with purpose. I am here to deliver maximum hurt. The Spear. The rest is just bullshit to me.

Tonight there were children backstage. I guess they were friends of X. It's their tour but to me, that's bullshit. I think it's fucking weak. I'm sitting on a chair with a towel across me and a little person walks by in the hallway. It's not family time. Perhaps I'm just a hard ass, or just a jerk. So fuck me.

The man who spat at me tonight missed. It made me fuck up a line in a song. I apologized to the audience and explained why I missed the line. Then I said there were no apologies to the man who spat who security were now escorting out. The security guys picked up on that and immediately walked over to the guy and walked him out. I hope he was at the show to see X. I hope he paid plenty and I hope he gets stabbed on the way to his car.

Past midnight: I ended up seeing the person on the guest list. They couldn't get backstage until after X played. They called me and I met them by the bus. I hired her at Haagen-Dazs before I was in Black Flag, that's how long I've known her. It's always great to see her and I was ok to talk to them by then. They showed me new pictures of their little girls, they are so beautiful. They also had a great picture of Guy Picciotto and his new daughter, another beautiful baby. So many people I grew up with are having kids now and they're all turning out so well. I am very fortunate to have known these people. One of the only times I am truly happy is seeing these people with their spouses. I don't want any of it for myself but I enjoy their happiness. It's all the happiness I can stand. For me, it would be a noose around my neck but it's not so bad to park next to it now and then. It was truly great to see them and I am glad we were able to get together.

Now all I want to do is start thinking about the next show. I am "happy" because I will be able to lift weights pre-show tomorrow. Today, there wasn't the opportunity. I can't wait to work out and then hit stage. This is what it's all about. This is all it's about.

Show. Protein drink, tuna, 2 protein bars, lime popsicles, water, coffee 1 cup.

07-29-06 Costa Mesa CA: 2231 hrs. On the bus. Show over. We played well tonight. It was an outdoor shed like we played on Lollapalooza. I have been playing very hard night to night and it's feeling good. At some point, I don't remember when, someone threw a bottle onstage. Chris saw it and said it landed between us. Nothing surprises me anymore. I don't care. Shit like this comes with the territory.

I guess X had a large guest list or something because after our set, there was a ton of people backstage. Moments after the set was over, people were all around me. They were all very friendly but it was a little much right after the show.

I got in a solid workout before the show and a bit of rack time after soundcheck. I spent a good part of the day sitting on my weight bench reading. I am still re-reading the Camus book and getting a lot of inspiration from it. Camus reminds me that I have to stay vigilant and always face down the enemy. The writing in the book is from the WWII era. The first section of the book is basically written to the Nazi Party but to me it reads like it is written to the Bush Administration. The way he so bravely stares down the enemy and tells them that they will be destroyed, the way he describes the bravery of Paris. His writing is poetic, describing tracer bullets and stars in the skies over the city. His writing is brilliant and powerful. He was so young when he was writing this stuff, it's too bad he didn't live very long. I have read some of his novels and they're great but it's the letters and other non-fiction stuff of his that are my favorite. Every sentence is packed with energy and intensity. I should learn more about Camus and perhaps re-read some of his books I read over 20 years ago. I might understand them better now.

That leads me to a subject I often wrestle with: is it better to keep reading new stuff and lunge forward or to perhaps read less and read it slower and take it in deeper? To read everything you can or to be a scholar on a certain writer, topic or period of history? I am greedy for information and want to do all those things. I am amazed by so much. Russian history and many of their writers and the Lost Generation Writers are of endless interest to me, especially F. Scott Fitzgerald and, if he can be considered part of the Lost Generation, Thomas Wolfe. The Cold War all the way up to the September 11th attacks are of great interest to me. And in between all that, there's so much great literature and poetry and essays and plays. You could read day and night for the rest of your life and not even read a fraction of what there is to be read. I want to re-read all the Knut Hamsun books I read years ago. I would like to re-read Celine, Miller and Leautreamont. I am definitely going to re-read Fitzgerald's <u>Tender Is The Night</u>. It took him nine years to write and it broke him when it wasn't a success. I owe it to him. Sometimes, when I drive by the apartment building he died in, I think about him haunting Hollywood bookstores and feeling like a failure. I would like to meet Matthew Bruccoli, the great Fitzgerald scholar.

I don't feel the same way with music. I have heard a lot, made a lot and played a lot. I am still interested in hearing more but it's more easily digested in a way as all you have to do is sit and listen. I have covered a lot of ground as far as listening to a lot of music and there's still a lot more to go but reading and traveling mean more to me.

Chest, abs. Show. Protein drink, hummus, pita bread, protein bar, lime pop-sicles, water, coffee 1 cup.

07-30-06 Agoura Hills CA: 1440 hrs. On the bus. Feeling pretty good. Chris and I came out with the crew. The rest of the band is in Hollywood at a hotel. They should be here soon.

We got into Hollywood very early in the morning. We dropped everyone off and I went back to the house. I got a few hours of sleep, not more than three.

We are in the parking lot of the Canyon Club. I really have no idea where we are. Somewhere in the San Fernando Valley, I guess. Across from the venue, a housing complex is being built. Canary yellow stucco-flavored anonymity looking out on the 101 Freeway. The parking lot of the mall across the street is full of SUVs. What the hell are these people thinking? You want to live in that? You're ok with driving that?

2335 hrs. Back at the house. We played about 30 miles from here and tomorrow is a day off in town. Tonight's show was good but the set needs work. Need to have less time between songs. People need to get their gear nailed down. I know Sim is having some of his stuff move around on him song to song so we have to get it nailed down. Melvin had some pedal problems but we have to get past all that and we can't be tuning after every song. All in all, it's good but it can improve, will improve, must improve. I am singing hard as hell and it feels good but I can play harder. I will take this first block of 4 shows as the means to hit it harder when we resume day after tomorrow in San Diego.

One of the things I have to start doing is standing up straighter and using more of the stage. I always go where it sounds the best so I can really zero in on the music but it feels at times that I am static, so I have to work harder. Wind is good. Legs are toughening up. Everything else feels good.

I am looking forward to getting out of California. I have no problem with the state or the people in the audience but it will be good to get out of the zone of the extended X family who populates the backstage area. They are friendly of course but backstage is not a fucking hang out to drink beers and attempt to hold semi-drunken conversations with me when I have just walked offstage. Like tonight. I am pacing back and forth in the hallway, cooling off, and these two useless friends of X start in with their idiotic bullshit. I politely answer and then they talk about the answer like I'm not even there. "Why did you wear shoes tonight and not last night?" I answer. They go into some dialogue and I am wondering why I have to listen to this bullshit and the only thing that makes sense at that moment was to haul out someone from X and tell them to clear their friends from the hallway or I will. As far as I'm concerned, it's my hallway and they can fight me for it and I know who's coming out of that one standing. But you know what? It's X's tour and it's X's useless friends so hey, it's cool. I just let it pass. Last night there was a ton of these people backstage. I am standing there just minutes after our set is over and there are people in my face with cameras, talking to me. It's unprofessional. I just hope their shows mean a lot to them because we are going to be traveling hard and we are to do a lot of playing and I know that I'm not going to let the fucking ball drop and if they do, the audience will know. I have to take my playing up to another level. That means I have to up the nutrition and training. I can do it. It's all I have to do all day so I have no excuse.

I read more Camus today and again, I was amazed and intimidated. The writing in the book is all from war time and it's so intense. Emotions are crackling and it's all life and death. No wonder he was feeling things so acutely. Some of the things I read today went over my head, the philosophy stuff but I could hang with a good deal of it. I am looking forward to getting work done tomorrow so I can have some hours to myself. I am feeling good about these last 4 shows.

Arms. Show. Yoghurt, eggs, hummus, tomatoes, onions, salmon, potatoes, water, coffee 1 cup.

07-31-06 LA CA: 2130 hrs. It's a night off. We're in LA. We're playing San Diego tomorrow night so we're leaving for that at 1100 hrs.

I spent today at the office working on stuff there and then came back here and worked on a radio show for later in the year. I figured I should get a jump on it. I am listening to a series of songs at the moment that might make for a good show.

Nothing eventful happened today. I talked to Janeane Garofalo for a little while today. She's a very funny woman. She always has some interesting reading suggestions. Past that, it was like many of the days I wade through when here. I worked at the office and now I am back at the house. I am very well aware I am on tour and am looking forward to tomorrow morning when I am back on the bus.

There's something about touring that feels like it's the right thing to be doing. I like working out in parking lots next to the bus and reading alone on loading docks. I like that so many things on the road are improvised. I like to establish myself in small locations for short amounts of time and then leave. I like that the bus moves all the time and we're always waking up somewhere else. A lot of the time, I feel life deals on me but when I am on the road, I feel like I am dealing on life. I like to see how primitive I can make my existence. The closer to the ground I get, the more pain I can take, the better the shows are and the stronger I am. When I am on the road, it's one of the only times I can stand being inside my skin. Every night is a chance to confront myself and the audience. Confrontation is truth. Dealing with the pain and the challenge of it all, over and over makes me feel like I am alive. When I am off the road, I am full of self-contempt and anger. I don't know where it comes from but it always builds up. When I am on the road, there's always the show to blow it out at.

It's been going pretty well so far. It needs to get better. I want to see the band more on it and into it. I think that will come with more shows down the line. Overall, the energy level has to come up. We can do it. It always has to be better. Rarely am I satisfied with my performance. I am going to raise the bar in the next week and push myself. I had the past four shows to show myself I can do it. Now that I know I can, there's no excuse for me not to push myself.

Last night, I couldn't sleep so I went looking around online to see if there were any interesting sites discussing F. Scott Fitzgerald's book Tender Is The Night. Years ago, when I first read it, I realized I had read a book that I was going to come back to again and again. It still haunts me. Of all Fitzgerald's work, <u>Tender</u> has captivated me the most. There are moments in all his novels and in many of his short stories that are so beautiful and alive that I sometimes stop breathing when I read a passage. No writer captures my attention like Fitzgerald. Thomas Wolfe, who I spent many months reading, is also great but writes by the truckload, a flood of words and images, where Fitzgerald is able to capture the condensation of things, the smell of a woman's perfume as she passes by. I have never read anything like him. For me, <u>Tender Is The Night</u> is his best novel. It took him nine years to write it because he never could sit down uninterrupted and work on it. Either his own lack of discipline, bad habits or family concerns kept him from it. When the book was finally published in 1933, it was largely panned by critics and ignored by readers. I think this was the beginning of the end for Fitzgerald. He came out here and tried his hand at writing screenplays and apparently had no good time of it. He died down the street from here at the end of 1940, only one year younger than I am now.

<u>Tender Is The Night</u> is a book I have to read again. I was looking around online last night to see if there was a Cambridge Critical Edition of the book as there are for some of his other books but I couldn't find one listed. I did find a set called <u>Tender Is the Night: The Diver Version, Pt. 1-5</u>. It has a total of 3500 pages over five volumes and is edited by Matthew J. Bruccoli, the Fitzgerald scholar. What the hell is it?! I looked all over for information on it but could find nothing. I was able to find two online. One in Chicago and one in England. They were both very expensive. I thought about it for awhile and then ordered the set that was located in Chicago. What the hell, life is short and if Bruccoli is involved, then it has to be worth it. In any case, it's on its way.

This throws me back into that same quandary I keep wrestling with. I could very well spend months re-reading <u>Tender Is The Night</u> and the companion notes to it or I could knock off the rest of the novels and plays of Bulgakov, something I have been wanting to do. I guess the best thing is to resign myself to permanent student status and get on with it. I would rather travel, learn and push myself than be in love, settle down or be normal. Perhaps I should take <u>Tender</u> out on the road with me and get back into it again. It's a heavy book. I think it's Fitzgerald summing up the failures, shortcomings and aspirations of his life. All the things he wanted to be, the heights he knew he wouldn't reach and the knowledge that those who reach them weren't always the better for it. I think it's now seen as a masterpiece. I wish he could see how many books he's sold and how much all his first editions (which were still sitting in warehouses at the time of his death) now go for. You want to spend a lot of money on a book? Check out any first edition or signed book by F. Scott Fitzgerald. If I were rich, all those would be on my shelf right now. I think it's time to go read a book.

Protein drink, salmon, spinach, hummus, rice milk, granola, corn chips, yoghurt, carrot juice, water, coffee 1 cup.

AUGUST 2006

08-01-06 San Diego CA: 2331 hrs. Show over. I am at the back of the bus listening to some music. I think tonight's show was the best one of the tour so far. This was the show were I stopped wondering if I could do it and just threw myself into it completely. Really great audience tonight. They were with us every step of the way. Sim went for some experimentation in the middle of *Liar* and it messed up going into the 2nd chorus but the audience was cool about it.

I have built up my confidence from the other shows to really ramp it up from here on in. I went out there tonight telling myself that I was going to start the set with at least 20% more energy coming off the blocks and take it from there. I knew I could do it. When I go out there really intense at the top of the set, it keeps me at a high level of concentration and intensity that is exactly what the songs need to realize their full potential. I am stoked that I made it around that corner and hit that level of kill tonight. From here on out, it's harder workouts and harder sets at night. Can't wait to take it to the next level tomorrow night. This is what it's all about. I have to kill it harder and harder.

The band was really good tonight. We had a meeting beforehand about trying to press the time out from between the songs as best we could and tonight was much better than the other nights. I want to stay on the audience and not give them a chance to catch their breath.

I said some crazy shit before *Civilized* tonight about how much I hated peace and harmony and how they were just a temporary rest-ing period before the next conflict. It was pretty fucked but I think it's true. I don't trust peace—it's just the moment when the bad guys are planning their next move. I would rather live in times of peace but in times of conflict, at least you know you are where it all ends up any-way, so you can stop wondering when the other shoe was going to drop. Dukowski used to say all kinds of insane stuff to the audience. I think it's good to communicate that kind of off-balance point of view in the middle of a set. It throws the whole thing into a new space. It sometimes leave the band members scratching their heads but what the hell.

I got on the bus post show and there were two females in the front lounge. I had met one of them on a previous visit to San Diego. I don't think she believed me when I told her I remembered her but I honest-ly did. Then, as politely as I could, I got them to leave. The last thing I want is people I don't know on the bus after the show. It's a very small space and people I am not familiar with makes the place even smaller. They left and I heated up a can of soup and ate in relative silence.

Earlier today, I read a good portion of <u>Tender Is The Night</u> and again, Fitzgerald just amazes me. I am going to try and get some more read tonight, between the workout and the show I am pretty tired but I'll try. I am feeling good about the show and looking forward to get-ting out of California and into America. Let's get this show on the road.

Shoulders pt. 1, abs. Yoghurt, protein drink, hummus, bread, protein bar, minestrone soup, rice crackers, water, Gatorade, coffee 1 cup.

08-02-06 Las Vegas NV: 2236 hrs. On the bus in the massive load-ing area behind the House of Blues. It's late and the temperature is still blasting hot. I thought the show was good tonight. I am liking the set and I think we're sounding good overall. Again, the audience was real-ly great and seemed to like us ok. It's an X crowd but they seemed to dig what we were doing. None of that matters to me as much as play-ing well. I would rather play well to an audience that is not all that concerned rather than play poorly in front of an enthusiastic audience.

After our set was over, I spoke briefly to Casey Chaos of Amen. I had him on the guest list. He's one of my favorite singers of all time. He's a maniac and Amen albums are so intense. I have played tracks from them on my radio show. He was looking healthy and it was good to see him. I respect him very much because he knows what it means to be a front man in a band. He gave me some CDs and I didn't get a chance to look at them until after he had gone. He was very generous. He gave me some Japanese imports of some Amen albums that have extra tracks. I had not seen these before. Being a fan, had I known they existed, I would have bought them as soon as I had seen them. I didn't get a chance to thank him. I wrote Heidi who has his e-mail address and asked her to thank him for me.

About half an hour ago, I went back into the venue looking for someone I had put on the guest list, Chris Petersen. His sister, Naomi, was the major photographer of Black Flag. Her photos are all over my book Get In The Van. She passed away three years ago. A book of her photographs is now in the works. Naomi always struggled with drugs and alcohol and it eventually got the better of her. It was very sad when she passed away. So many people in that book are gone now. I had never met Chris before so it was good to tell him how much his sister meant to the band. She also took a lot of pictures of me and Ian. He had a stack of photos to show me and one was of me and Ian that I had never seen before. I had seen others from the same roll but not that one. He gave it to me. It's summer 1984 in Ian's room at Dischord House.

There is more sadness and loss from those days than anything else. If there were good parts, I can't remember them, or they have been overshadowed by the darkness of the many bad parts. The years in Black Flag left a permanent mark on me. I only play to kill. I don't know what the others are into and don't really care because I am not them and they are not me. For me, it's all kill and that's it. I don't want to hang out and laugh and joke around. I don't want to socialize with motherfuckers after the show. I want to hit it, quit it and reset for the next one. That's all there is for me. The rest is lightweight fluttering around the lamplight. I want to be The Spear.

There's a little time left before we hit the road. I am going to the parking lot and read <u>Tender Is The Night</u> in the desert heat. <u>Tender</u> fuses Fitzgerald's greatest inspiration and his greatest heartbreak at once. I can't imagine what he went through to complete the novel. I have read quite a bit on him. I am going to wade back into the biographies and look over the notes I made about the time period in which FSF labored over <u>Tender</u>. I am interested in too many things, too many writers and too many parts of history but I think that pursuing a deeper understanding of FSF and <u>Tender</u> will be worth it. It will be a lot of work but knowing how much he had riding on the book makes me all the more curious. Of all the writers I have ever read and researched, F. Scott Fitzgerald is the one who fascinates me the most.

`Shoulders pt. 2. Show. Protein drink, hummus, pita bread, salmon, salad, lime popsicles, Gatorade, water, coffee 1 cup.`

08-03-06 Salt Lake City UT: 2325 hrs. It's a night off and I am sitting on the bus. I have been in my room once. I would rather be on the bus. I have some music, a cup of coffee and the bus all to myself. I will most likely sleep in here. I like the bus better than the room when I am on tour. I don't know why. I like hotel rooms a lot but I always prefer the bus to a hotel room.

Earlier today, I went to Sam Weller's Zion Bookstore on Main street with Chris and Melvin. They like bookstores and I knew they would like this one. I always go when I am in town. It's not as good as Powell's in Portland OR, but it's really great for used books. I found a book on Fitzgerald that I don't think I have. It has some pictures in it that I didn't recognize so I got it. I also got some Proust and a collection of letters of Max Perkins. Perkins was an editor at Scribner's who worked very closely with Fitzgerald, Hemingway and Wolfe, among others. A. Scott Berg's biography, <u>Max Perkins: Editor Of Genius</u>, is one of the best books I have ever read. Anyway, the book about FSF has some pictures of him shortly before his death. This is a period of his life I am very interested in knowing more about. I don't remember what I learned from Bruccoli's FSF biography <u>Some Sort Of Epic Grandeur</u> so I should re-read parts of that at some point, especially since there is a new edition of it. I should also check out the James Mellow biography, <u>Invented Lives: F. Scott And Zelda Fitzgerald</u>, that I have not spent much time with. As I remember, in his biography, Bruccoli spent a good deal of time detailing FSF's struggle to complete <u>Tender Is The Night</u>. I guess none of this would be of any interest unless you read <u>Tender</u> and liked it. The more you know about FSF, the more interesting <u>Tender</u> is. The main character, Dick Diver, seems to be the man FSF wanted to be and the man he ultimately became. There's a lot of FSF's life in the book. His actual life was very turbulent and sad at the end. It's that tragedy, along with the beauty of his writing that is so interesting to me. It's the perfect combination. Sometimes when I read about the end of his life, I feel like a morbid voyeur. The fact that he died so close to where I live in LA also makes me feel closer to him in a way. I know that sounds strange.

Not much happened today. I enjoyed the bookstore. Being around books puts me in a good mood. I don't think you can have too many books around. I wish I had some more out here with me. I was thinking earlier that I should have brought some Andre Breton and some Alfred Jarry with me.

I didn't do much today except some press and reading about things online. I value my mind and my ability to think more than anything. Even if I were in prison, I would still have my imagination and the ability to have my own thoughts. Touring puts me very deep into my mind. So much of performance is mental for me. I admire great thinkers, speakers and writers. Melvin, who is always reading something interesting and usually ten miles over my head, scored a few books today. They are sitting on the couch across from me, I'll get them out now. Ok, he got <u>The Ambidextrous Universe</u> by Martin Gardner, a collection of essays called <u>The Myths Of Information: Technology And Postindustrial Culture</u> and <u>Umbundu: Folk Tales From Angola</u>. I don't even know where you find books like the first two. I spent some time reading from the <u>Myths</u> book, a study called *The Political Economy Of Social Space* by Andrew Feenberg. I am determined to finish it. It's only about 20 pages but the 4 I got through, where he talks about theories of social space according to Marx, Heidegger, Husseri and other people I don't know a damn thing about, left me in the dust. Also while reading this, I came across a word I am not aware of ever reading before: Phenomenology. I went online and looked the word up and there is a page of definitions according to Husseri and Heidegger. I read through it and still don't know if I understand it. Now, what Mr. Melvin Gibbs is going to get from this is beyond me but I am very interested to find out. I also read some of the folk tales from the <u>Umbundu</u> book and really enjoyed them. Melvin is one of the more interesting people I've ever met. And what did I get at the bookstore? Proust! When Melvin saw the book, he hugged me and said he hoped I would cheer up soon. This is an interesting band to be in.

The late afternoon was beautiful here. The air was dry and it wasn't too hot. The air here is clean and the views of the mountains are fantastic. One of the many reasons I would rather live on the road than in any fixed location. I can be in all kinds of weather all the time. I like the extremes of weather the best. Really hot or really cold, lots of rain, snow, etc. It's a little strange to consider the weather lately, I don't think the incredible temperatures we're enduring now are natural but man made. A conservative douche bag wrote me the other day and called Gore "Gore the Bore." The douche bags don't want to know about Global Warming because it's not happy news. They don't like real news. Only happy news, like our great successes in Iraq and how we're winning the war on terror over there. My great nation, run by cowards. Stay happy!

Minestrone soup, carrot juice, sushi, hummus, bread, water, diet Coke, coffee 1 cup.

08-04-06 Salt Lake City UT: 2331 hrs. I am sitting on the bus. We hit stage tonight at 2130 hrs. and played very hard. The temperature in the venue was a bit on the cool side so I never got the sweat going the way I wanted it but I hit it hard anyway. It is of the utmost importance to play hard. The songs will not register as true unless I am pushing myself physically. Physical intensity is the most important factor for me onstage. The more I get into the playing on that level, the less everything else matters. The amount of people at the show, the venue we're playing—nothing matters but the songs and how hard I can throw myself into them. I think I will achieve many nights of fierce intensity on this tour. It's what I have been training for all these months and now that we have a few shows done, I know I can do it. From here on out, I am only interested in how fucking hard I can smash it every night.

I got in a good workout on the loading dock of the venue earlier today. It's good to workout in the desert heat. Not a great deal happened today, I got some reading done and soon enough, it was time for soundcheck and the show. I will get some work done when we hit the road again tonight. I seem to be getting more done at night on this tour. Tonight, I don't know how much I am good for. I am pretty wiped out from the workout and the show but I'll see what I can do. If I am not working or doing something, I feel like I am losing ground.

Our venue is across the street from a massive venue where some Country and Western acts are playing tonight. Faith Hill and someone else. Tons of people walking by the bus after the show let out. White people. Lots of cowboy hats and jeans. As the audience for our show was being let in, I watched these people walk by and give our audience some very long looks.

I came out here as soon after the set as I could. I kept hearing someone yelling my name outside the bus so I put down my rapidly cooling bowl of soup and went out to see what I was needed for. There were two people. A male and a female. The female told me she had seen me some years ago here in Salt Lake and then said something about rubbing my leg at the show and that I was a lot grayer now. I just nodded. I shook their hands and went back inside the bus. I try to be cool to everyone no matter how tired I am or whatever the situation is. People are very cool to me and I don't want to be anything less back to them. So far, people have been very accommodating of us on the X bill and I appreciate it. Tonight, the audience was great.

Another amazing sunset here this evening. The view of the mountains was spectacular. I am not looking forward to the show tomorrow night. I want to do it of course but the Ogden Theater isn't the best place and there's always idiots in the crowd who throw shit, spit, whatever. I am always happy to be leaving that place. I will play hard and they will get the best I have. What they do with it is up to them. What will happen to me, I am not particularly concerned about.

Chest, abs. Show. Granola, rice milk, protein drink, protein bar, tomato soup, hummus, pita bread, carrot juice, water, coffee 1 cup.

08-05-06 Denver CO: 0233 hrs. Sitting in the back of the bus as we climb into the mountains. Before the bus left, I sat on some rocks next to the parking lot and looked across the street. Bordering a park, there were a row of trees and between the trees were street lights very similar to the ones I used to see in DC. The more I looked at the leaves of the trees back lit by the street lights, the more it looked like an old Hollywood set where they would use those massive painted backgrounds that didn't look real but looked almost more beautiful than real. The lights in the trees made them look superimposed against the night sky and the buildings behind the trees. The more I looked at it all, the more it looked like DC. The night air was dry and very cool and almost reminded me of autumn. As soon as it occurred to me that it felt like autumn, I started to think of that time of year when summer has exhausted itself and its furnace has no more to burn but is not yet ready to succumb to the cold hands of winter. Those long fall afternoons when all is still and sad, yet joyful. It is that time of the year that is the most beautiful and meaningful to me. For a few moments, I was right there.

As I sat there on the rocks, looking into what I was pretending was DC, I wondered why this time of the year holds such meaning for me. As far as the calendar is concerned, it's just another part of the year. Perhaps to many people it is just that and nothing more. For me, it is

A Dull Roar

so much more, it is life itself. I also wondered why I think of things like this. Is it because of the way I was raised? Is it because of all the afternoons after school delivering newspapers or playing in the park alone as the smell of wood burning fires and dead leaves filled my nose? Was it the sunsets that beautifully painted the bricks of the buildings fueling my early awareness of isolation and loneliness? I don't know why just looking at some trees and some street lights at night in a city is so powerful to me, how it can dominate my thoughts for so long afterwards. I don't know but I am glad of it.

I would rather be sensitive than not. I would rather be melancholy than happy. I would rather be alone than not. If I have to love, that is to say, if the feeling of love occurs to me, I would rather love that which is not alive than that which is. I would rather love October than a person. I would rather love the Night than a woman. I don't need to be loved by a human or an animal or the Night or October or Alone. I don't need them to tell me anything. I don't need them to be true to me. They are going to happen as long as I am alive and that is all I need.

1623 hrs. Sitting in the bus outside the venue. Soundcheck is done, it sounds good in the theater. We always do good shows here but the audience always has some surprises. This is an X tour. We are the middle slot so we go where X goes but if this was our tour, we wouldn't be playing here. I don't like shows where I have to pay attention to the audience to avoid a bottle or whatever else. People who throw stuff at bands should be handcuffed to a radiator and worked over with a lead pipe.

The Ogden Theater sits on Colfax Ave. It has been a rough part of Denver for a long time. There is not any time of day when you won't see homeless men and women walking up and down the street, limping, pushing shopping carts, whatever. Some of these people are really hard. They are as hard as it gets. I have been watching them for hours. I remember the first time I came to Denver, in 1982 I believe it was, and there were dozens of homeless people walking around in front of the venue even then.

We'll see what happens tonight, you never know, it might be a great night with no hassle. I forget what year it was, perhaps 2004, where I got into it with a drunk in the lobby after the show. I forget how he started it. I think he pushed me or something. I remember the last time we played here with this line-up, it was a bad night. Again, the audience. I am hoping for an eventless evening audience wise. I just want to play the songs as hard as I can.

2315 hrs. Set done, back on the bus. We went on at 2100 hrs. People seemed to be ok with us playing. No one threw anything. At one point two guys looked to start fighting and I yelled for them to kill each other and then they made up and I told them to fuck each other. I played hard like last night and I think we had a good show. There's not a lot to report about the show itself. I am playing so hard that I don't remember much of it after the show is over. About a minute after the set was over, I grabbed my bag and Road Manager Mike and I bailed out the side door, up the alley and to the bus that was parked across the street. I figured I would catch a shower on the bus and get out of the venue as there was no reason I wanted to be in there any longer than I had to be. It was good to walk right out the door and be done.

I read from the Camus book earlier today and tonight I will try and continue with a project I have wanted to do for some time. I need to see more films. I don't see enough so I am trying to watch one a night. Last night I watched <u>Junebug</u> which I really liked. Amy Adams was fantastic. Great performances all around I thought. I got the DVD some time ago but had not taken the time to see it. Tonight, if I can stay awake, I am going to watch Michelangelo Antonioni's <u>The Passenger</u>. It was recommended to me by one of the people who works on the IFC show named Rick, who knows a lot about film. I always ask him to recommend films to me. He said that <u>The Passenger</u> had just been released on DVD and I should check it out. Jack Nicholson and Maria Schneider star. I don't know what it's about. I am trying to learn new things and this is part of that effort.

I don't know where the rest of the band is, there is no one else on the bus. Tonight we drive to Omaha NE and I am looking forward to it. Colorado is not one of my favorite parts of America and I will be glad to be heading out of here. I've seen too many fucked up things happen at shows and I get too much conservative douche bag mail from this state to ever enjoy myself here. I am cool to the people who are cool to me and I play as hard here as I do anywhere else but I'm glad to leave when it's over and done.

Show. Granola, rice milk, minestrone soup, protein drink, ice cream bar, peanut butter, crackers, hummus, pita bread, water, coffee 1 cup.

08-06-06 0215 hrs. At the back of the bus. I have watched a good deal of <u>The Passenger</u> and like it but I'm so tired, I can't stay with it and will finish it when we get into town. I did a little reading about the film online to learn how it was received when it came out over 30 years ago. There have been some great scenes so far, Nicholson and Schneider walking around the Gaudi structure was a great touch and some of the wide shots from the African desert scenes are great as well. Looking forward to seeing the rest of it. I don't know how long I can keep up watching a film a day but we have some good ones out here so I will have some options for sure.

I met a few people outside the bus when we pulled in front of the venue to load the gear. They were all very friendly and I was friendly back to them. I don't know how long tonight's drive is and I don't know where the venue is. I remember there being a good used bookstore in Omaha but I don't know if it will be open on a Sunday but I will see if I can find it. I like doing shows in Omaha.

2335 hrs. On the bus. Not a lot happened today. We were not really near anything so we just hung out in the parking lot next to the venue. I finished watching <u>The Passenger</u> and liked it very much. It moved very slowly but I didn't think it was boring. I thought the dynamic between Nicholson and Schneider was great and the last shot of the film made watching the whole thing worth it. I want to check out more of Antonioni's films. Tonight, if I can stay awake, I am going to start in on Georges Franju's <u>Eyes Without A Face</u>. I forget how I came upon this one. Maybe I was on Amazon.com and saw it referenced by a different film I was looking at. It is on the Criterion series and I know they don't mess around with bad films so I went for it. I read some reviews to get an idea of what I was in for and am looking forward to it.

The show tonight was good. It was the first show on the tour where it was hot onstage. Usually in the summer almost every venue is a sweatbox but on this tour, there's been a lot of cranked air conditioning. Tonight's show was at an Elk's hall or something. No air conditioning and a lot of people. The daytime temp was in the 90s and then it rained so it felt like a sauna. I liked it. I like playing in heat. It forces me to see how well I have trained for a tour. All the training I have done for the tour has been worth it. I played hard for the entire set. The audience was friendly towards us. One fat fuck piece of shit in a Pantera shirt threw water on me twice but I didn't say anything even though it was distracting. I am The Spear and water will not alter my path. After the show I walked to the bus to get a shower and change up. Some people were walking out to their cars, not staying to see X. I talked to a few of them but didn't want to stay outside long because I didn't want to alter my body temperature, I am trying to keep it fairly constant. I am sleeping in a thermal shirt, pajama bottoms and socks. I learned this from David Lee Roth and it has served me well. We leave soon to go to Sauget IL which is near St. Louis MO I am told. I have gotten a few letters complaining about the venue we're going to be playing at. It's an X tour, not a lot I can do about it and as far as I'm concerned, I don't give a fuck where I play. I am just happy to be out here doing it every night. I feel bad for the audience if the place is no good though.

Arms, abs. Protein drink, protein bar, minestrone soup, rice crackers, peanut butter, crackers, water, Gatorade, coffee 1 cup.

08-07-06 Sauget IL: 2323 hrs. Sitting in the bus, waiting to leave. Incredible heat today. It was around 98 degrees at noon and it felt hotter later in the day. Now and then I would go outside and sit by the railroad tracks behind the venue and read. There was a particular smell out there that took me a second to recognize but soon enough it hit me. It's what I smell every time I'm in Africa or Thailand or parts of the Middle East. It's a combination of burned rubber and garbage. I like the smell because it brings back the memories of being in all those places. Most of the time I am alone in those places so I associate the smell with being alone. I read a good part of <u>Tender Is The Night</u> until the heat got me. Later on, after soundcheck, I went out and read some more from the Camus book I have been hammering away at. As always, I learned something from my Camus experience. I like Camus when I can understand him. A good deal of the time, I think he's way over my head but still, I try and hang in there. I have spent a lot of time with French writers. As far as non-American writers go, it's the French who interest me the most. I think it was Henry Miller's book <u>Time Of The Assassins</u> that got me interested in French writers. I don't know how I got a copy of Leautreamont's <u>Maldoror</u> in my hands but I did and that book really did a number on me. Baudelaire's <u>Paris Spleen</u> amazed me and around then came Rimbaud, Celine, and Camus. From there, Breton, Jarry, Vian, Gide and at least a couple more. I still read and re-read these writers.

The show was a good time. I look forward to these shows now to show myself how hard I can lay into the music. Tonight, I gave it all I had. I usually don't notice anyone in the audience unless they're fucking with me and then I have to keep track of them so I don't lose an eye or something. Tonight I noticed two young people, one male, one female, who stood at the front and looked at us as if they were watching paint dry. They seemed to go out of their way to show no expression. I don't care, they can do what they like. The female came up to me after the show and said hello. I was very polite as usual. Our drummer said, "You're the girl who couldn't have been more bored!" She said something about the show being two hours and something else I didn't catch. She gave me a CD of her band and walked away. I just put it on the ground near the bus, maybe someone will take it home and she'll have a new fan. People are funny. I met all the people who were in front of the bus and they were all cool as usual. One female asked to hug me and I said no and just shook her hand. Same thing happened last night. It's a smart policy that I will stick to for as long as I meet people in public. I don't want to run the risk of having a female say that I touched her inappropriately and then trying to sue me. It has never happened, nor have I ever done anything like that, but I always need to reduce the chances of getting fucked with. Females ask me to hug them all the time. I bet about 99.9% of them are sincere and only mean the best but I can't run the risk. I would rather not do that kind of thing anyway. No one needs to hug me, come on.

We are going to Minneapolis tonight. We have a night off there tomorrow. It's a good neighborhood for a day off, with some good restaurants, stores and theaters. I will try and get some reading done, do some book editing stuff and work on some radio show broadcasts.

I have to keep moving. I have to keep working. It's the best thing for me.

Show. Protein drink, tomato soup, minestrone soup, rice crackers, popcorn, carrot juice, water, coffee 1 cup.

08-08-06 Minneapolis MN: 2132 hrs. In a hotel room down the street from a venue called 1st Avenue. It's one of the first places I ever played with Black Flag. Earlier today, I walked by the venue and stood next to the side door and remembered watching Joe Cole getting arrested in 1987 for mouthing off to a cop. I walked past the door and looked at the side of the building and remembered how I sat on the sidewalk with my back against the building in 1981, waiting for the show to start. I remember sitting there realizing that there was going to be a lot of waiting around if I chose to stick it out as a member of the band. We're not playing 1st Ave. tomorrow night which is too bad. I have done so many shows there.

Audiences are great in this town. They were great to Black Flag and they have always been great to this band. They always show up for the talking shows too. I am looking forward to the show tomorrow night. I wish we had played tonight but it's good to take a night off from the shows. We have a string of five-in-a-rows coming up and that might start to get hard on the throat, so I'll take any time off I can get. Body is feeling good for the most part except my left shoulder is in a good deal of pain. I don't know what I did to it but it's been hurting like a bastard for three days now. It's always been something with this training cycle.

I came up with some good ideas for two radio shows and started working on them. One will be a broadcast of all B-sides of singles. That should be good. As far as my record collection goes, I think it's mostly the British who have made the B-side of a single into an art form. Several songs came to mind but many of them I had played before so I had to think more. One good one is Public Image's *The Cowboy Song,* which was the B-side of their first single. I have a 7″ of it. Ian and I used to play that song more than the A-side, which is a great song too. I went looking to see if the song exists on CD and found it on a box set that's out of print. Several hours ago, I wrote to Martin Atkins (PIL's drummer) and asked if he could supply me with a CDR of *The Cowboy Song.* He got right back to me and said he would bring it to our Chicago show. He's a cool guy. The original line-up of PIL was one of the most dangerous bands in the land. The Sex Pistols were great but to me, the best thing John Lydon ever did were those first two PIL albums. There's nothing like those records anywhere. The other idea I had was to make a playlist comprised of songs from John Peel BBC Sessions. Peel had so many great bands play for his show over the years, I am almost spoiled with so much to choose from. That list came together rather easily but I wanted to make it more than what people who listen to the show would usually expect, more than just The Buzzcocks, Damned, Ruts, Wire, etc. In my letter to Martin, I also asked if he could supply a copy of the Peel version of PIL's song *Poptones.* The Peel version, which I don't have a copy of and have not heard in some time, I remember as being really good. He said he has it on a tape somewhere and will source it. I also wrote Ian MacKaye for permission to play a track from the Fugazi Peel Session. They did a four song session many years ago and the standout track is the version of *Glue Man.* It's not released but it's all over the internet. I didn't want to play it unless Ian was cool about it. He wrote back and gave me the ok so that will make the show all that much better.

That was pretty much how I spent the evening, working on the radio shows, getting broadcast dates of the Peel Sessions and information on the singles I want to play. I also zapped some typos in this book. Every morning I lie in my bunk and have a few thoughts on my own and then start thinking about this book and all the things I have to do: my workout that day, the show and all the rest. My stomach clinches up and then I am very awake and nervous. That's how my day starts.

F. Scott Fitzgerald was born in St. Paul MN in September 1896. I thought about that a bit as I walked around today. His birthplace doesn't mean as much to me as where he died. I don't think I'll get a chance to read from <u>Tender Is The Night</u> tonight. I feel too distracted to do anything but write, stretch and do push-ups. Nights off make me nervous. Around 0400 hrs. I will shower, shave, leave this room and sleep on the bus. Same thing I did on the last day off. The maids must love me, so little to do to get my room ready for the next customer. I sleep better on the bus on nights off. I want to stay connected to the tour.

I will have to gauge what the damage is to my shoulder in the morning and see what kind of workout I can get in the afternoon. It will be a relief to have a show tomorrow night. I get very depressed on nights off. I am going through a pretty bad spell of it tonight. I will be better tomorrow with a show to work towards. The show at night is so true, it forces complete obedience from me. I want to do great shows every night. I can do it if I just stay focused.

Push-ups, abs. Protein drink, enchiladas, rice, beans, peanut butter and crackers, diet Coke, water, coffee 1 cup.

08-09-06 Minneapolis MN: 2321 hrs. So glad the night off is over and we're back on tour. I got a lot of work done yesterday so I'm glad about that. I went back to the bus around 0438 hrs. and slept for a few hours. I didn't do a lot today except work on the radio shows and get ready to play. I did another calisthenics-only workout today and that proved to be very effective. It's a lot harder for me than weight training and it's hard to stick with it but it's worth it. I am going to start doing a lot more push-ups and on the floor ab work in the next few weeks and see where it gets me.

Tonight's show was good. The audience was really great and I think it was one of the best shows of the tour so far. We're playing very well. Nothing out of the ordinary happened during the set, no one threw anything or spat on me so I just concentrated on the playing and that was it.

Within minutes, I was out of the venue and on the way to the bus. I figured there wouldn't be anyone out there but there was. I put my stuff on the bus and came out and signed everyone's stuff and took pictures with people. They were all really cool. It's interesting that so many people leave after we play, they're missing a good band by not seeing X. I came back in here and heated up my last can of soup and sat down for the first time in hours. My left shoulder is giving me a lot of problems right now so I don't mind not moving around much after shows.

I fell a little behind on my film watching schedule but last night I managed to finish off <u>Eyes Without A Face</u>, which I liked very much. The use of black and white was great and the actress who was the mangled daughter had great movement. A little corny here and there but worth seeing. After I finished that, I watched a documentary called <u>Maxed Out</u> which I don't think is out yet. The editor of the film gave it to me months ago. It's about credit debt in America, credit card companies, debt collectors and the people who fall behind. It was really well done, incredibly powerful. I wrote the director and asked if he might be interested in coming on the IFC show next season and he wrote back and said yes. In any case, it would be good to get the word out when and if the film hits screens or DVD. I recommend it. There were some moments that were very sad and really moved me. Not to give anything away but there are some people interviewed who either fell behind on their payments or were related to people who fell into credit debt and the outcome was devastating.

The documentary reinforced what I have been thinking for a long time about America: It's a great place but it's not your friend. I love America. I have been all over the world and I know how great we have it here compared to so many other places. That being said, it's still a dangerous place. I don't think the Government is there for me and I don't trust the courts, the law or the police. I don't count on insurance policies or Social Security. I don't trust the banks or the economy. I am on my own in America. It's one of the reasons I work all the time. I am going to survive America. It's a test for me to see if I can live in a country that wants to kill me. I truly believe that America will take me for all I have if I don't save and dodge and take cover and do all I can to outrun it before it hunts me down. America is full of greedy, cowardly liars. America has a money problem. American money lenders don't care who they destroy and many Americans can't or won't live within their means. I will always live below my means and save all I can. Money is ammunition to fend off America. America will not break me. America will not lull me into a false sense of security. I don't trust America at all. I love the place but it's like keeping a crocodile. It's not a pet. You don't hug the damn thing—it's a fucking crocodile.

And now, the douche bag letter of the day:

Oh Henry, What happened to you man? You were always one of my teen age heroes until I recently heard you spewing gay mafia-sell out shit on your show ...."my neighbors were buttfucking and I put on my Dio album to assist them"???? - what a complete Homowood kiss ass you are! You talk about "pepper spraying people driving hummers" but sell out to the Miata mob on national T.V. I hope it is worth it to pretend you like something you despise deep down inside. Artistic integrity / conviction was always your strength, please keep this in mind Bro because you make a horrible Ryan Seacrest. --Big Rick

Boy, sure going to lose sleep over that one. What happened to me, besides getting idiotic letters full of misguided hatred from homophobic conservative douche bags, you mean? I don't know, just living my life. I wonder how ol' Rick was able to send me an e-mail from underneath Dick Cheney's ball sack?

Another female asked for a hug tonight and again, I just stuck out my hand for a handshake. Another female put her arm around me for a photo and I kept both hands in plain sight of the camera. So many times I have put my arm around the person who put their arm around me in a photo situation and looking back, I see how foolish that was. You can really let yourself in for a lot of trouble if someone accuses you of something improper. Years ago, there was a female on the tour bus. She walked off and when her foot hit the ground, she stumbled, fell on her ass, got up laughing and with her friend, who saw everything, walked away. Later on, I got a letter from a lawyer saying that his client, this female, claimed that I had pushed her from the top of the stairs of the bus, causing her to fall and hurt her leg. Her friend said that he witnessed it. Our bus driver and I also witnessed it and there was no pushing of anyone at any time. They quickly figured out that they would get their asses kicked in court and there was no way I was going to give them money or something so they eventually fucked off. It was around then I reckoned that people are cool for the most part, but you shouldn't take any chances. I like the audiences and I am always cool to them as they have been to me for so many years but the fact is that I don't know what is on their minds and must act appropriately. I am both close to them and very distant from them at the same time. It's a strange way to live but I am used to it.

Show. Push-ups, abs. Protein drink, 2 protein bars, tomato soup, rice crackers, water, coffee 1 cup.

08-10-06 Milwaukee WI: 2335 hrs. In the bus. Another show done. I went for it hard tonight. The audience just stood there. It doesn't matter to me. I do what I do, they do what they do. Every night there's people in the front row who just stand there, expressionless. One guy tonight just looked at us catatonically and then talked on his phone. I don't care about light weights. I hit it and they can do what they want. I used to care what the audience did and didn't do. Now I don't. I know I am delivering. When they applaud, I know why. We trained for this tour and the result is we kill it every night. I don't play to them, I play at them and through them.

After the set was over, I walked out to the bus. People had formed small groups outside the bus and at some point, one of them knocks on the door. It's been happening all night. They're very friendly but it's a little much. It's been happening a lot on this tour as people leave before or during X's set. One guy told me that this show was basically presented as X being the opening band as far as the press attention and then he showed me the ticket and it looked like we were the headliner. He was mad we didn't play longer. We're playing well and I'm looking forward to playing in Cleveland tomorrow night.

Very depressing to watch the news today and see what happened at Heathrow Airport in London. It's great that the plot to bring explosives on airplanes was foiled but too bad that the world is in such a bad state. Also depressing to watch Bush on television saying that the alleged terrorists are a reminder that we are at war with people who hate our freedom. They don't hate our freedom or anyone's freedom. They hate Bush and his policies. Bush always tries to make it an "us" thing when it's not that at all. It's him and his gang of criminals. I wonder what the future will be with all this stuff. Probably soon, you won't be able to take your laptop or iPod on any flights. What terrorism has done to the travel industry might be its most damaging effect. I can't imagine what could have happened if these terrorists hadn't been caught. I guess there will be more information on all of that stuff in the days coming up if, in fact, there was really a plot to blow up airplanes at all. One thing I have learned from Bush and Blair is that they lie all the time and can't be trusted. Like a lot of conservative douche bags, they lie and smear and abuse. The truth is out there somewhere but I don't know if I'll ever get a piece of it. I am hopeful.

I watched almost all of Goddard's Breathless last night. Thought it was great and will finish it tonight and start in on another film. I read a lot of Proust after soundcheck. Really enjoying his writing.

Show. Shoulders pt. 1, push-ups. Protein drink, 2 protein bars, popcorn, ice cream bar, water, coffee 1 cup.

08-11-06 Cleveland OH: 1912 hrs. I am sitting in the back of the bus. Sim just came back here and said that he had nothing to do, so I suggested he start a fanzine for the bus. A bus-zine. He thought it was a great idea and vowed to get on it. We'll see what he comes up with. We play at 2100 hrs.

I didn't do a lot today. I have been getting more work done after the shows rather than before. I am always behind on something so tonight, after the show, I'll be back here and working on a couple of things. I finished <u>Breathless</u> last night and really liked it. I have liked all the films I have watched over the last few days. I know it makes me sound like I am into anything on DVD but it's true, all the films I have watched on this tour I thought were great so far. I got about an hour into <u>Cobra Verde</u> last night. It's been a long time since I've seen it and this time around, I am picking up on more things than the first time I saw it. I like watching Klaus Kinski work. What a maniac that guy was. My favorite stuff of his are the films he did with Herzog. They're all epic and insane. No one will ever make films like Herzog or Kurosawa did. I have not seen <u>Seven Samurai</u> for a few years, I should watch it again. I have seen it at least 4 times and it's never boring. I like films, books and music better than people. I know it takes people to make all these things but for me, good art is the human race's greatest hits and I'd rather check out the best of the best rather than slog through the drudgery of the commonplace. The drugs, the hatred, the lies and oppression, the sadness and pain created by those at the top who never have to really deal with what irrevocable harm they cause to the people below them. I don't want to deal with it but of course I have to and whenever I can, I opt for the aforementioned. The world is full of good things but the bad parts are speaking very loudly these days.

There's so much to look forward to. The NYC show, which for some reason is in a 2500 seater, is at about 750 tickets sold, which is pretty bad for the promoter. I also found out that the ticket price is pretty high and the guaranties are high and it's all too much in my opinion. I don't know how that one will go.

Tonight is show #3 of a 5 in a row. Voice is feeling good so far. Perhaps it's because we're only doing an hour set that I've been able to be consistent every night vocally. We'll see how it's going weeks from now. The tour is far from over and there's a lot of variables to deal with in terms of heat, moisture, sound systems, etc.

I have to start getting ready to play.

Show. Shoulders pt. 2, push-ups. Protein drink, protein bars, shrimp, rice, lettuce, popcorn, ice cream bar, water, coffee 1 cup.

08-12-06 Cincinnati OH: 1816 hrs. Sitting in the back of the bus. I didn't get a chance to write more last night. I finished the show and soon after was in my bunk. I guess between the workout and the show, I used myself up.

During the first song last night, I cranked my lower back really hard. It hurt like a bastard but I had to stow it and keep playing. It might be from the workout I did before the show. I did a bunch of over head presses on a slight downhill. The show could have just made it worse. It hurts a lot as does my left shoulder, the combination has me moving in a lot of pain. I'll be alright for show time though. I'll play hard and pay later. I definitely have to reduce the shoulder workouts.

Last night's show was a great time. Audiences out here are some of the best you'll ever have. We played hard and the audience went off hard, it was a good night. After the show, my body just quit. I ate a little food afterwards but didn't have much appetite. I should have eaten more. I am going to start working on post-show recovery, getting some nutrition in as soon as the show is over. I need to start getting some nutrition quickly after shows if I'm going to play as hard as I want to. It's tricky pushing my body hard at this point. It's like a good car with a lot of miles on it. It's dependable but needs constant upkeep.

Tonight should be a good show. Cincinnati is one of the better audiences you get on a tour. Whenever we get here, there are usually already people in the parking lot waiting to get something signed and get a photo taken. They're always very cool so it's no problem. Today was no different, there have been people hanging around in back of

A Dull Roar

the venue all day. We're about two hours out now. Tonight is going to hurt for a few songs and then I'll be in it and nothing will matter but the music.

Late: On the bus waiting to head out for Chicago. It was a good show tonight but it was a drag that a barricade kept the audience so far from us. It's just the way they work it here but still it felt like they were very far away. It was a great crowd like last night and I think we played well. I am very tired and very sore. Left shoulder is in a lot of pain. I will have to lay off it for a little while.

I stood outside after the show and talked to the people who had gathered at the back of the venue. They were all very cool, a lot of them have seen me on my own and with the band many times. Some drove great distances to see the show tonight. I wonder if there would be enough audience to make a tour like this work if we had an album out. That might not be sustainable and that would mean there would be no tour. For something that is so heavy duty and seemingly hard to kill, it's remarkably fragile and unstable, these tours. I am the one in the band who sees and has to deal with all the numbers and make the decision. President Bush calls it being "the decider." The tour has been such a good time so far and the band is playing really well. I don't know if anyone would go to see us if we toured again. There's a lot of good parts of touring but there's a lot of worry that comes with it. It's not for the band to worry about though.

Show. Abs. 2 Protein drink, clam chowder 2 cans, rice crackers, popcorn, carrot juice, water, coffee 1 cup.

08-13-06 Chicago IL: 1732 hrs. Sitting backstage at the House Of Blues. Early show tonight and we go on at 1910 hrs. I don't mind an early set time. Maybe that will get us on the road a little earlier and that could mean more time in DC. Tonight is the first time I will do five shows in a row on this tour. Soundcheck sounded good and one of the upsides of a HOB show is that the PA and monitors are always really good. Last night, the sound was a little washy up there but I got through it. It doesn't really matter what level of monitor I get or how the place sounds when I'm playing, that's all the choice I get and I get by.

I am looking forward to the day in DC and the chance to walk around the streets of my old neighborhood. It's a ritual of mine to walk those streets over and over every year. It forces me to keep bringing myself back to where I started. Some might say this is regressive or not living in the present but I disagree. It's a way of keeping things in perspective. I walk by a house I lived in for a few years and look at the tree I used to climb up to the window of my room and it makes me see very clearly where I am and where I'm going. I also like walking the old streets because it forces me deeper into myself and reminds me that I am on my own. I can't allow myself to ever forget that. I like to do things that smash me into myself, things that remind me of how I'm no big deal. I never want to forget walking around on those streets not having a fucking clue as to what I was going to do with my life. It only hardens my resolve to never quit. The more I immerse myself in myself, the purer I become. For me, it's like tempering a blade. I have to get ready to play.

2225 hrs. Back on the bus. That was a good time. I like playing in this town. I don't think the House of Blues is really the place for us but that's where we were. The audience seemed to like us alright. One young man threw a beer can onstage. I gave it back to him after the song was over.

After the show, I went back to the dressing room, grabbed my stuff and Road Manager Mike took me out of the venue to the bus. On my way out, I ran into Martin Atkins who was on his way into the backstage. I told him I'd try to come back up and say hello to him but once I got here and got a shower and ate, I became too wracked with body ache to get up so I wrote him a letter thanking him for the PIL tracks he gave me for the radio shows I am putting together.
Show. Protein drink, protein bar, salmon, shrimp, water, coffee 1 cup.

08-14-06 Washington DC: 0211 hrs. We are going down the road. I don't know where we are. We've been moving for a couple of hours

A Dull Roar

now. A few moments ago, I went to the front of the bus where everyone else who's awake are sitting. They are trying to watch a film and I tried to watch with them but I couldn't last more than a few minutes. A few of them are just talking loudly through it and it's very frustrating. For some people in this traveling group, it's like their last chance to drink beer before the world's reserve runs dry and every night I retreat to the back so I don't have to listen to middle-aged men be drunk. They're adults and they can do what they like but to me, it's weak and really fucking boring to be around. So, I am back here with the ear plugs in listening to music and as far as I know, there's no one on this bus but me and Tim the driver. If this is what touring will be like with these people, I might not be doing any more. I love them all dearly but I want to kill, not fuck around. From here on out I am going to check in with them for soundcheck and shows and tune out the rest of the time so I don't lose track of why I'm out here. I worked too hard for this tour to do anything that's not going to make the shows as good as they can be. Every hour of sleep, every workout, every bite of food, every thought and attitude all show up onstage, you can't hide it.

1904 hrs. In DC. We got here around 1400 hrs. I put down my bags and walked down to a coffee place I always go to when I am here. I sat and wrote in my journal and took in the view. It was hot but not humid. I looked across Wisconsin Avenue at the sidewalk and thought about the time 25 years ago that I walked up that very sidewalk to go to the train station to go audition for Black Flag. I looked at the storefront that used to be the pet shop I worked at many years ago. Whenever I am in this neighborhood, I always take a good long look at that place. There was not a lot of activity on the street at the time and things were relatively quiet. Some of the older structures from my youth are still there, simple ground level storefronts wedged in between newer, taller buildings. It makes the strip look mixed and matched. The vantage point I have from my hotel room lets me see the roofs of all these buildings. All around the buildings and for as far as you can see are explosions of trees. They look like dense, green clouds of smoke frozen in motion.

I was enjoying being on my own, looking out at the street and thinking about the walk I was going to take past my old house when the phone rang. It was Ian. He was finishing up work at Dischord and was about to leave. We made plans to meet up around 2015 hrs. Right after that, Ian Svenonius of The Make-Up and Nation Of Ulysses walked up and said hello. He's one of the more interesting people I've ever met. He's an intense intellect and always has something interesting to say. We talked for about an hour. He has a new book out that he promised to send to me. I can't wait to read that. His liner notes for his albums are incredible. I am very excited about the book. He is someone who should write all the time. At one point, we heard a helicopter and saw Dick Cheney's chopper rise out of the trees. We were sitting about a block from the VP's quarters. Ian remarked that if you had a shoulder mounted ground-to-air missile, it would be an easy target. It's true. I wonder what kind of security they have in place for that. I wonder if they just hope some psycho is sitting there waiting every day with his finger on the trigger. I don't want Dick Cheney to get assassinated. I want him to be alive and well so he can stand trial for war crimes. Keep breathing, Dick.

I went from the coffee place to Whole Foods and got some salad and then took a walk around the old streets. It was a perfect afternoon. I walked down Benton St. which is lined with row houses and large trees. There is hardly any traffic so you can walk in the middle of the street and think you have the entire neighborhood to yourself. A woman with a small child and a man walking a dog were the only others I saw on the street. There was little noise other than the cicadas making their engine sounds and the breeze making the trees hiss. The sun was setting and the air was cool and dry. It was like walking through a painting. I walked to W St. to go by a house I lived in for a few years with my mother in the mid-70s. The street has huge trees on either side that form a tunnel of leaves and branches. I walked around the block and down the alley behind the house, where the real view is in my opinion. The alley itself is little more than a path that cuts through seemingly impenetrable trees and undergrowth. The light filters in and makes it look like you're in a glowing tunnel of leaves with every possible shade of green you can think of. I walked up the stone steps to a field where I attended a public summer camp in the early 70s. It's a large, rough, oval shaped field that is almost entirely surrounded by trees. I counted 22 dogs running around with their owners. I stood for quite awhile and just looked at the field, remembering being no older than 9 or 10 running around where the dogs were now running. After awhile, I walked back down the steps, the same steps I have been walking down since those days at summer camp, walked down the alley and looked at the back of my old house and the tree in the back yard. I walked back up W St. and wound my way through the small and quiet streets back to Wisconsin Ave. It was a great walk. If I were a better writer, I could detail the way the sun hits the streets and the trees. I have been all over the world and seen many great sights but some of the most beautiful are these streets. I don't know what I would do day to day if I lived here but I always look at the houses with the "for sale" signs in front and pretend I live there as I walk by. You can never go home again, of course, but there's a familiarity with this area that makes me feel pretty good.

A lot of people talked to me on the street today. All very friendly. One guy told me he saw my old band SOA many years ago. I walked up and down the avenue looking at things, I went to the CVS store and bought some notebooks. I always buy notebooks at this same CVS so wherever I go, I always have something from the old neighborhood.

Tofu, pasta, water, coffee, seafood, noodles, diet Coke, water, coffee 1 cup.

08-15-06 Washington DC: 0323 hrs. Just finished folding my laundry. One of my day off traditions. Tonight was one for the books. Ian picked me up here around 2050 hrs. We were driving up Wisconsin Ave. and he told me that Party Line was playing at Fort Reno and we should go check them out. We went up there and caught most of the set. Fort Reno is a great place to see bands in the summer. Bands play for free all during the summer season. Ian's sister Amanda books the bands. Party Line were really great. Guy Picciotto, Amy Evens, Amanda and Katie MacKaye were there. Great to see them. I talked to Alison Wolfe from Party Line after the show. I always get a kick out of her, she has got a lot of charisma. It was great to see her play. Standing there amongst people and watching the show made me feel like this was the place I should be. I should be going to shows at Fort Reno more often. I should be in this town more often.

Ian and I went to the Thai place we always go to and ate some good food and then went down to the neighborhood. We went for one of our epic walks. It was a great one. The only thing more beautiful than the neighborhood is the neighborhood at night. All the trees lit by the street lamps, there's nothing like it. The sidewalks are like walkways underneath these massive, leafed canopies, up lit by the street lamps. It's like a series of tunnels. The row houses have their lights on and it's all very quiet and secret. I saw only about three cars on the street the entire time we walked around. There is a quality to the air here at night that is beyond my ability to describe. It is a combination of humidity, smell and temperature. I have been all over the world and have never walked through any night like a night here in DC. I was remarking to Ian about the nights here and asked him if he could detect by smell, in the most minute quantity imaginable, the onset of Autumn. He said he could. It was there, the leaves are starting to dry. Even though August has not yet released the city from its grip, it is beginning to show signs of weariness, a loss of tenacity. The nights will be cooler now as we head towards September. Ian and I talked about a lot of things. It's always good to talk to Ian and hear what's on his mind and what's happening in his world. He's always got a lot of things happening, he's working all the time. He gave me some great CDs I can't wait to play: The new French Toast album, Joe Lally's solo album, some other new releases on Dischord and at the top of the pile, the new record by The Evens. It's called <u>Get Evens</u>. It's not coming out until November. I can't wait to play it. It's too late to play it right now so it will have to wait for the drive up to NYC later tonight. I can't wait to hear it!

Show. Push-ups, abs. 2 Protein bars, 1 protein drink, humus, pita bread, veggie burger patty, water, coffee 1 cup

08-16-06 Washington DC: 0205 hrs. In DC, sitting next to the venue waiting to leave. It was a good show tonight. Played hard and had a good time. It's always a good show at this place. The audience was great and we went for it hard. After the show I went out to the bus as soon as I could. The venue is really loud and there's nowhere to get away from the PA in that place. I talked to some people out by the bus and they were cool. I spent some time talking to my USO rep. We talked about hopefully getting me out to Iraq and/or Afghanistan. I hope it happens. I am tired as hell and I need to rack as soon as I can. NYC is always a high pressure show. I had a great time hanging out with Ian. I am too tired to write more. Will try to get at it again tomorrow.

Show. Protein drink, protein bar, fish, egg salad sandwich, ice cream bar, water, coffee 1 cup.

08-17-06 Sayreville NJ: 1751 hrs. Sitting in the bus outside the venue. Last night's show was good. I felt some basic body exhaustion part way through so I am going to up the protein intake during the day and see if that helps the shows. The NYC crowd was very good to us. It's an X crowd for the most part every night we're out there but they're very cool. Not much to say about the show, it was a good sounding venue and when the production is good, I tend to just hit it without much distraction. I am not remembering much of these shows after I come offstage. I play hard and get all the way into it, every song feels like an entire show in itself. Last night I played as hard as I could and dragged myself offstage. I am pretty beat after these shows. I am glad to get the NYC and DC shows done. It's not that I don't like to play these places but when there's a large guest list and there are familiar faces backstage, it's more distracting than anything. I like locations like the one we're playing tonight the best. We are in the middle of nowhere. It's not familiar. It's a show during the week in America. I like that.

I did have a good time in NYC before the show. I met up with Janeane Garofalo for lunch. We hung out around the corner from the venue at a restaurant. She's a very funny woman, very smart and very quick. After the show we walked around and talked some more and then she went home. I don't hang out with people all that much but she was cool to hang out with.

We had hotel rooms last night as today's drive was so short. I didn't sleep much, my shoulder kept me up. Not a lot else to report. The tour is now at that point where it's not exactly a routine or a grind. There is a sense of regularity now that things are pretty set. There hasn't been time to listen to the new Evens record yet. I am going to try and listen to it tonight. I am very eager to hear it but there was no way I was going to get to it in NYC with all the activity. The more I think about it, the more the NYC show seems somewhat anonymous. The venue was so clean that it was completely forgettable and the barricade kept us pretty far from the audience. It was a good show playing-wise and the audience was great but it sure seemed to be over quickly. I guess that's it. It's the shortness of the set. It's sometimes hard to get all the way dug in. I don't feel like we're really inside the thing until the last three songs. It's not that we don't play well before that but right when the 2nd wind kicks in and we're really killing it, then it's time to leave stage.

2333 hrs. Sitting on the bus. We played and they watched. I had all my stuff on the bus so when the set was done, I walked out the back door and onto the bus. I showered and then met a few people outside the bus and have been here ever since. X are ripping it up, I can hear them through the wall. Those first four albums are pretty bomb-proof. I have played them so many times over the years. They have a lot of fans.

Not a lot on my mind. Mostly just exhausted from the shows and the locations. DC and NYC are stressful locations to play. On this tour, those were the two most stressful shows and they are behind me now.
Show. Chest, abs. Protein drink, protein bar, salmon, water coffee 1 cup.

08-18-06 Philadelphia PA: 2328 hrs. Back on the bus after the show. I liked this show a lot. We had some strange sounds up there, something with one of Melvin's basses was giving him trouble and it sounded like Chris went a little out of tune during *Alien Blueprint*. My increased protein intake closer to the show was a good idea. I felt the difference tonight. I stayed on it hard for the whole set. I am doing all I can to make sure I am 100% for the shows and when anyone is distracted or in any way dragging onstage I get pissed off. I am starting to see things here and there on the tour that are getting me mad. I don't expect any of them to be able to keep up with me, I don't even expect them to be close but I want everyone to take what we're doing seriously. Sometimes I make mountains out of mole hills.

We have an early show tomorrow. As much as I want to stay up and work, I have to try and hit the rack as soon as I can so I can start recovering my voice. I don't understand why anyone in this band wouldn't be thinking the exact same thing. If there's a song you are having difficulty with onstage, shouldn't you be practicing that song all day? If you're out of shape and it's hindering your playing, shouldn't you utilize the day to work on that? Shouldn't you watch what you ingest, knowing that you are performance bound? The show is the only reason I am in this town. It's my only reason for going to Boston. I am not going there for my fucking health. I only go out to kill it and leave and that's what I do. I kill it and then I leave the venue. If it were perfect, I would not meet or see anyone after a show. I don't have anything against the people I meet after the show and I always sign whatever and answer every question. I don't mind it at all but I really don't have anything to say to anyone post show. I can't think of one person I want to speak to after a show. I am not trying to be a jerk but to me, it's all about landing on it hard and then leaving. There is nothing to say afterwards. The more people you talk to, the more your cell phone rings, the more you hang out at a bar talking to a bunch of people, the less intensity you will be able to bring to the mission. I know I'm right.

Today, I did a lot of push-ups and sit-ups. Damn that's hard stuff. Hard and boring so I better do more of them. I am going to do push-ups and sit-ups every day at soundcheck now along with whatever workout I have planned. I will up the protein intake to compensate for the exertion and take this whole thing to another level.

Show. Push-ups, sit-ups. Protein drink, protein bar, cheese sandwich, tomato soup, carrot juice, water, coffee 1 cup.

08-19-06 Boston MA: 2336 hrs. Show has been over for some time. We went on at 1920 hrs. I was afraid that I was going to have a hard time vocally, not having enough time to get my voice rested but I was ok up there. That was five shows straight. We have another tomorrow and then a day off. I am fine with playing every night but I think my voice and body will be ready for a night off.

I can't say enough good things about the Boston audience. They were great to Black Flag, they have been great to this band and they always show up for the talking shows. They were great tonight, too. I play very hard these days and am not always aware of what is happening in the audience. I am the Spear. I am not onstage to entertain so I am not looking at individuals that much but tonight when I looked out I saw so many people singing along. On one song, I messed up a word because I was watching a guy singing when I should have been singing myself. The stage was smooth tile and even with shoes I was sliding around which makes me think about my feet when I want to only be thinking about the songs, so that took calories to deal with. It's all calories up there, if I am having to brace my legs so I don't patch out, that takes a lot of effort. I was feeling it tonight towards the end of the set. My left leg was on fire and my right foot was numb. I come offstage so spent after these shows. I am putting all I can into it. Sometimes I can feel immense pain in my chest from trying to push out all the words in a line of a song with the same intensity, like with *Civilized* and *Volume 4*. To do them correctly, I have to almost pass out it seems. All the abdominal work I have been doing has really helped keep the energy up for the whole set. I can feel it. Where I used to feel no control abdominally halfway through a set, now it's tight and I can

A Dull Roar

almost aim my voice from my waistline. It also allows me to get the note I want and not overdo it. The slippery stage was problematic tonight but all in all, I think it was a good show. I talked to people after the show and as always, they were really cool. People are very good to me. I am lucky. I run into the odd jerk now and then but most of the time, people are great to me. It's not wasted on me, I am grateful but it has become harder to talk to people after shows as the years go on. On this tour, I get out of the venue as soon as I can and get to the bus. I just want to be alone. The people I meet are cool and I am cool back to them but it's easier to be back here with no one. It makes sense to be alone after a show. I feel like a weapon after use in a battle, it should be cleaned and put away until the next time.

There is a lot on my mind right now. I don't think I can concentrate enough to put any of it down tonight with any clarity so I will back off from it for the moment. I have been thinking a lot about war and I think it's just part of the human condition. Everything having to do with human interaction causes friction. I want to write more about this but it's a little late and there is distraction on the bus. That's another thing that's weighing upon me. The same bullshit as last night. As it stands at this very moment, there is no fuckin' way I will sit in a room with these guys and even try to write songs with them. The shows have been very good but considering the mood I am in now, I see doing the last show in LA and saying thatwasgreathaveagoodtriphome and never thinking about it again.

Show. Push-ups. Protein drink, protein bar, minestrone soup, rice crackers, popcorn, water, carrot juice, coffee 1 cup.

08-20-06 Boston MA: 0132 hrs. Sitting in the back of the bus as it rolls over the tortured streets of Boston MA. I want to get to sleep as soon as I can as I think it's going to be a loud one on the bus. It's the same bullshit every night. I am listening to the new Evens record at the moment. As I mentioned earlier, Ian gave me a copy with instructions to keep it under wraps as it doesn't come out until November. It will be as if I don't have it. I am on my second listen and to me, it is better and different than the first album, which I liked very much.

This was recorded at Dischord House in the basement on multi-track and then taken to Inner Ear Studios and transferred to 24 track 2". Some vocals and other things were added and then it was mixed. <u>Get Evens</u> is fantastic. I will be playing this one a lot. So far, my favorite track on the album is a song called *No Money*. There's a breakdown section where Amy's vocal is just incredible. She really sings great on this album. I can't wait for it to come out.

0307 hrs. Still up. I have no idea where we are. I should get to my bunk but I don't want to just yet. I am now listening to a mix file I put on the iPod of assorted tracks by The Damned. I never get tired of listening to this band. I have been gathering interesting clippings of the band to add to the next volume of <u>Fanatic!</u> which I will work on for a couple of hours right now to get myself out of the pissed off mood I'm in. Work makes everything better.

2323 hrs. Sitting on the bus waiting to leave. Set was a little loose tonight. It was slow in a few places. The audience was great. There was no barricade so they were right up front and the people in front of me sang all the words which actually screws me up because they never sing on time and I end up singing along with them because I can't get away from the sound of their voices. It's cool though, I just gave them some room and went over to the guitarist's side.

The bands are playing well and the audiences have been great but all the promoters have been losing money so they all probably hate us now, which doesn't make my life any easier out here since I come to all these places on my own on the talking tours. Most likely, if we toured on our own it wouldn't go very well. There's always a certain amount of negativity that goes along with band tours. The playing is always good but there's always something bad happening on one of our tours. Once it was different—more than a decade ago! I don't think if we did an album and toured next year that it would be any different than it is right now attendance-wise. It would probably be a disaster. That's life!

Show. Arms. Protein drink, protein bar, minestrone soup, rice crackers, water, coffee 1 cup.

08-21-06 Norfolk VA: 2250 hrs. A night off after six shows. It's a good thing too. Some of us needed a night off the bandstand to get ourselves together and I only hope the others take this night to get in touch with their god or whatever the fuck they have to do to get their shit together. It had just better be intact when we hit it tomorrow night. Last night pissed me off. I don't want to think about it too much. We have ten more shows on this tour and as it stands right now, my mind set is that the last show will be the last show. I do not have 100% confidence in the unit. It's not that I hate anyone or that anyone sucks, it's just that I am not feeling that the unit is what it needs to be to really tough it out. I wish some members were a little more intense and focused. I'll know more in the shows to come.

Norfolk isn't all that far from DC so the weather and basic look of the place is similar. It was great to walk around at different times of the day. I spent a good part of the day working on upcoming radio shows.

I have been watching Spike Lee's HBO documentary about the Katrina disaster called <u>When The Levees Broke</u>. It's so well done. I can't stand his movies for the most part but his documentary stuff is great and this is his best one. Everyone knows that America dropped the ball on Katrina but the documentary shows the catastrophic day after day brutality people have to live with because of the negligence. It seems like the Bush Administration just didn't give a fuck about the 9th Ward at all. At the beginning of the doc. they talk about how the hurricane actually moved away from the city, it was the levees (that everyone knew were not sound) that broke almost as if planned. That's what struck me, the levees were never fixed properly so when the next hurricane came anywhere near Lake Pontchartrain, you get this catastrophe almost like you had scheduled it. It was a way to get poor people killed off and out of New Orleans. Racism is alive and well in America. Katrina is the perfect window into one of America's most awful problems. Freedom is only for some people and everyone else can just feel free to figure it the fuck out, get what they can and deal with what happens. For many, the system is set up to fail. Think about this: people are living longer lives than in generations past. Sounds good, you hope it's going to be you but even if a small percentage of people live longer, everything changes. If people retire at the regular age but need healthcare for an average of three more years than usual, there will be no money to cover that. Only the rich will be able to live longer. It will come to the point where good health will be a privilege. Literacy is almost a privilege too and if you look at the way Katrina was handled, just being alive in America is a privilege. Some think this is great, that this is how it should be. If you can't afford America, then just die off. The banks will collect the things they lent you and then lend it to the next person. Through war and savvy design with disaster in mind, the top 1% elite white America is slowly taking the country away from everyone else. African Americans are being hunted down to be replaced with more gentle and obedient Hispanic people to clean, bow and scrape. Black people were getting too hard to deal with so they're being killed off. It's very telling that on Fox News, they call Liberals with ideas "The Cultural Elite" as if the Conservatives are the "common man." Ironic isn't it that, try as you might, you can't see any Fox News personality ever really being able to deal with the real world at all? Corporate jets, events and high lifestyle is their world. It's almost a rule of thumb: whatever they accuse someone of being, they are in fact themselves. They call people who voted for Ned Lamont "insurgents" when they are the insurgents. The President was flappin' his gums today saying all kinds of dumbass bullshit. He said that our occupation in Iraq is "straining the psyche of our country." It's insulting that he used the word "our." It's not his country at all. He went on to talk about giving the Iraqis the freedom they want, blah blah blah. Like he gives a fuck about the Iraqi people's freedom. He just wants them to do what he and his administration wants Americans to do: shut the fuck up and do what they're told. Hezbollah save us all!

On a different note, even though it's only August, I have started to think about Autumn. I think it was that night in DC last week when I could smell it in the air that did it. It was great to walk up the alley behind my old house by myself in the afternoon and then hours later, with the street lamps on, to walk up the alley again with Ian. That is perfection. Right time, right place, right everything, so rare. I love Autumn so much that I get an early start on it. I used to start living in October while still in September. As the years go on, I have been starting earlier and earlier. As far as I'm concerned, Summer is over by August 10th or so. It's very hot then but it's Summer's last roar. Everything is better in the Autumn. Even music sounds better. So, I'll have that to look forward to if I'm in America to enjoy it; if I'm not, oh well.

You never know exactly what you're going to get when you go out on the road. You can train and practice and plan but the only truth is when you're out there doing it. I know I am playing hard and not letting anyone down but I don't feel as if everyone in the unit is going for it as hard as they need to and I have to make some decisions about that. I have to give myself a few days to cool down temperwise and assess things with more clarity than I can right now. Right now, I'm not feeling like it's got the heaviness to endure into next year. The audiences are getting great shows, no doubt about that, but there's something going on inside the machine that's not working. I'll know more tomorrow. Perhaps part of it is me wanting this to be so great and putting too much into it. I don't know any other way to do it. How could you go on a stage in front of an audience who trusts you to give them the real thing and not do everything in your power to make it completely kill? I put the show before myself and that's probably the thing I'm not getting from everyone. I don't expect them to be like me and it's not for me to tell adults how to be.

Protein drink, tuna sandwich, hummus, chips, sushi, ice cream, popcorn, water, diet Coke, coffee 1 cup.

08-22-06 Norfolk VA: 2310 hrs. Sitting on the bus. I can hear X playing all the way out here. They've been playing really well. Their drummer, DJ, is such a cool guy. They've all been great on this tour. They're easy to tour with. They show up and hit it with no drama. We played well tonight. Much better than two nights ago. People were very into it tonight. I went out of the bus twice tonight and met people who had accumulated outside the bus door, they were all very cool. I wonder why they don't stick around for X.

I am glad the day off is over with. I got a lot of good work done for some upcoming radio broadcasts and I got some reading done too but I was thinking about this show the whole time. I need a day off now and then to rest my voice but sometimes it makes my vocal chords tighten up and the first show after the day off is a little tough. Also, once the body thinks it's done with the nightly beating, the pain threshold drops and I have to jump it back into the gang again so to speak. It's good to have a day off but I am relieved to have done the first show after it's over.

I read a lot of Fitzgerald today. The older I get, the more I appreciate him. Reading <u>Tender Is The Night</u> again has been a great experience. He's one of the writers I read in Autumn. I am starting my Autumn early this year. It's my favorite time of the year so I might as well start it in my mind. It's been great being on the east coast for the last few days. It's been hot but not too bad and the nights have been really great.

After shows, the bus is sometimes a hard place to be in. It's crowded and people are loud. I get along with everybody but I don't want to listen to anything anyone has to say. The bus is pretty empty at the moment but soon people will start straggling in and the noise level will escalate. I am not good around people in close quarters. Just having to listen to someone eat is hard to handle. I've never been good around people and it's only getting harder. Sometimes people in the band say something to me and I don't even bother to answer. Most of the time, there's nothing to say. Some of the band members have become high maintenance and when that happens, I tune out until it's time to play.

Show. Push-ups, sit-ups. Protein drink, minestrone soup, rice crackers, protein bar, tofu, vegetables, water, coffee 1 cup.

08-23-06 Charlotte NC: 2310 hrs. The show was pretty good

A Dull Roar

tonight but Sim blew out in a couple of places and that made it hard to concentrate because I never knew if he was going to blow out again. So, it was a hard show for me to get all the way into because I didn't know if the music was going to go south on me. There were some strange rolls and some endings of songs I've never heard before, I'll have to see what deal is with him. I'm not happy with the last three shows, I don't think they had the intensity and tightness of the ones that came before it. It's not coming from my end. I came to play. I trained for this and I am 100% onstage every night. There's no fucking way I am going out with this outfit again. It's been a good run of shows but now I am just hoping the band can get through the last 8. The drummer's playing has been a shot to my morale and very destabilizing. I don't look forward to the set at night now because I don't have confidence in the band being able to get through the songs. All the training and preparation I did is just being laughed at so there's no point in thinking about any further work with this line up. There's no way I'm going to feel like this any longer than I have to.

I didn't do much before the show. The venue isn't really close to anything so I worked out and stayed to myself. It's hard to be around the band members because of all the stuff I just mentioned. I like them all but it's hard to be around them.

Show. Deadlift, shrugs. Protein drink, granola, rice milk, protein bar, minestrone soup, rice crackers, carrot juice, water, coffee 1 cup.

08-24-06 Atlanta GA: 0205 hrs. En route to Atlanta. Just came back from the front lounge. When I walked in, I heard the guitar player saying basically all the things I had been thinking about the drummer. The soundman was there and expressing his frustration at the situation. The drummer is not on the bus tonight. He's with the opening band, I have no idea what they are up to but it makes me nervous about tonight's show in Atlanta. From what they were saying, the problem is worse than I thought. We all feel bad about it but there's not a lot you can do with an adult. I take it all personally. When someone doesn't deliver onstage, they have sold out. They have cheated the music and I am done with them. Like on the 1992 tour when the bass player would go onstage and go out of his way to fuck the band up. He was dead to me at that point. I never saw or spoke a word to him after the last show of that tour. Since I have been disrespected, the music has been disrespected, the rest of the band has been disrespected, I'm done with him musically. I still like him but the relationship has changed. I just talked to Road Manager Mike and asked him if we should pull the last two shows and he said no, that the drummer would be fine. I am now in survival mode. I want to play really well at these last shows and not let the audience down, I just hope we have the band to do it. Eight shows doesn't seem like a lot but in these circumstances, it's a lot. It's 8 shows in 10 days. It's going to take a long time.

2322 hrs. On the bus. One of the better shows of the tour. Whole band was on tonight. I knew it was going to be a good night about two songs in. The audience was fantastic. They were going off. It was great to look out there and see all that activity. The drummer was really on tonight. I spent a lot of time slipping in my sweat. I kept wiping it off the stage and finally just left a towel up front. We have 7 shows left to do. I hope we can keep up this momentum. I can do it if they can. It would be great to finish strong on this run.

I didn't do much today and took all the opportunities I could to get some sleep here and there. I didn't sleep all that well last night because I was so bummed out about the state of the band. I need to watch my throat now and the best thing for it is sleep so I am getting all I can.

I got some reading done in the parking lot today, more Fitzgerald. I kept to myself mostly, the less I talk the better and I want to be on my own to stay focused on these last shows. I did spend some time talking to Melvin, the bass player, he's a very interesting guy, very smart.

I'm in a better mood now than last night because the show was really good. That's all I want out here, to play as well as I can every night, that's the only reason I am here tonight. I am wearing down a bit with these entries, I know. The shows flatten me out and shut me up pretty much. Not a lot happens during the day and I have not been wandering around much before shows like I sometimes do. I have been very focused on the show itself and feel chained to it in the hours leading up to when we go out onstage. It's a confinement I know well. It is hard for me to even lose sight of the venue before a show. I want to be close to the place until the work is done and then I want to be gone. I have to go do some radio show interview tomorrow. It's Bubba The Love Sponge so I don't mind. He's a good guy so it should be alright. I have a lot of radio show writing I should do tonight but I don't know if I will be able to do it, I'm pretty tired and flagging a little mentally.

Show. Push-ups, sit-ups. Protein drink, protein bar, fish, vegetables, minestrone soup, rice crackers, 2 cookies, water, coffee 1 cup.

08-25-06 St. Petersburg FL: 2323 hrs. What a night. The weather is typical Florida summer. Earlier today I did an hour on Bubba The Love Sponge's show. That was a good time. I have been doing Bubba's show for about ten years or more. I like the guy because he's honest and really funny and he doesn't care what anyone thinks of him. He always talks up our shows when we come down here.

Tonight's venue is outside so you get to play in the night air which is really great. The place was packed out and it being Friday and all, there were a lot of people who were pretty drunk. As I write this, I can hear people standing outside the bars that line the sidewalk yelling and screaming. It has nothing to do with us, it's all about alcohol. Earlier, I went outside the bus to meet the people who had gathered by the door. X had just started and people were leaving. People were leaning in really close to me, putting their arms around me, very drunk and loud. Sometimes people get their thing signed and do the photo but they don't leave, they stand next to me and keep talking, so the group never seems to dissipate. Then there's the bar population who sees something happening outside and decide they need to investigate, so now there's drunken fingers punching into my chest, "who are you?!" Minutes go by and the same people keep coming up to drunkenly shake my hand for a third time. It's hard for me to be around drunks. I don't like their slowness, their rudeness, etc. It sucks that meeting people sometimes turns into a test of endurance and restraint.

The show itself was pretty good. It wasn't always easy to hear onstage because of the way the stage is laid out but once the show starts, none of that matters to me. Bottom line, never complain, just hit it. The band was solid tonight and the drummer was really good. I am not optimistic about the remaining shows and am taking them one at a time but he's been playing great the last two nights so I am hoping for the best. I don't know what else to do. He's not on the bus tonight, he went to hang out with the opening band. One less person on the bus makes it a little quieter though.

Earlier today, I went back and forth with the USO rep about a potential tour in early November. I asked for Iraq and/or Afghanistan and she said there might be something happening in the UAE. Not all that interesting but if I can help out, I am good to go. She said it was only being talked about so there's nothing solid but at least we're talking about it and that's good. I told Road Manager Mike and he said he's good to go if I want him to come along. Even though he's not going to do the tours anymore, it would be great to still do the USO tours together. He's been on every one of them with me.

Show. Push-ups, sit-ups. Protein drink, protein bar, water, coffee 1 cup.

08-26-06 Orlando FL: 2323 hrs. In the bus, show over. I spent a good deal of time today working on the foreword for a photo book called Punk Love. The book is a collection of photographs by a woman named Susie J. She was there at the time when The Teen Idles and Minor Threat and bands like that were happening in Washington DC. Some of her photos are pretty well known. The first ever Dischord records release, The Teen Idles Minor Disturbance EP, features one of her photos as does the first Minor Threat single. Some of her photos can be seen in the Banned In DC book as well. Punk Love will feature only her photos and it's a great look at the early days of the DC Punk Rock scene. I have a PDF file of the book on my computer and have been enjoying looking at the photos. She asked if I would do the foreword and I said yes but with some apprehension. It's not that I don't like her and her work, I do, it's just that I don't want to disappoint her and this is one of those things that I take so seriously. I am just afraid of not delivering. It's the same feeling I got when Ian asked me to do the liner notes to the Dischord box set. I did it but I sweated bullets over that thing and then Jeff Nelson, co-owner of the label, changed some of my words at the last minute. I still think it's a good piece of work. So, today I worked on Susie J's thing and sent it in to her and she liked it. I let it sit for several hours and then came back to it and re-wrote it and sent that one in to her and Ian as well. I hope to hear from her soon. I have a little while before my deadline so we can go back and forth if she wants but I think it's a nice little piece of writing that gets across what I wanted. When I have to write up stuff like this it makes me see just how unable I am to get what I want onto the page. It's done for now, I'll see what Susie J and Ian say about it.

I had a good time playing tonight even though the venue, the Hard Rock Café, is a bit sterile. It was a good show even though the venue itself is boomy and doesn't seem built for music. Doesn't matter, once you're up there you adjust, the audience adjusts and everyone gets into it. I did have some difficulty onstage, slipping in my sweat again. I had to have a towel at the front of the stage to mop up between songs to get some traction. The drummer held again tonight and played very well. He's been good the last few nights. I am still uneasy onstage but it's been better and I think he's really trying. He's a good guy.

After the set was done, I went out to the bus. There is no access to the back so no one was waiting by the bus for autographs. I really wanted to get back to work on Susie J's foreword.

Tonight we roll to New Orleans for a partial day off. We'll get in late and stay several hours so the driver can rest up for the drive to Houston. We'll do the last three shows with X and then the last two on our own. The tour has gone very quickly and I am satisfied with the playing overall. I wasn't expecting many people to show up and I

was right about that part but it is what it is: old music played by old people. As good as it may be, it's not the hottest ticket in town. All I can do is play with extreme ferocity every night in front of the people who decided to show up. I don't care about good or bad reviews or the number of tickets sold, I am free of all that. All there is to do is play as hard as possible every night.
Show. Veg. burger patty, pasta, salmon, 3 cookies, ice cream sandwich, protein drink, water, coffee 1 cup.

08-27-06 New Orleans LA: 2320 hrs. We have been here for a few hours. We head out for Houston soon. I walked around, did my laundry and worked on the radio show. A little while ago, I sat on a bench and watched the Mississippi River. The air was extremely humid and the cicadas were roaring away. I love the Mississippi River. I don't know what it is but I've always had a thing for rivers. A few years ago, I spent a week on the Nile River, that was great. Last year, I had a hotel room in Cairo that overlooked the Nile and at night, I would stare at it for hours. I definitely want to do another Egypt trip. The last time I was there I was told there are multi day hikes one can take and sleep under the stars, that's what I want to do.

Not much happened today. We drove and stopped here for a little while so the driver could sleep up a little. The air here is very humid. We are parked right off Decatur, near the House Of Blues. Walking around here, it's hard to imagine that the Katrina disaster hit this town. I know that this area was relatively untouched but it's still strange to see everything pretty much business as usual around here: white people walking in and out of bars. I don't remember exactly when I was here last but as far as this part of town, I didn't see anything out of the ordinary. I am a little burned out on anything besides staying focused on the last five shows. Days off are distracting. I want to get back into it and rock these shows. Texas is great for shows, I'm looking forward to getting to Houston.
Protein drink, soup, rice crackers, protein bars, water, coffee 1 cup.

08-28-06 Houston TX: 2331 hrs. Glad that the day off is over. I don't like getting too far away from the shows. Earlier today, I got in a good workout on the sidewalk next to the bus. I am feeling it now. Between the workout, the show and the heat, I am pretty dead. I will be in my bunk soon. Tonight's show was good. The drummer delivered and the band was good. The barrier was pretty far away from the audience and that wasn't great but I had a good time all the same. As much as I don't like days off, tonight I could feel the difference a day of rest made. There are 4 more shows on this tour. I am not looking forward to the tour being over but I do want to get through these shows and get onto the next thing.

Interesting watching Katherine "Douche Bag" Harris' public disintegration. I saw her quoted on the news today saying that the separation of church and state is a lie and that our forefathers never meant it to be that way. Why are these people so nuts? What compels an educated adult like Ms. Harris to say such things? There are, no doubt, many people who avidly support her. People cried in the streets when Stalin died, so what are you going to do? What would America be like if these people got their way? I can't imagine how awful day-to-day life would be. It's useless getting mad about it but at the same time, it's unwise not to take these maniacs and their threat to Liberty very seriously.

When people come on the bus and start talking, it's immediately too loud for me. I don't want to hear them. I don't want to listen to beer talk. It's the same every night. There are some people on this tour that drink every single night. There's no way I'm putting myself in this environment again.

Show. Chest. Protein drink, protein bar, tomato soup, rice crackers, cookies, water, coffee 1 cup.

08-29-06 Dallas TX: 2337 hrs. I liked the show tonight. I started very hard and stayed there the whole night. Some nights, it feels like one song. I like to hit the first one really hard and stay at that pace if I can and tonight I did it. I don't know what it looks like to the audience, they probably think I'm nuts. The set went by really quickly and all of a sudden we were done and I didn't feel tired. I walked off the stage and out a back door to the bus. The back door at this club has a pretty cool story behind it. Robert Plant did a show here and said there had to be a back door for him to leave by or he couldn't play the place. So, they put a hole in the wall and built him a door. It sounds like a little much but what the hell, it's Robert Plant!

I like Texas. I don't know if I could live here but the audiences have always been good to me and they were good to Black Flag too. It was one of the first places I played when I joined the band. Earlier today, I sat outside and marveled at the heat. It's hotter than Los Angeles but it feels different. Texas looks like it's built for heat and LA looks like a city inconvenienced by a sudden heat wave. The heat feels malevolent in LA, like it's set up by the county to make things harder than they have to be, whereas the heat in Texas seems almost innocent, like a fact of life. I know that sounds strange. Perhaps it's the way Texans wear the heat. LA residents look like they're in denial with the way they dress in heat and people here look like they've accepted it as part of life.

I completely fell off the film watching regimen. I have been too tired after shows to concentrate. I did get through a good bit of <u>Sir Henry At Rawlinson End</u>, which the guitar player lent me. It's one of the more insane films I've ever seen. It's Pythonesque and incredibly funny. It's a DVD-R as there's no official DVD of it so far. When that one hits DVD for real, I will be there.

At the beginning of the tour, I felt different about things and while I'm not looking forward to the tour being over, fatigue and depression are taking their toll on me. There's always a degree of both for me on tour but this one has a lot of baggage and emotional intensity. I don't know if I will ever see some of these people again.
Show. Sit-ups, push-ups. Protein drink, protein bar, soup, rice crackers, water, coffee 1 cup.

08-30-06 Austin TX: 2347 hrs. We played tonight at Stubbs. It's an outdoor venue and it was a hot day today so I was wondering what the stage temperature was going to be like. I felt nervous before the show. I am unsure as to how the band will play these last shows.

Earlier today, the guitar player asked me what my thoughts were as to where we were going from here band-wise. I told him that I am out. I don't want to continue with the present line-up. It's not that I hate anyone, I just don't want to go on with this any further. The band feels like a car I can't depend on that I'm stuck driving anyway. It's not a good feeling. I was thinking about all this right before we went onstage tonight and it wasn't a good feeling to go out there with but the show was good, the band was solid.

I finished the show and came back to the bus. I went outside at one point and met some people in front of the bus, they were all really cool. I came back on the bus and have been here ever since. I am not in a very good mood because the tour is ending and while we played well, I don't see it going anywhere. I don't think it was a waste of time but I don't think it was an entirely positive experience. It is what it is, that's all there is to it. I had no illusions but it's distressing to see some people still stuck in the same groove they were in when you were last with them.

Two more shows to go. I think we'll deliver, although I don't think there will be many people there to check us out. Apparently the advance ticket sales for the last two shows are at about 100 each. Yay! All I can do is play my guts out. I can't do anything about how many people show up so I'm not bothered by it. It was an interesting ride though. I am so deep into this thing, I can't think of much else. I have been living on this bus for weeks and don't really remember when the tour started. I have been very focused on the shows and have not thought of much besides the next show. My cell phone has been turned off for about two weeks. I have been living in a tunnel in an effort to give all I can to the shows at night. I talk to as few people before and after shows as possible to save my voice and stay intense. I don't see any other way to do it. Fuck it.
Show. Push-ups, sit-ups. Protein drink, soup, rice crackers, coffee 1 cup.

08-31-06 El Paso TX: 2323 hrs. It's the end of the day off. We pulled in here several hours ago and have been basically just hanging out. I spent a good part of the day working on the upcoming radio show for Tuesday. It will be the first live one in several weeks. I also thought about the end of summer and the start of Autumn and I felt pretty good about that. By the time August is almost over, I am also done with summer and am ready for the next season. I spent a lot of time thinking about the shows and the band. There have been moments in the last few weeks when I have been really mad at some people in the band, times where I felt somewhat betrayed and disrespected. It's not an anger I hold onto for long though. I like all the guys in the band, I have known them a long time. In any band there's frustration, I have never been in a band where there wasn't. I have been trying to figure out what has been nagging at me all day long and I think I know what it is. Being on tour with X was kind of like having training wheels on. It was a tour but it wasn't. It was a semi-tour. It wasn't a full set, there were a lot of people around and a certain amount of distractions that kept us away from each other and our problems. Those last two shows, it will just be us. I have been thinking about it and have come to the conclusion that we'll play fine. I never had my hopes set too high for this tour. I did not at any time think we would be greeted in the streets as liberators. I expected pretty much what happened: fair sized audiences, good playing and a lot of stress. I want to play well at these shows and I want to be done with it. I have been focused on this tour for five months now and I am losing perspective. It would have been impossible for me to have approached it any other way. It would have been stupid to have underestimated what it would take for me to be able to do the music justice. I was right to fear and respect it, to dread it and to prepare for it with the intensity that I did. And this is where some of my anger lies. I guess I wanted more out of certain members of this band. They all gave what they were capable of giving and that's why I am unable to stay angry for more than a few moments. Doesn't mean I want to do this again. It's been a strange mindset to be in for all these days. I don't get lonely, I don't miss anyone and there's nothing I'm looking forward to especially. I am just in the present, doing it and not stray-

A Dull Roar

ing from the objective. As soon as the tour is over I have to get onto the next thing, whatever it will be, as soon as I can. I think it is best when completing a tour, to treat it like a magazine with no more bullets and eject it from the weapon and reload with the next thing and not look back. But until we walk off the stage in LA, the shows are all there is to think about.

Granola, rice milk, cheese quesadilla, shrimp salad, squid, more shrimp, protein drink, potato chips, water, coffee 1 cup.

SEPTEMBER 2006

09-01-06 Tempe AZ: 2322 hrs. That was one of the better shows of the tour I think. It was the first show without X and we got to play longer and I think that actually made us play better. The audience was great. They went off for the whole show. We have had some great audiences at the shows on this tour but tonight stood out. We played *Shame* tonight for the first time on the tour and it sounded good. I like playing that song. I was very nervous about this show, all through the afternoon my stomach was knotted up from thinking about it. A few songs in though, I figured we were going to be alright. Soon we will head to LA for the last show.

On Monday I will have the office to myself as it's a holiday. I am feeing good about tomorrow night's show seeing how good tonight's was. I wish I could trust us to be able to deliver every night but at this point, I just can't. I am going to try and get a few hours of sleep so I can get some things done before soundcheck. I want to start getting stuff put away, get laundry done and start separating myself from the tour. I feel pretty depressed about the tour ending. I wanted it to be more than what it ended up being. I knew there could be some difficulty getting back together with the band. We have known each other a long time and are very close, there's a lot of baggage that comes with that.

Show. Push-ups. Pasta, bread, protein bar, soup, crackers, water, coffee 1 cup.

09-02-06 LA CA: 1914 hrs. At the house. I went to soundcheck at 1700 hrs. and thought I was going to stay there but I didn't like the place so I came back here for some chow and a nap. I will go back there soon. We go on at 2215 hrs. I ran into the Mother Superior boys at the venue, it was good to see them and they are looking forward to the show. I am too but again, as yesterday, I am nervous about it, nervous about my voice, which seems fine but still. Also, I just don't like playing in LA. Once we're playing though, I think it will be fine.

I spent the day between the house and the office, cleaning and getting all my tour stuff put away. It's almost all done. I will do the rest tomorrow. I want to leave right after the show but I guess I had better stay and say goodbye to everyone. I would like to just walk out the side door to my car and bail because I think that hanging out afterwards will be kind of sad. I'll have to see how it feels when I get there. Last night, with that audience, it felt right. Playing with an audience that was partly there for X was distinctly different than last night. The audience was only there for what we do and it wasn't watered down. The X audience is a more sedate crowd and they had to sit though us, which I am sure for many of them was a drag. The point I was getting to is this: it felt really great last night and made me feel like it would be great to go on with the band. It hit me while we were playing. I think that's probably me just wanting things to work but I don't think they would in the long run. It's sad and that's one of the reasons I want to get out of the venue as soon as I can. For me, there's a lot of pain involved with working with these people. I have a lot of feelings for them and it makes things confusing. I should get going back to the venue. Tonight is going to be a tough one.

Show. Protein drink, spinach, salmon, water, carrot juice, water, coffee 1 cup.

09-03-06 LA CA: 0124 hrs. A good way to end it. We played well, the audience was into it and all in all, it was a great night. We used Theo's camera and took a group shot in the dressing room afterwards. It was the only group shot we took since we got back together. I went out of the venue to the parking lot and met some kids who were hanging out there. I did photos with them and then got in my car and drove down Sunset Blvd. I drove by the Whiskey and saw a bunch of kids hanging out and it took me back to the times I used to hang out in front of the Whiskey when I first joined Black Flag. We stood in front of the place because we never had enough money to get in. We lived down the street from there and had nothing else to do at night. It hit me that all the kids I drove by tonight weren't even born when I was hanging out there, listening to bands like Agent Orange, China White and Social Distortion through the front door. That block used to be pretty beat but now it's all upscale. Things change. I checked my e-mail and already people have written in saying very nice things about tonight's show. I don't know when I'll see the band members again. Tonight was so good, it made me want to do more shows and work on new stuff but I don't think it would sustain itself. To go the distance, you really have to want it bad and I am not convinced that all 5 of us are on the same page there.

After the show was over, I stayed in the dressing room for a little while and all of a sudden the weight of the tour kind of hit me. I was very hungry and very tired and wanted to leave. So now I am back here, alone. I have not eaten anything for several hours, I wanted to be very empty onstage.

0725 hrs.: I am feeling too depressed and smashed up to sleep so I came here to the office to work on Tuesday's radio broadcast. I still have a lot of work to do on it but it's going to be a good one. My body aches from head to toe and whenever I stand up, I get dizzy and almost vomit. This happens sometimes at the end of tours. My body knows it has crossed the finish line and lets me know what I have been doing to it. I hope I don't have to do 24 hours on my back like I sometimes do after tours. I really need to get onto the next thing. I have been working here for hours and am now going to try and get some sleep.

2200 hrs. I went back to the house and managed to sleep about 90 minutes and then I was up again. I have been working on the radio show and other stuff. Too sore to work out. I've been in a bad mood most of the day. Tours are hard to come down from. This one is proving to be very hard to get away from. I should be onstage tonight. I should be in harness, getting ready to play or getting to the next show. I don't know what to do with myself now. It's hard to go and go and go and then just stop. Being in a band is very hard for me. I feel the pressure of each show. I never walk out onstage thinking it is going to be easy or that it will be fun. I always think my voice will blow out or something else will go wrong like I'll run out of gas or somehow be unable to complete the set. This happens every night. Last night was really hard before we went on. I felt sick from the weight of it all and then I went out there and tore into the set like it was meat. Now I'm just sitting here without purpose. I went to the grocery store earlier today. A woman came up to me and said, "I think you're great, not just sexually, I also think you're really interesting." I politely said thank you and went on my way. That was the only conversation I had today besides thanking the cashier for my change. It's all the humanity I could take. It takes me a few days to adjust to not being on the road. It's a hard and painful transition to make.

It's September. Summer feels like 100 years ago. I'm glad it's over. I want to feel the cool air of late afternoons and hear dead leaves rustle on trees. Wrong coast for that. Today was an oven. It is in the Autumn that I feel most human. There's something about this time of year that makes me not exactly lonely but showing cracks and signs of heavy use here and there. I guess it's weariness before the 2nd wind kicks in. I will be pretty much going flat out until the end of the year after this pause in September. Later on tonight, if I can keep my eyes open, I will read some Thomas Wolfe. Wolfe is one of the September to November authors I read.

I have been writing in this journal for so long that I don't want to stop. I feel redundant now, like a broken piece of furniture. Being back with the band was a mixed bag. We have known each other for so long. There were moments where I felt like we had never stopped playing. Towards the end I saw how we had changed over the years and how, for better or worse, we hadn't.

I love playing live onstage with a band. It's in me. It was great to train hard for a single purpose. It was great to play hard every night.

None of this stuff is a casual endeavor to me. It's all intense and it's all real. It's all that matters.

2006 Rollins Band Tour Dates

July 2006
27. Cabazon CA
28. San Francisco CA
29. Costa Mesa CA
30. Agoura Hills CA

August 2006
01. San Diego CA
02. Las Vegas NV
04. Salt Lake City UT
05. Denver CO
06. Omaha NE
07. Sauget IL
09. Minneapolis MN
10. Milwaukee WI
11. Cleveland OH
12. Cincinnati OH
13. Chicago IL
15. Washington DC
16. NYC NY
17. Sayreville NJ
18. Philadelphia PA
19. Boston MA
20. Johnson City NY
22. Norfolk VA
23. Charlotte NC
24. Atlanta GA
25. Tampa FL
26. Orlando FL
28. Houston TX
29. Dallas TX
30. Austin TX

September 2006
01. Tempe AZ
02. Los Angeles CA

A Dull Roar